BEAUFIGHTER BOYS

By the same author

Men Behind the Medals
The Buccaneers
Men Behind the Medals – A New Selection
Shot Down and on the Run
Shot Down and in the Drink
Royal Air Force Day by Day
The RAF's First Jet Squadron
The Battle of Britain Story
The Sowreys
Buccaneer Boys
Airmen Behind the Medals
Forever Vigilant
Royal Air Force Day by Day 100

BEAUFIGHTER BOYS
TRUE TALES FROM THOSE WHO
FLEW BRISTOL'S MIGHTY TWIN

AIR COMMODORE GRAHAM PITCHFORK MBE, FRAeS

FOREWORD BY
AIR CHIEF MARSHAL SIR DAVID COUSINS KCB, AFC, RAF (RTD)

GRUB STREET · LONDON

First published in 2019 by
Grub Street
4 Rainham Close
London SW11 6SS

Copyright © Grub Street 2019
Copyright text © Graham Pitchfork 2019

This paperback edition first published in 2021

A CIP record for this title is available from the British library

ISBN-13: 978-1-911667-16-2

Formatted by Caroline Teng

Printed and bound by Finidr, Czech Republic

This book is dedicated to
All those who flew and serviced the Beaufighter
Remembering those who failed to return

CONTENTS

FOREWORD

I first became aware of the Beaufighter shortly after arriving at the RAF College Cranwell in 1961 to begin officer training. A fellow cadet and good friend was the son of Air Vice-Marshal (as he later became) Desmond Hughes who was a gallant and high-scoring night-fighter ace in World War Two. He had boundless admiration for the Beaufighter and his reflections leave one in no doubt that it was a workhorse of the skies.

Iconic aircraft like the Spitfire deservedly attract heroic adjectives and other worthy synonyms. But when military aviators use the word 'workhorse' it takes on a very special meaning. It invariably implies that the aircraft can carry out a number of roles. It also implies a rugged aircraft that can absorb a great deal of punishment and damage and still bring the crew home safely. It suggests an aircraft that can carry a formidable amount and variety of weapons. *Beaufighter Boys* reinforces all those attributes. It even goes further and confirms the aircraft's vital contribution to the lethality of air power in World War Two that it so richly deserves. The vivid personal reminiscences of those who flew and operated the aircraft also demonstrate the deep admiration and affection in which they all held the aircraft, despite the high-attrition rates.

This book, however, offers more than that. Military aircrew can be tribalistic. They invariably develop passionate loyalties for the aircraft they flew and those they flew with. Indeed, these admirable traits have been reflected in the success of Grub Street's 'Boys' series.

Military aircrew also have other shibboleths. They can believe they invented the wheel when it comes to the development of tactics. As one who thought he was breaking new ground in flying Lightnings on interceptions at low level at night over the North Sea, and then low-level attack sorties in the Buccaneer, it was salutary to discover that the Beaufighter crews - across a significant array of roles and in different theatres - had done it all in what was a truly multi-role aircraft of its day.

Indeed the author, Graham Pitchfork, who has a very extensive background with the Fleet Air Arm and Royal Air Force Buccaneer force, drew on the Beaufighter Strike Wing experience in formulating contemporary maritime attack tactics - an experience which coincidentally created his lasting interest in the Beaufighter. The aircraft must surely serve as the genesis and concept for later aircraft - like the Buccaneer and Phantom and Tornado - with its ruggedness and versatility and two-man crew concept.

For those with an interest in aviation and iconic military aircraft, this book, written and researched and compiled with such thoughtfulness and thoroughness and insight by Graham Pitchfork, is an essential page-turning read. I hope you enjoy it as much as I did.

Air Chief Marshal Sir David Cousins KCB, AFC, BA, RAF (Rtd)

INTRODUCTION AND ACKNOWLEDGEMENTS

In 1965 I began a long association with the Buccaneer strike-attack aircraft, initially in the anti-shipping role. It soon became apparent to me that we were following in the footsteps of the RAF's World War Two Strike Wings of Coastal Command. I became fascinated by how the tactics had evolved and how the Beaufighter was so effective. As a result, I began to see the similarities between the Beaufighter and the Buccaneer and the men who flew the two aircraft. Both came from the same breed.

As we developed the tactics for the Buccaneer, so we followed the principles of the Strike Wings. First send in a section for defence suppression followed by the attackers with their dedicated weapons – torpedoes for the Beaufighter and air-to-surface missiles, in our case MARTEL, for the Buccaneer. Later in my time on the Buccaneer, when operating over Norway in the long-range interdiction role and attacks against amphibious forces, so the similarities between the two aircraft became even more apparent.

All this led me to look in much greater detail at the activities of the wartime Beaufighter crews. After retiring from the RAF in 1995 I became involved in the Aircrew Association as its archivist and this gave me the opportunity to meet many ex-Beaufighter Boys and form firm friendships. I admired their modesty and stoicism – "we were only doing our job" – and I decided that their exploits should be recorded. Hence this book is a tribute to them and their ever-faithful ground crew.

I have many people to thank for helping me to bring this book into being. I am very grateful to my old friend and fellow 'Buccaneer Boy', Air Chief Marshal Sir David Cousins for his eloquent and moving foreword.

Many Beaufighter veterans sent me their stories and memoirs. Sadly, the majority have now passed away but I remain forever grateful for their support and generosity. Jack Anderson RAAF, Freddie Baldwin, David Bellis, Jim Blake, Jackie Briggs DFM, Roy Butler DFC, Keith Collett RAAF, Des Curtis DFC, Tony Day RCAF, James Denny, Bill Dickinson, George Dowding DFC, RCAF, John Edgar DFM, David Ellis DFC, Les Fitton, Jeff Forrester, Pat Fry DFC, Arthur Hall DFC & Bar, Bill Higgins, 'Hilly' Hilliard DFC, 'Spike' Holly, Jack Howe CGM, Air Commodore Peter Hughes CBE, DFC, Harry Humphries, Stuart Legat, Geoff Long, William Mann DFC, RAAF, Joe Marquis DFC, Jack Meadows DFC, RCAF, Peter Montgomery, Roy Nesbit, Bernard Nicholls, Bill Powell DFC, Ray Price DFC & Bar, Air Vice-Marshal Michael Robinson CB, Bill Rogers RCAF, Bob Sterling, Atholl Sutherland-Brown DFC, RCAF, Ken Waldie RCAF and Peter White RAAF.

Michael Allen DFC & 2 Bars and Bob Willis MBE, DFC had their memoirs published and they gave me permission to use extracts from their books. Richard Pike kindly allowed me to adapt excerpts from his biography of his father and Woodfield Publishing gave permission to use extracts from Dennis Spencer's book. These four books are listed in the bibliography.

I am also very grateful to numerous families who sent me accounts, photographs and logbooks of their 'Beaufighter Boys'. My thanks go to Mary Bite, Terry Dowding, Helen Evers, Miranda Freer, 'Paddy' Hughes, Kate Masheder, John Milne, Sue Rawcliffe and Ian Spencer.

As always, my aviation writer friends answered the call and thanks go to Tony Buttler, Ian Carter, Don Clark, Mike Dean, Ken Ellis, Chris Goss, Chris Granville-White, Frank Haslam, Tony Holmes, Jeff Jefford, Fred Langan, Ian McIntosh, Simon Parry and Andrew Thomas.

It was always my intention to include chapters relating to the operations carried out by Beaufighter squadrons of the Royal Australian Air Force in the South-West Pacific Area. In addition to Australian members of the Aircrew Association whose names appear above, I have been given a great deal of help by Wing Commander David Fredericks RAAF who provided invaluable advice and help and put me in touch with Steve Allan, Brendan Cowan, Flight Sergeant Daryll Fell RAAF, Martin James, Michael Mirkovic and Sebastian Spencer who all helped me with photographs. Ian Madden, the historian of the 31 Squadron Beaufighter Association, helped with photographs but also offered valuable suggestions and amendments to the chapters dealing with 31 Squadron.

In addition to receiving photographs from the 'Beaufighter Boys' and their families, I have, once again, been given immense help by Lee Barton of the Air Historical Branch whose encyclopaedic knowledge has discovered photographs to fill the gaps.

Finally, John Davies and his great team at Grub Street have given me every encouragement and assistance and I thank them.

Graham Pitchfork
Gloucestershire

AUTHOR'S NOTE

Given the period setting of this book, imperial rather than metric standards have been used to retain the historical context.

At various times and in different locations, the terms airstrip, airfield and aerodrome were used to describe the same establishment. Similarly, aeroplane, airplane, plane and aircraft were used during World War Two. Since the book is built around individual accounts of those who served at that time in theatres across the world, I have retained them.

Throughout the development and operational use of the Beaufighter, the second crew member was described as radar operator, observer, navigator/wireless and navigator. Again, I have retained the terms used in the original personal narratives since the description was that used at the time and in that particular operational scenario.

Every effort had been made to ensure the correct spelling of people's names and the names of places. However, given the time period since these events took place, it has not been possible to check every name mentioned. Some names have been misspelt in individual's accounts and also in some official documents. In certain parts of the world, not least the Far East, there are several spelling variants of places.

Readers will find a small amount of duplication in some chapters but I have tried to limit this as much as possible. However, where it does occur, I felt it had to be included to make each contribution stand on its own as a comprehensive account of that individual's experience.

Finally, I have tried to trace copyright holders of the photographs. However, if I have unwittingly transgressed, I apologise and, if informed, will make corrections in any future edition.

CHAPTER ONE

THE BRISTOL BEAUFIGHTER

The Bristol Beaufighter has often been described as one of the RAF's most valuable and versatile aircraft to serve in the Second World War. It gave distinguished service in all theatres of war, in a number of vital roles and operating in every kind of weather. With its massive rotary engines thrusting forward of the cockpit, the Beaufighter's sturdy profile portrayed a sense of power and aggression.

The Aircraft Development

The arrival of the French Hispano 20-mm cannon in the mid-1930s created a new opportunity for the development of a heavily armed fighter for long-range escort and night defence duties. By late 1938 it was apparent that the delays in developing the cannon-armed Westland Whirlwind were proving too long and Air Marshal Sholto Douglas, the Assistant Chief of the Air Staff, was anxious to have such an aircraft as soon as possible.

The Bristol Aircraft Company were aware of this need and the design team under Leslie Frise suggested using the existing strong wings, tailplane and undercarriage of the Beaufort and converting it into a Beaufort Fighter (Bristol Type 156), a name soon to be shortened to Beaufighter. Armed with four cannons and fitted with more powerful engines, Frise believed the aircraft might be suitable for a fighter. Sholto Douglas favoured this idea and work to convert two Beauforts began almost immediately.

L. G. Frise – Head of the Bristol design team. (Ken Ellis Collection)

The Air Ministry requirement included using the Hercules VI engine with the aircraft capable of reaching 350 mph at 25,000 feet and it had to be equipped with four 20-mm Hispano cannons. After the production of the first fifty, six 0.303-ins Browning machine guns were fitted in the outer wings, four in the starboard wing and two in the port.

Progress with the airframe was rapid but delays in developing the Hercules VI engine resulted in a decision to use the Hercules III as an interim measure. The prototype (R2052) first flew on 17 July 1939 with Bristol's chief test pilot, Cyril Unwins, at the controls. He reported that the aircraft 'handled better than our other types [the Blenheim and Beaufort]'.

Owing to further delays with the Hercules III engine and the need for some fuselage modifications, the first aircraft did not reach the RAF for service trials until June 1940. The war situation dictated the need to curtail some of the standard testing procedures in order to get the aircraft into squadron service as soon as possible and it was finally cleared for RAF service on 26 July 1940.

Beaufighter prototype. (Ken Ellis Collection)

The Hercules III engines did not provide sufficient power and delay in the production of the superior Hercules VI prompted the Air Ministry to decide that Merlin XX engines should be fitted until the teething problems with the Hercules VI were resolved. Eventually, almost 500 Beaufighter Mk. IIs powered by the Merlin were produced for the night-fighter role. By the spring of 1943 it had become obsolete and was largely used for training.

The increased availability of the Hercules VI engine in 1942 led to the development of the Beaufighter VI, which was basically a Mk. I with a few modifications based on the experiences of operating the earlier models, the most obvious being the twelve-degree's dihedral tailplane to improve longitudinal stability.

The Hercules VI engine offered greater high-altitude performance and Fighter Command's Beaufighter VIf had the improved AI, the Mark VII centimetric radar, which used a dish in the nose in place of the arrowhead aerials.

Early in 1942 the Bristol Company suggested the development of a Torpedo Beaufighter to replace the Beaufort. Trials by the Torpedo Development Unit in May proved successful and the Mk. VIc modified for torpedo dropping was released for operational use in August 1942. The Torpedo Beaufighter became the TF.Mk. X, which was a Mk. VIc modified to carry the torpedo externally beneath the fuselage. Two 250-lb bombs or eight of the formidable and very effective three-inch rocket projectiles (RP) could be carried beneath the outer wings instead of the torpedo. The six Browning machine guns could be displaced by an extra 72 gallons of fuel. A single Vickers Gas-Operated (VGO) 0.303-inch machine gun was mounted in the observer's cupola for rear defence. AI Mk. VIII was installed in a nose ra-

Beaufighter II with Merlin engines. (Author's Collection)

dome for ASV work. The Beaufighter TF. X became the standard equipment for the Coastal Command Strike Wings and over 2,200 were built.

By the end of the war, 5,546 Beaufighters had been built in England and 367 in Australia.

Night-Fighters

The Beaufighter If (F for Fighter) entered squadron service in September 1940, initially with 25 and 29 Squadrons and then 219 and 604 Squadrons. Unlike later aircraft the first fifty were not fitted with the intended six machine guns but had only four cannons. All were equipped with AI Mk. IV air intercept radar. The Beaufighter became the first truly effective radar-equipped night-fighter to be operated by the RAF.

Initially, success came slowly for the Beaufighter night-fighter squadrons but matters began to improve significantly in the spring of 1941 by which time there were six squadrons in Fighter Command. By the end of the year a further five had been formed including 406 (Lynx) and 409 (Nighthawk) Squadrons of the RCAF, 456 (RAAF) Squadron and the Polish-manned 307 (Lwowski) Squadron. Six more squadrons appeared in 1942, the last to form being 488 (RNZAF) Squadron.

With the Luftwaffe increasingly committed to the Eastern Front, the need for so many night-fighter squadrons based in the United Kingdom decreased and some began intruder operations over the Continent. Others left for the Middle East and by September 1943 there were just six fighter squadrons based in England including the two Canadian squadrons. By April 1944 the last of Fighter Command's Beaufighter squadrons, 406 (RCAF), had re-equipped with the Mosquito.

Coastal Command

As the Battle of the Atlantic grew in intensity during 1941 Coastal Command recognised the value of the Beaufighter as a long-range fighter and anti-shipping strike aircraft to support operations off Norway, over the North Sea and in the Bay of Biscay. The wing-mounted guns were removed and replaced by 50-gallon fuel tanks and a DF aerial replaced the camera gun on top of the fuselage. Designated the Mk. Ic (C for Coastal) the aircraft entered service with 252 Squadron based at Chivenor in Devon becoming operational in April 1941. The build-up of Coastal Command squadrons was rapid and included 404 (Buffalo) Squadron of the RCAF.

By the spring of 1942 many Coastal Command squadrons had re-equipped with the Beaufighter VIc. Bellows-operated dive breaks were adopted for the aircraft but the standard Hercules VI engine did not offer the best performance at low level. Modifications to the engine and fitment of special propellers improved range and better single-engine performance and the engine became the Mk. XVII.

In September 1942 the Air Ministry finalised an agreement that the Beaufighter was to be adopted as Coastal Command's principal strike aircraft with ten squadrons available by April 1943. Five squadrons were to carry a Mk. XV torpedo filled with Torpex, giving rise to the nickname of 'Torbeau', with the remainder as fighter or anti-flak aircraft. Three Beaufighter Strike Wings were eventually formed each with a torpedo squadron and two fighter/anti-flak squadrons.

April 1943 saw Coastal Command's North Coates Strike Wing mount a major attack on a convoy off the Dutch coast and this was the prelude to an increasingly effective campaign against the convoys sailing down the Norwegian coast and off the Frisian Islands to the Dutch North Sea ports carrying crucial raw materials to feed the massive needs of the industries in the Ruhr. In March 1944 the Strike

Beaufighter VIc interim torpedo fighter JL 832/A of 144 Squadron at Tain. (Air Historical Branch CH 9753a)

Wing's eight squadrons, 143, 144, 235, 236, 254 of the RAF, with 404 (RCAF), 455 (RAAF) and 489 (RNZAF), began operating from Scottish bases against targets off Norway.

As D-Day approached some moved south to combat the E-boat threat with one based at Davidstow Moor in Devon to deal with targets around the Brest Peninsula and down to Bordeaux. Once this threat was over the four remaining Beaufighter squadrons (others had converted to the Mosquito) returned to Scotland to form the Dallachy Wing where they remained until the end of the war.

Mediterranean and Middle East

The arrival of 252 Squadron in Malta in May 1941 heralded the beginning of a build-up of squadrons in the Middle East. No. 272 Squadron arrived at Abu Sueir in Egypt and became heavily involved in strafing operations against ground targets including enemy forward airstrips and convoys and in support of Allied shipping. No. 227 Squadron began operations from Malta in August 1942 and provided escort for anti-shipping operations against convoys carrying supplies to Rommel's Panzer army in North Africa. Beaufighters of 89 Squadron arrived in November 1941 to provide an air defence capability for the Suez Canal areas and in May 1942, 46 Squadron arrived and began operations. After the Eighth Army had begun its advance from El Alamein in October 1942, some Beaufighter squadrons moved to Malta to continue harassing shipping and attacking targets in the desert.

Following Operation Torch, the Allied landings in Morocco and Algeria in November 1942, a number of Beaufighter squadrons deployed from England including 153, 255 and 600 with 219 Squadron arriving in June 1943 to reinforce the night-fighter force. The four squadrons had the crucial role of intercepting German aircraft attempting to halt the advancing Allied armies and they wreaked havoc among German transport aircraft carrying reinforcements. By early May 1943 ten squadrons of Beaufighters were based in the Middle East with two others, 39 and 47, giving up their Beauforts at Protville in Tunisia to re-equip with the 'Torbeau' for operations against shipping.

The defeat of Axis forces in Tunisia on 11 May 1943 allowed the Beaufighter squadrons to turn their attention to attacking targets in preparation for the invasion of Sicily and defending the ports where invasion forces and supplies were being assembled. Together with Beaufighters operated by the USAAF's 12th Army Air Force, RAF squadrons provided night air cover for the landings in Sicily.

As the Allied armies advanced in Italy, the night-fighter squadrons were very active and three Beaufighter squadrons, 39, 16 SAAF and 19 SAAF joined the newly formed Balkan Air Force for operations over Yugoslavia, Greece and Albania. Others, operating from airfields in Egypt and Libya began a major campaign attacking shipping in the eastern Mediterranean and the Aegean Seas where 603 and 12 (SAAF) Squadrons had arrived to bolster the attack force against enemy shipping.

The end of 1944 saw the transfer of numerous Beaufighter units to other theatres, some converted to the Mosquito and others returned to the United Kingdom.

Burma

The Allied gains and successes in North Africa allowed long-overdue reinforcement of RAF units operating in Burma. Beaufighters of 27 Squadron mounted their first attack against Japanese forces on 24 December 1942 and it was fully operational in February 1943. Within days of the second squadron forming (No. 176), Flight Sergeant Arthur Pring shot down three Japanese bombers as they headed for Calcutta on a bombing mission. No. 177 Squadron formed in January 1943 and, together with 27 Squadron, was in constant action flying interdiction missions deep into Japanese-held territory.

Operations were mounted almost daily to attack every form of transport links including road, rail and river traffic. The brunt of these attacks was born by 27 and 177 Squadrons until 211 Squadron reformed in August 1944. During 1944, 47 Squadron was transferred from the Middle East and 22 and 89 Squadrons, which had been based in Ceylon, soon joined the force. The constant harassment of Japanese supply lines continued to give crucial support to the British XIVth Army as it advanced towards Rangoon.

The final months saw 27, 177 and 211 Squadrons continuing their devastating attacks. The end of the conflict in August 1945 saw some squadrons disband, others converted to the Mosquito with just 89 and 176 remaining and by June 1946, 89 Squadron had converted to the Mosquito and 176 Squadron had been disbanded.

South-West Pacific Area

Eighty-seven Beaufighters, the first seventy-two being the Mk. 1c, were sent from the United Kingdom to Australia from mid 1942 for operational service with the RAAF in the South-West Pacific area. By the end of the war, 217 had been delivered, the last arriving in August 1945. In the meantime local production began in Australia in 1943 and the first Mk. 21, powered by Hercules XVIII engines, made its first flight in May 1944. Eventually, 365 Australian-built Beaufighters entered service with RAAF squadrons.

The first squadron, No. 30, was formed with the British-built Mk. 1c and moved to Port Moresby in New Guinea in September 1942 and was in action almost immediately. Shortly after, 31 Squadron was formed and moved to Coomalie Creek, south of Darwin and was in action in November over the Timor Sea. These two squadrons were to remain the only RAAF Beaufighter squadrons on operations for almost two years before 22 Squadron, which converted to the Beaufighter in early 1945, joined them.

Beaufighter VIc of 22 Squadron RAAF. (Ken Collett)

By the end of 1944, 30 Squadron was operating from Morotai and 31 Squadron had moved to Timor where the two squadrons operated with 77 Wing of the First Tactical Air Force attacking targets in the Celebes, Ambon and North Malaku. In January they were joined by 22 Squadron, which had recently converted from the Boston. A fourth squadron, No. 93, was formed in January but it was not until early August 1945 that it saw its first action and shortly afterwards the war against Japan was over. Within a year, all four squadrons had been disbanded.

Post-War

In 1946 a limited number of ex-RAF aircraft were refurbished to serve with the air forces of Turkey, Portugal, the Dominican Republic and the Israelis who used four.

The Beaufighter continued in limited service with the RAF for a further fifteen years. In late 1946, 45 Squadron exchanged its Mosquitos for Beaufighters and moved to Negombo in Ceylon, later moving to Kuala Lumpur where it saw action during the Malayan Emergency. It was the last operational Beaufighter squadron in the RAF and re-equipped with the Bristol Brigand in late 1949.

Beaufighters flew in small numbers for a brief period in 1949 and again in 1951 as anti-aircraft co-operation units in the United Kingdom. For another ten years, a small unit flew the aircraft for target-towing and army co-operation exercises based in Singapore – the last sortie being flown by a Beaufighter TT10 from RAF Seletar on 16 May 1960.

CHAPTER TWO
A MAN FOR EVERY THEATRE

Warrant Officer Jim
Blake. (Jim Blake)

Jim Blake spent over four years as an observer in the Beaufighter world and may be unique. He began flying operations in the UK in late 1940 when he joined the first Costal Command squadron. He went on to serve on squadrons in the Middle East and in Burma before returning to fly with the North Coates Wing until the end of the war. His experiences provide an ideal introduction into Beaufighter attack operations, which will be covered in more detail in later chapters.

Shortly after Christmas 1940 I was posted to Chivenor in North Devon where I met up with 252 Squadron, which was equipped with the Beaufighter Mk. If initially before we received the Mk. Ic in March 1941. It was a long-range fighter with Browning machine guns firing forwards from the wings and four Hispano cannons mounted underneath in the body of the fuselage. The Beaufighter was a bulldog of a warplane, immensely tough and able to withstand any amount of damage. Its quiet engine earned it the nickname 'whispering death' in the Far East.

Our sojourn in Devon was not to be a long one. Our squadron had only been newly formed and was now in the process of working up to operational readiness. We had a number of teething problems but we were soon carrying out operational sorties over the Channel. After a few weeks the squadron was sent to Aldergrove in Northern Ireland to fly patrols in the hope of intercepting the Luftwaffe's Condor aircraft that were causing serious problems to the Atlantic convoys. Our flight commander, Flight Lieutenant Bill Riley DFC, raised our morale when he shot one down. This was good but our pleasure at his success was short-lived.

With our troops being evacuated from Greece, and the need to bolster RAF forces, half the squadron, with the most experienced crews, were sent to Malta, leaving the rest of us to be reformed at Dyce near Aberdeen. I was now unattached, my pilot having moved on, so I was sent to Catfoss in East Yorkshire where I made up a crew on the operational training unit (OTU) with a New Zealander, Pilot Officer Derek Hammond.

After a few weeks we were sent to re-join the squadron at Dyce, which had been re-numbered 143 Squadron since the crews that had gone to Malta remained 252 Squadron and continued to serve in the Middle East. I was to re-join them later on.

It was now September 1941 and we had done a few sorties over the Norwegian coast but my pilot had other ideas. He had heard that there was more action in the Middle East and he invited me to go with him. Nothing daunted, and I did not want to lose a good pilot, so I fell in with the idea. Before long we were away, first to RAF Kemble to pick up a Beaufighter, and then to Portreath in Cornwall to await a favourable wind to take us down to Gibraltar.

The trip was uneventful and the famous Rock of Gibraltar looked magnificent. I felt relieved to see it after such a long flight. We enjoyed a few days' rest while our aircraft underwent some maintenance, and then we were off on the next leg of our trip to Malta. My navigation over the Mediterranean was spot on and soon the island hove into sight.

Within days I suffered awful pains and I soon lost my appendix and a first-class pilot who was given a new navigator. After some three months I finally returned to 252 Squadron, which was now based at Idku near Alexandria. We used to take off and fly north out to sea for about thirty miles before turning onto a westerly heading. After reaching enemy territory, we would come in low over the coast to surprise the Germans before attacking troops, tanks, and motor transport on the main coastal roads. Sometimes we attacked aerodromes or supply columns – any target that looked worth a shoot-up.

Beaufighter Ic of 252 Squadron at Idku. (James Pelly-Fry)

On several occasions I flew with an Australian called Nettleship but nicknamed 'Battleship' due to his aggressive approach. He was a real press-on-regardless sort. Whenever our operational duties were over he would ask me if there was any ammunition left. If I replied yes, he would then go into action entirely independently and beat up anything worthwhile. We always seemed to return with bullet holes in the airframe or bits of telegraph wire hanging from the wings.

Crash landings in the desert were fairly common. On one occasion Battleship and I were together in such a landing. I was a bit apprehensive about landing without an undercarriage but slithering along the sand with no obstacles in the way was no great problem.

On some sorties we would fly south towards the Qattara Depression, a vast expanse of rocky ground and salt flats below sea level. This proved ideal cover for our approach to attack the enemy from their southern flank.

There was so much going on at this time with our sister squadron No. 272 that everyone was exhausted. Casualties were heavy, with over half our squadron being written off. I lost one of my closest friends from my time at Yatesbury when Tom Coles and his pilot 'Smithy' were shot down near Derna. Another loss amongst the many was a young officer called Reed, the son of the boss of Austin Reed, the Liverpool-based outfitters.

I was now getting weary of the desert, so when volunteers for Burma were asked for, I immediately stepped forward to take up the challenge of stemming the Japanese advance towards India.

It was now November 1942 and the guns at El Alamein were booming all day and night and I left my desert camp for Cairo, having been posted with others to form 27 Squadron in the battle zone between India and Burma. On arrival at the transit camp we learnt that we were to fly by civil aircraft to Khartoum where we would pick up a Beaufighter and fly to India from there.

We were called to a briefing and while we were standing around I noticed a flying officer called Bunny Horn who I had met briefly at Dyce. He was a no-nonsense daredevil character, but I knew from experience that if you wanted to live flying Beaufighters it was best to have an aggressive, make up your mind quickly type of pilot who also had instinctive reactions. So, I walked straight up to him, introduced myself and discussed some previous operations. After a time I asked him if he was free and needed a navigator and I offered my services. He accepted and we teamed up. It was a lucky break that paid dividends through the year ahead.

The next day we boarded the civil airliner and landed at Khartoum. We were now crewed up and ready for the long journey but first we had to test our aircraft. A few days later we were issued with maps and a route plan to Cuttack near Calcutta.

Our route took us over the Red Sea at 10,000 feet and we headed east to land in Aden. The next stop was Salalah in the Oman where we refuelled before heading for Masirah Island just off the Oman coast where we stayed for a few days. It was then on to Karachi and a night's rest before setting off the next day for Allahabad to refuel and then to our destination at Armada Road, Cuttack near Calcutta. We completed the long journey on 4 December without incident but some of the other crews were less fortunate and were left behind to wait for spare parts. However, we were warmly received by 27 Squadron's ground crew who had been shipped out via Durban and were now glad to have some aircraft to service.

There was the usual spell of building up the squadron for operations, and with the arrival of more crews, we were ready. However, after a few sorties it quickly became apparent that we were in the wrong area for operations along the River Irrawaddy, so we moved to Agartala near the Indian-Burmese border. At last, after intensive preparations, in February 1943 we began our assault on the advancing Japanese. The form our sorties took was usually to take off an hour before dawn, climb over the Chin Hills to 10,000 feet before descending as dawn was breaking in order to surprise the targets. We attacked sampans, river steamers, railway engines and wagons, oil depots, aerodromes and any road traffic. We flew in pairs and at the target, one crew would travel south and the other north to do a fifty-mile sweep each. We were successful and caused a lot of damage to the supply columns and other targets. The Japanese, however, were not slow to retaliate. They may not have had anti-aircraft batteries but they were very clever at stationing small arms at strategic spots ready for our attacks. They were surprisingly successful, as we seemed always to come home with bullet holes, while other crews were not so lucky. After one attack I noticed a small tear appear at the rear of the wing in front of me. I knew what it was, but didn't think to mention it. It was only on landing with one tyre punctured that I realised that I should have told Bunny where the hole was and what to expect. As usual, he took the lop-sided landing in his stride. These routine operations went on and on and were my fare for the next ten months and proved to be a hectic time. We lost quite a few aircraft during this period but the job went on.

In July our commanding officer Wing Commander H. Daish was tourex and Bunny, who was now a flight commander, took over until Wing Commander J.B. Nicolson VC arrived to be our new leader. After getting into his stride he decided that the remaining Middle East crews had done enough and should be posted home. Meanwhile, my pilot had been awarded the DSO, so I was very pleased to have had a share in the honour.

After a long sea journey home and a month's leave, I left for the OTU at East Fortune, near Edinburgh where I was to be an instructor. In mid-September 1944 I was posted back to a Beaufighter squadron, my fourth. This time it was 254 Squadron at North Coates. I was a bit apprehensive and wondered what was in store for me as I had done all this flying over the North Sea before in 1941 and knew what to expect.

Top: Attack on Burma railway. (Air Historical Branch C4119)
Bottom: North Coates Wing attack a convoy off Den Helder on 25 September 1944 and encounter heavy anti-aircraft fire.

Joining a well-established squadron can be a bit daunting. One has to break the ice with the crews and settle in. Who I was going to fly with was another question always crucial for the navigator's peace of mind. I need not have worried. I met the CO, Wing Commander David Cartridge DFC & Bar who made me feel very welcome. Within a few days I was programmed for my first operation with a sergeant pilot called Joe Chapman .

After my experiences of pilots with their different approaches to flying in action, I was hoping for someone more experienced; Joe had told me that he was still a new boy. This was a bit disconcerting but 'orders is orders' and I had to get on with it. However, after the first few ops I was pleased to find that Joe may have been inexperienced but he had what it takes and was obviously going to be a top-class operator.

Just as we were settling down together, the flight commander's navigator was posted away and the CO decided I should take his place. So, to my disappointment I had to accept the change and I spent the remainder of the war flying with Squadron Leader Archie Freedman DFC.

The Germans were finding deliveries of raw materials from Sweden down the Norwegian coast and the Frisian Islands had been made very difficult by the attentions of the Beaufighter squadrons. These had been formed into Strike Wings and were very far removed from the individual efforts of single or small flights of Beaufighters roaming about looking for targets. The Strike Wing was made up of three squadrons. One used cannon to suppress the enemy's return fire, a second carried rockets and the third, my 254 Squadron, would come in at sea level to drop a torpedo. This was the theory and in practice it worked well.

The Germans became acutely aware of the damage being inflicted and, as the Strike Wing improved its tactics and firepower, so the Germans had improved their defence systems. Each convoy was well armed and protected with many escorts carrying anti-aircraft guns and every convoy had the protection of two Sperrbrecher minesweepers. These were large 7,000-ton ships, very heavily armed with tremendous firepower and they also flew balloons to deter attackers. They were a formidable opponent and suffered heavy losses. The

Rocket and cannon attack on a **Sperrbrecher** off Ameland. (Air Historical Branch C 4312)

Beaufighters too didn't get off lightly with many damaged and we too suffered high losses.

The new year brought continued activity and sometimes we flew to North Scotland to bolster the Dallachy Wing attacking targets in the Norwegian fjords. I had a brief, and unexpected, few days away in March when I was summoned to attend a commissioning board and a couple of weeks later, the station Tannoy summoned 'Pilot Officer Blake' to attend the officers' mess.

In the final months we remained very active and were confident of our superiority and final victory. With our CO Dave Cartridge leading our operations, we were sure of success. We continued on operations until the end of the war. The Germans were using every means available to escape the oncoming Russian forces by sailing across the Kattegat to reach neutral Sweden or Norway where they hoped to hold out. Some of their U-boats were also trying to escape into the Atlantic.

During the afternoon of 3 May, seventeen of us, armed with cannons, took off with twelve rocket-firing Beaufighters of 236 Squadron and headed for the Kattegat. We were briefed to fly over Denmark and to attack anything afloat. We were escorted by Mustangs and in the Great Belt we found a surfaced U-boat and attacked it. It appeared to explode and soon sank. We then searched out for any vessel and attacked at least twelve, raking them with cannon. About seven were sunk and others were damaged. Unfortunately we lost one crew, the last from the North Coates Wing. We landed at Helmond in Holland and stayed the night.

The next afternoon we headed back to the Kattegat in search of other targets. We attacked a destroyer then found no less than four surfaced U-boats heading for Norway and we sank them all. We then returned to North Coates. The next day the war was over.

A few days later I was told that I had been mentioned in despatches. I think Dave Cartridge had looked at my record and decided that having survived flying in Beaufighters in all the war zones since 1940 and being still alive, I should get some recognition.

Over the next couple of weeks we flew VIPs to see the devastation over Germany and we also accepted invitations from the other Beaufighter Wings to visit them. I arrived at Dallachy to find that a New Zealand squadron was having a disbanding party and the CO was none other than my pilot from way back, Wing Commander Derek Hammond DSO, DFC & Bar. He was now pushing the boat out before leaving for New Zealand after a magnificent career and war service with the RAF.

At the end of September I said goodbye to all my colleagues and went off to the demob centre and there had another extraordinary co-incidence. While taking my turn to try on an overcoat, who did I see in the mirror behind me but my old pilot with 27 Squadron in Burma – Squadron Leader Bunny Horn DSO, DFC.

CHAPTER THREE
NIGHT-FIGHTERS OVER ENGLAND

The Beaufighter's operational debut came on the night of 17/18 September 1940, writes **Graham Pitchfork**, when the CO of 29 Squadron, Wing Commander S.C. Widdows, and his radar operator, Pilot Officer Watson, flew the first sortie in squadron service. Taking off from Digby near Lincoln, they had an uneventful patrol. The Beaufighter's first success came on the night of 25 October when Sergeants A.J. Hodgkinson and Benn of 219 Squadron destroyed a Dornier 17 in the Kenley area. The type's first AI radar-assisted success was achieved on 19 November 1940 when Flight Lieutenant J. Cunningham and Sergeant J.R. Phillipson of 604 Squadron shot down a Junkers 88A near Chichester.

Cunningham's success brought to an end the long period of Fighter Command's ineffectiveness against the Luftwaffe's night-bombers. Initially, further success was slow but a steady increase in Beaufighter strength, allied to a build-up of ground control interception (GCI) sites, better servicing and improved training set the foundations for a welcome improvement in the efficiency of the RAF's expanding night-fighter force. An important element was the establishment of the first twin-engine night-fighter operational training unit, No. 54 at Church Fenton, equipped initially with AI Mk. III Blenheims. Training in the technical trades improved and many of the radio and radar tradesmen subsequently became radar operators (R/O) and joined up with pilots at the OTU where some partnerships were formed that endured for the rest of the war. Without doubt, one of the most successful, and lasting, was that of John Cunningham and his R/O Jimmy Rawnsley.

John Cunningham joined the de Havilland Aircraft Company in early 1935 on an aeronautical engineering apprentice scheme. Soon after, he joined 604 (County of Middlesex) Auxiliary Squadron based at nearby RAF Hendon. An aircraft hand on the squadron was Jimmy Rawnsley who worked his way up to become an air gunner on the squadron's Hawker Demons and he regularly flew with Cunningham.

With the outbreak of war, the Auxiliary Air Force squadrons were mobilised and 604 moved to North Weald and soon started to replace its Hawker Demons with the Bristol Blenheim. The squadron flew from Middle Wallop during the Battle of Britain but success eluded the inadequate Blenheim night-fighter force. By the end of September, the first of the Beaufighters started to arrive on the squadron and Cunningham, now a flight commander was one of the first to fly the aircraft. Initially, he flew with Sergeant Phillipson as his R/O.

Cunningham, again with Phillipson, achieved his second success on the night of 23/24 December when he shot down a Heinkel III. These rare night successes at the time of the Blitz were a great morale booster and the press published photographs of Cunningham. The public and the press were unaware of the Beaufighter's secret 'magic box' so his success was attributed to having night vision like a cat and so they nicknamed him 'Cat's Eyes Cunningham', something that the modest Cunningham found embarrassing. However, it did serve the important purpose of making the public aware that the RAF now had a night-fighter force. At the end of January he was awarded the DFC.

In mid-February 1941, Rawnsley finally managed to re-join Cunningham and they had their first success together when they intercepted and shot down a Heinkel III off the

A youthful John Cunningham meets the King at Middle Wallop in May 1941. (Air Historical Branch CH 2659)

Dorset coast. Successes began to mount rapidly and by the end of April Cunningham had been credited with destroying eight enemy bombers and damaging others. This period of success included the destruction of three Heinkel IIIs on the night of 15/16 April. He was awarded the DSO and Rawnsley the DFM.

On 7 May, King George VI visited Middle Wallop and met some of the crews including Cunningham and Rawnsley. As he left, the crews changed into flying kit and Cunningham and Rawnsley took off to patrol over the English Channel. Meanwhile, the King was driven to Sopley GCI site to watch the evening's activity. A bandit appeared on the controller's screen and Cunningham was immediately vectored in behind it when Rawnsley picked it up on his AI radar and took over control and the Beaufighter closed in. It was a moonlit night and, mindful of the silhouette he would present to the enemy air gunner if he closed over the moon-bright sea, he delayed his attack and the two aircraft flew towards Sopley. The controller advised the King that if he left the control caravan he would almost certainly see the interception.

Cunningham positioned the Beaufighter below and behind a Heinkel III and, still unnoticed, he fired his cannons and the Heinkel started to burn. The fire spread rapidly and the enemy bomber curved earthwards and crashed. It was Cunningham's twelfth victory. Unfortunately, it proved to be his last success in his own Beaufighter, 'R' for Robert (R2101). Later that evening another crew flew the aircraft and the return fire from a Heinkel forced the crew to bale out.

By early June Cunningham's total had reached thirteen but with the withdrawal of many Luftwaffe units to the Eastern Front, interceptions became more sporadic. In August he was appointed as the commanding officer of the squadron but only three more successes would be achieved by the end of May 1942 when he and Rawnsley were rested. By this time, Cunningham had added a Bar to his DFC and would receive a Bar to his DSO shortly afterwards. Rawnsley, now commissioned, had already received a Bar to his DFM and he received the DFC.

This signalled the end of their time on the Beaufighter but before the war was over, flying the Mosquito with 85 Squadron, their total had risen to twenty making Cunningham the second highest night-fighter pilot in the RAF. He was awarded a Second Bar to his DSO and Rawnsley was awarded the DSO.

After the war, John Cunningham went on to have a glittering career as the chief test pilot at de Havilland where he tested the early jets but the pinnacle of his test-flying career came with his association with the Comet jet airliner.

Night-Fighter Squadron Commander

Wing Commandeer **Tom Pike**, a regular officer trained at the RAF College Cranwell, arrived at Tangmere in February 1941 to take command of 219 Squadron and here relates his experiences.

The squadron had been operating the Beaufighter If for three months but results had been disappointing. The key to a successful night engagement was the Airborne Interception (AI) Mk. IV system and the co-operation between the AI operator and the pilot. After a few familiarisation sorties on the aircraft, it was time to start operations.

Unlike day-fighter squadrons, when entire squadrons are sometimes scrambled, the night-fighters operated as individuals. The duty operations officer managed a rota system with crews ordered into the air in rotation as and when they needed to respond to enemy activity.

Aircrews had no inkling when they might be required; they had to react as instructed by radar controllers at the sector operations room when an enemy approach had been identified. Sometimes the crews were not needed at all and this uncertainty added to the tense atmosphere in the crew room. Wearing the dark adaption goggles to acclimatise to the dark added to the melancholy atmosphere as the crews waited.

For the first evening on standby on 11 March, Flying Officer Duart, one of the squadron's most experienced AI operators, was detailed as the second member of the crew.

Eventually the scramble bell rang and it was time to rush to the aircraft, which had already been checked and prepared

Top: Beaufighter If. (J. Oughton)
Bottom: 219 Squadron crews at readiness, some wearing night goggles. (Richard Pike)

and where the ground crew were waiting. Each climbed into their individual cockpits and the Beaufighter soon headed for the runway marked by 'dimlights' (a mix of paraffin flares and battery-operated 'glim' lights). After take-off the fighter controller, based at Durrington with the call sign 'Flintlock', gave orders to patrol over the airfield at 16,000 feet. Eventually he called "standby for trade" and gave directions towards a possible target thirty miles away. He then started a running commentary to put the Beaufighter a few miles astern of the target.

As the range reduced, the controller told Duart to "flash the weapon" and he immediately started searching for the target. Eventually he gained contact and took over the interception. At 350 yards the dim shape of a Heinkel III appeared and when the range reduced to 250 yards it was time to open fire with the cannons. Wreckage came from the target but, with the rapid closing speed, it was necessary to break away. In taking emergency avoiding action, the Beaufighter almost stalled and then both engines stopped in turn. The situation rapidly became critical but, with quick reactions in taking the stall recovery procedures, together with a build-up of airspeed, it was possible to restart both engines and slowly recover from a potentially disastrous situation. At the debriefing the squadron intelligence officer agreed that a 'probable' could be claimed.

Three nights later the scramble order came just before midnight. After checking in with Durrington, the controller gave directions to fly south at 15,000 feet and Duart almost immediately picked up a contact but was unable to hold on to it. The controller then took over to position the Beaufighter five miles behind the target. As the range closed, Duart called "Tally Ho" (in contact) and took over until visual contact was gained at 500 yards. A Junkers 88 was clearly revealed by the moonlight.

After the first burst, two fires, one near the cockpit and another in the starboard engine, appeared. The machine started to bank away, slowly at first, and then it steepened and started a long downward spiral to the sea below.

After landing, the required post-operations routine was to debrief with the intelligence officer who completed the combat report and he confirmed the claim for one as 'destroyed'.

At midnight on 16 April the order to scramble came and, once in the aircraft, the night-adaption goggles could be dispensed with. After take-off the controller vectored the aircraft towards a target and Sergeant Clark, the AI operator on this sortie, soon made contact. Then began a series of heading changes, which could best be described as a 'night-time dogfight'.

Clark hung on to the manoeuvring target and kept up a running commentary and eventually brought the Beaufighter in to a range of 350 yards where the dull glow of the target's exhaust flames could be seen. Without ambient moonlight these became the main reference. Finally, at 200 yards the target was engaged with the cannons. It soon became necessary to take evasive action to avoid some falling debris as the intruder's angle of bank steepened and fires started to break out. His rate of descent increased and an attempt to follow him down was made but it was difficult to match his descent. Shortly after there was an explosion as the intruder hit the ground near Guildford.

After reporting back to the fighter controller, an immediate return to Tangmere was received as poor weather was closing in. Approaching the airfield, a number of bombs exploded nearby and Clark returned to his AI radar and soon picked up a contact on a southerly heading. The controller confirmed that it was hostile and an interception was set up when Clark started to call out the range. During the chase the enemy started to evade but Clark continued to give instructions until the bandit's exhaust flames could be seen. At 250 yards it crossed the dim moon giving a better view when it was time to open fire. There was an explosion and the intruder started to turn when there was a bigger explosion followed by a violent flash as an object hurtled towards the Beaufighter and a thud was felt. Power and the aircraft instruments were checked just as Clark called "look out" as the enemy aircraft exploded and debris hurtled towards the Beaufighter. There appeared to be no damage and a diversion to Middle Wallop was made where the intelligence officer confirmed the destruction of a Junkers 88 and a Heinkel III.

On the night of 3 May, Sergeant Austin was detailed to be the AI operator. After take-off 'Flintlock' gave orders to head south of Worthing and hold. The anti-aircraft guns around London had opened up and smoke was drifting across the sky but the controller gave instruction to remain over the beacon at Worthing. Finally, after almost an hour, directions were given to head towards London.

Austin gained contact and as he counted down the range a silhouette appeared, which became more distinct as the range reduced and at 800 yards a Junkers 88 was identi-fied. Careful use of the throttles brought the Beaufighter closer when the bomber's slipstream was felt. Fire was opened at 200 yards but surprisingly there was no return fire. There was the usual crashing sound from the cannon and the strong whiff of cordite. There was a flash from the bomber's starboard engine before it started to swerve and decelerate causing a near collision. Suddenly, return fire was encountered and, in banking steeply to avoid it, sight of the enemy was lost but shortly afterwards there was an explosion on the ground not far away at Petworth.

Wing Commander Tom Pike with Sergeant Austin at dispersal. (Richard Pike)

A week later, a Heinkel III was inter-cepted. It was not quite dark and Austin controlled the interception but a visual sighting was soon made, which confirmed the R/O's instructions. Initially, the bandit made no attempt to evade but eventually he saw the danger and started to turn towards it, making it necessary to judge carefully when to counter. A deflection shot was needed. Austin kept up his commentary and, after opening fire, the allowance for a deflection shot had to be increased. Smoke appeared and two of the crew baled out and the aircraft eventually crashed near Eastergate.

A Junkers 88 was engaged the following night when two strikes were observed on the starboard engine. The Ju 88 took violent evasive action and efforts to follow it failed before it disappeared into a cumulus cloud. Only a claim for a 'damaged' could be made.

After this engagement there was a very quiet period with little action. Then, on the night of 15 June came a scramble and orders to fly south and orbit over Selsey Bill. 'Flintlock' soon had some trade and gave vectors to an easterly heading. Picking up a contact proved difficult but the controller kept giving slight changes of heading until Austin got a contact. A visual on a Heinkel III was soon achieved but the target immediately started to evade but two bursts from the cannons started a fire in both engines. Efforts to follow failed, as his final dive was too steep before it crashed into the sea.

There was no further trade so it was back for a landing at Tangmere.

A 219 Beaufighter If takes off from Tangmere. (Richard Pike)

In the event, Tom Pike was not to know that this was to be the last combat flight of his career. During his period in command of 219 Squadron, he was credited with destroying six enemy bombers, probably destroying two others and damaging one. He was twice awarded the DFC. The citation for the Bar to his DFC commented, 'he has displayed outstanding skill and keenness....' By the end of the war he was serving as an air commodore at the HQ Desert Air Force and after a long career he became the RAF's Chief of the Air Staff. He then served as the Deputy Supreme Allied Commander Europe and retired in 1967 as Marshal of the Royal Air Force Sir Thomas Pike GCB, CBE, DFC & Bar.

Four in One Night

On 18 January 1943 the Air Ministry News Service issued Bulletin No. 9013. One of the reports was titled 'Night-Fighter Pilot's Record Bag'.

Wing Commander C. M. Wight-Boycott and his observer, Flying Officer E. A. Sanders, were in the air in their Beaufighter for six hours last night. They made three patrols. On their first, between 1840 and 2040 hours they destroyed a Dornier 217. They saw no enemy aircraft on their second sortie and on their third flight, which began shortly before 4 a.m. they shot down two more Dornier 217s and a Junkers 88.

Wing Commander Wight-Boycott, who is aged thirty-two, comes from West Somerset and is the CO of 29 Squadron. His observer, who is thirty-four, lives in Norfolk. Both were at school together at Marlborough, but they had not met until they paired up as a Beaufighter team.

After a few hours sleep this morning, the wing commander told the story of his record-breaking fights.

"Our first Hun last night exploded somewhere in the middle of the fuselage when I began firing. It went down in a steep dive and we saw it blazing on the ground when the bombs appeared to explode.

Wing Commander C. M. Wight-Boycott and Flying Officer E. A. Sanders photographed in January 1943 after their success on the night of 17/18 January. (Air Historical Branch CH 8208)

"We didn't meet a thing on our second patrol but shortly after 4 a.m. we took off again and after about half an hour's flying, we saw another Dornier 217, which was jinking violently. The pilot was obviously scared of night-fighters. I got in a fairly long burst and he went down in flames. We could see him burning on the ground.

"By this time I was getting rather tired, but when we saw another Dornier 217, I managed to get in a long burst which hit him amidships. There was an explosion and the Hun went down. I found, by the way, that my tiredness was due to the fact that I had turned off my oxygen by mistake and as soon as I switched it on again, I felt fine.

"Our fourth Hun of the night was a Ju. 88, when fires broke out in both engines. The fire spread along the wings and back along the fuselage and lit up the sky so clearly we could see the black crosses on the aircraft. We watched four members of the crew bale out, one after the other, and then the aircraft went down, exploding in a brilliant flash.

"It was a grand night for night-fighting for the moon and cloud made conditions almost ideal."

Wing Commander Wight-Boycott was awarded the DSO. After taking command of 25 Squadron he was awarded a Bar to his DSO in November 1944. His observer, Flying Officer Sanders, was awarded the DFC for his role in the action described.

CHAPTER FOUR

BOMBER SUPPORT OPERATIONS

Michael Allen of 141   Harry White, Allen's
Squadron. (Michael Allen)   pilot. (Michael Allen)

When Michael Allen crewed up with Harry White in August 1941 it was the beginning of a four-year partnership that would see them become one of the most successful RAF night-fighter crews. By the time they joined 141 Squadron in June 1943, they had flown many operational home defence sorties in the Beaufighter and later in the Douglas Havoc, the latter carrying a searchlight in the nose known as Turbinlite.

Allen and White had previously served on 141 Squadron but on their return, the squadron was pioneering tactics to provide support for Bomber Command's strategic bomber offensive. The squadron's Beaufighters were equipped with new specialised electronic equipment, which allowed the navigator to home on to the signals emitted by an enemy night-fighter's radar emissions.

By mid-1943 the German air defence system had been developed to its peak efficiency and with the bomber offensive also reaching 'maximum effort' the electronic war over the skies of Occupied Europe was reaching new levels. Allen and White became notable participants in this new and absorbing dimension to air warfare.

Michael Allen takes up the story.

On our arrival, the squadron was commanded by Wing Commander J. R. D. Braham DSO, DFC & Bar who, with his AI operator, Flying Officer W. 'Sticks' Gregory DFC, DFM, had already made a name for themselves in the night-fighter world. Before the end of the war, they were to become a legend.

When we arrived at Wittering, the squadron adjutant told us about the new Operation Serrate. In essence, 141 Squadron would be flying freelance high-level intruder sorties over Germany and Occupied Europe to try and find and destroy

German night-fighters who were themselves trying to find and destroy the bombers of Bomber Command.

Early in 1943 the Telecommunications Research Establishment at Malvern developed a receiver or homer, which could pick up the impulses from the German night-fighter's AI radar, this was codenamed 'Serrate' due to the display looking like a serrated herring bone. Serrate indicated direction at ranges up to 80/100 miles but it did not indicate the exact range to the target. For this our AI was needed. The Serrate signal would also indicate that the target was an enemy.

The key to the new operation lay in the homer. This was an additional 'black box' which matched up the frequency of the Serrate receiver with the frequency used by the Luftwaffe night-fighter's AI radar.

I found that I could pick up the herring-bone pattern of the Serrate signals when the target was fifty to sixty miles away. Harry and I were most impressed.

There were different tactics to be learned. Sometimes we would be flying near to the bomber stream, sometimes over the target area, and on other occasions with a spoof raid attempting to draw the Luftwaffe night-fighters away from the main target. For the immediate future, we needed to go to RAF Drem in Scotland as quickly as possible and complete the special training necessary for Serrate interceptions. Then, all being well, within days of returning to Wittering we would become operational and have the opportunity of putting our years of training into practice.

Wing Commander Bob Braham (right) and his radar observer 'Sticks' Gregory photographed later in the war with their Mosquito. (Air Historical Branch CH 13177)

On our return from Drem we flew seven more exercises practising with Serrate and I also learned how to use our new navigational aid, the 'Gee Box'. In the months to come, Gee would assist in checking our point of entry over the enemy coast and again, on our way out but, once over the other side, the Germans were able to jam it effectively as the radio and radar countermeasures war became more intense. By the end of June we were considered 'operational'.

Our first operation was on the night of 3/4 July when Bomber Command carried out a raid on Cologne. The CO briefed us on all the details of the raid, including the bomber's route, the time of the attack, the Pathfinder tactics and marker flares and our own patrol areas. We flew to Coltishall to refuel and took off again at 2340 hours in our Beaufighter VI. We headed towards Eindhoven where we sighted a white tail-light 500 feet above and 300 yards ahead. Harry identified a Messerschmitt 110 and he opened fire at 200 yards with a two-second burst. Strikes were seen on the starboard engine but the range was closing rapidly and Harry dived violently to avoid a collision and we overshot. We did not see the enemy aircraft again.

In our excitement I did not see that the range of the target was diminishing far too rapidly. In the back of the Beau, as we overtook the Messerschmitt, I could hear the thudding noise of the four cannons firing and the lighter, quicker fire of the machine guns. Then I felt the shaking and yawing as Harry 'pulled everything back' and wrestled with the controls to avoid colliding with the twin fins of the 110. Bounced around under the cupola in the rear, I still had my head stuck in the AI set and was peering at a large blip, disappearing inside minimum range. We had come in too fast and did not give ourselves time to steady up and put in an accurate burst of four or five seconds. We had let a 'sitter' off the hook.

When we taxied in and Harry switched off the engines, we climbed down. Our ground crew greeted us excitedly. They could see that the canvas patches that normally cover the gun muzzles (to keep out dust and dirt) had been blown away. This could only mean that we had fired our guns and I heard shouts of "Did you get anything?" We had to tell them that we had only got a 'damaged', but they seemed pleased enough and were happy for us that we had got something on our first trip. We were lucky to have the same ground crew for many months and – no matter what hour of the day or the night – they always gave us tremendous support and encouragement.

Before leaving for our first sortie 'over the other side' there must be a word said about navigation. I don't remember what other AI operators did on the Serrate sorties but Harry and I decided at the outset that I should keep my head in the AI set for virtually the whole trip, and certainly for the whole time that we were over Occupied Europe. Only by doing this could we be sure that we would not miss the chance of investigating any aircraft that came within range of our radar equipment and which could be hostile. Harry would look after the navigation!

At briefing, Harry would mark out the track to our patrol area and the track of the bomber stream, to and from the target, on a 'captains of aircraft map'. He would then, with a red crayon, put in the defended areas, add the time of 'H' Hour over the target, fold his map and stuff it into the top of his right flying boot and off we would go. It was there, handy in his boot if needed when we were wandering about over the Third Reich in a few hours' time!

On 9/10 July we went to Gelsenkirchen but had no joy. We had better luck on the 15/16th. We flew down to West Malling before taking off in support of the raid on Montbéliard. Near Rheims I picked up a strong Serrate signal and the herring-bone pattern on the two cathode-ray tubes was getting stronger by the minute. I switched across to the Mk. IV AI and there was the blip on the tubes.

The signals on the Serrate were coming from a Lichtenstein AI and, as the blip was already well down the time race, it showed that we were within a couple of miles of a German night-fighter. The weather was fine and Harry spotted the silhouette when the enemy aircraft (another Me 110) was half a mile ahead. We had learned from our combat of 3 July so did not close too fast. Harry opened fire at 250 yards as we closed slowly. This time, as we watched the Me 110 go down in two burning pieces and hit the ground, there was no need for me to keep my head in the box.

Harry and I had just one minute of self praise before some searchlights started looking for us and the flak opened up but we managed to get back safely to Wittering.

Over the next few weeks we flew a number of operations but had no luck. On the night of 10/11 August Bomber Command attacked Nuremberg and 141 Squadron sent seven Beaufighters to Bradwell Bay to refuel. We took off to patrol the German night-fighter airfield at Juvincourt in France. Just after crossing the coast near Dunkirk, Harry saw four lines of tracer going into a bomber, which blew up at 7,000 feet and crashed. We could not find the enemy aircraft although we had a fleeting glimpse of an unidentified aircraft but we were unable to engage before it dived into cloud.

That night as so often in the months ahead, when we were equipped with Mosquitos and could range further into Germany, we saw a British bomber attacked and shot down, without us being able to do anything about it. We always flew back to Wittering disheartened.

We must now turn our attention to one of the great raids of the war - the Peenemünde operation and the small, but significant, part played by 141 Squadron. On the night of 17/18 August 1943, 600 aircraft bombed the German research and experimental station located on the Baltic coast. Here, under a tight blanket of secrecy, Hitler's so-called secret weapons were being designed, developed and tested.

Before ten of us took off from Wittering we had the usual briefing. The bomber track looked an incredible distance as it stretched across the North Sea, on over Denmark and then still further on into the Baltic until it was just past Rostock. The target must have been all of 600 miles away. It was pointed out to us that it was an exceptionally important target and success was vital. Wing Commander Braham told us that if the attack was not successful, we would have to go out again the next night.

The plan was for our Beaufighters to patrol to the north of the Frisian Islands, thus positioning ourselves between the German night-fighter bases in northern Holland

and north-west Germany and the bomber stream as it passed on its way across the North Sea heading towards Denmark. It was anticipated that once the bombers were picked up by the Freya long-range location equipment, the waiting Me 110s and Ju 88s would be scrambled and ordered to fly north to intercept them. We were also tasked to patrol in the same area to cover the bomber's return journey after bombing Peenemünde.

Our small force was split into two; five Beaus taking off at five-minute intervals from our advanced base at Coltishall between 2000 and 2026 hours with the other five taking off around midnight to cover the return. They could then escort them on the long seaward crossing back to their bases. All ten Beaufighter crews were hoping that they might be able to come between the defending German fighters and their prey. Harry and I were amongst those on the second wave and we took off at one minute to midnight.

As we skirted the Dutch island of Terschelling, I saw a contact on the Mk. IV AI but thought it was too soon for us to be picking up any German aircraft. I assumed it must be one of the other Beaufighters operating in the area or even a stray bomber off track so I never bothered to intercept it properly! At the last minute I saw that the range of the blip on my tubes was decreasing rapidly and that we were on a converging course with the other aircraft, which would mean that we would pass in close proximity and at completely the wrong angle to take a good look at him. The blip disappeared into minimum range on my AI and Harry got a fleeting glimpse as we overshot and he slipped in behind us. He was presented with a 'sitter' and opened fire and I drew Harry's attention to four lines of tracer going over our heads with the Anglo-Saxon observation to the effect that some bastard was firing at us to which he replied, "I know" as he pushed everything into the bottom right-hand corner and we fell out of the sky.

We lost a lot of height as we peeled off and out of the way of the unpleasant attention of the gentleman behind us. We must have been down to 10,000 feet before Harry decided it was safe to pull out. We clawed our way back up to 18,000 feet and almost immediately I found an AI contact. I switched across to the Serrate frequency and there was the distinctive herring-bone pattern pulsating away very strongly with every indication that the enemy night-fighter was in front of us and only a mile or two away.

Sure enough, when I switched back to the AI time trace there was the blip that, in azimuth and in elevation, matched up with the Serrate signals. We had only to finish off the interception carefully....bring him to minimum range....obtain a visual....and we would have him and be able to atone for the earlier fiasco.

The Me 110 proved to be faster than us and, with full throttle pushed right through the 'gate', we simply could not catch him. Eventually, Harry was forced to open fire at very long range. There were strikes, like fireworks, flecks of flame and a dull red glow as the Messerschmitt dived steeply away. We followed but lost sight and we could only claim a damaged. It might have been destroyed but we couldn't be sure.

Our third combat came about through another Serrate interception and we again had difficulty in overhauling our target and bringing it within firing range.

We sighted a Ju 88 above and to starboard and we followed it visually for five minutes at full throttle as the range decreased to 250 yards. A three-second burst was fired from dead astern, strikes were seen and a fire in the starboard engine spread through the fuselage to the port engine. After another three-second burst there was a blinding flash and the aircraft dived to the ground where it exploded. We then returned to base.

There were two sequels to our sortie. Post-war research had shown that our first victim had in fact been destroyed and the second was also a Messerschmitt 110, not the Ju 88 we had identified. The German pilot survived.

In these early days of bomber support, our Beaus did not have the range to accompany the bombers all the way to most of their targets. We were given enemy night-fighter airfields for patrol areas as the most likely places to make contact

A night-fighter crew head for their aircraft. (Richard Pike)

with the enemy. But, we were freelance and we usually flew with the bomber stream towards their designated target either just below, or just above or to one side of the stream. We used our Serrate and AI radar set as soon as we left the English coast and were over the North Sea. Our experience on the Peenemünde operation also illustrated our lack of speed to match the German night-fighters. We were operating at long range and had sufficient fuel for about five hours of flying time but lengthy stern chases at maximum speed wasted our fuel reserves.

During this period the squadron suffered many 'early returns' due to equipment un-serviceability, the majority due to failure of our Serrate equipment. The Mk. IV AI and the Serrate homer were prone to failure at height and we operated up to 22,000 feet. Harry and I had three aborted trips owing to AI set failures. We were briefed to come home if the set failed and not to run the risk of losing an aircraft with its top-secret Serrate equipment by coming down and attempting to operate as a low-level intruder.

On the night of 6/7 September Bomber Command carried out an attack on Munich with 404 aircraft. Seven of us flew down to Ford on the south coast to refuel. Two went unserviceable and the rest were split to cover the outward and return route over northern France. Harry and I took off from Ford at 2045 hours and we had been briefed to patrol over the Rheims area and in the vicinity of Juvincourt, the German night-fighter base. At about 2205 hours I got a strong Serrate contact, which I was soon able to match with a blip on my AI tubes. We completed the interception and Harry saw four very bright exhausts of an otherwise unseen aircraft flying east at 17,000 feet and turning port. We followed and, turning in behind as we closed the range, Harry identified it as a Ju 88.

It will be recalled that on the night of the Peenemünde raid we had identified a Me 110 as a Ju 88 but this time it really was a Ju 88 and I remember glancing up from my AI set and turning round to take a good look at it. I could see the tail-fin, rudder and tail wheel all quite clearly, and the large Swastika emblem on the fin.

The enemy aircraft was doing about 160 knots and was evidently quite unaware of our presence. Throttling back and getting behind at the same level, we gave a two-second burst of cannon and machine-gun fire from 200 yards. There were many strikes on the fuselage and on the starboard engine, which burst into flames. Streams of glycol covered our windscreen. We gave the enemy aircraft another two-second burst with all guns. The enemy climbed steeply, straightened then dived enveloped in flames. We watched it strike the ground where we could see it through the haze burning fiercely.

On the same page of my flying logbook in which I recorded the destruction of this Ju 88, there is another entry; 'Harry awarded the DFC'. In the same issue of the *London Gazette* that announced the award, the CO was awarded a Bar to his DSO, and his title and style thus became Wing Commander J. R. D. Braham DSO & Bar, DFC & two Bars.

Although I was not similarly decorated, perhaps this is an appropriate time to discuss awards in general and mine in particular, because it had some significance for the other nav/rads on the squadron. The story, which came out later, was that Wing Commander Braham had put both Harry and me up for an award at the same time, conscious, as he was, of the part played by nav/rads in the Serrate operations. When nothing came through for Harry's navigator (me), the CO was extremely put out because of the detrimental effect this might have if other navigators on the squadron felt that there was little chance of their efforts being recognised in a similar manner to those of their pilots.

Years later, I learnt from our former intelligence officer that Wing Commander Braham got on to 12 Group HQ and made this point to the AOC, with happy results for me in November and for other navigators in due course.

At the end of September our inspirational boss, Wing Commander Braham, was finally rested and sent to a staff job at HQ Fighter Command. The loss of our CO was tempered by the prospect of being re-equipped with the de Havilland Mosquito. With its greater range we would be able to reach Bomber Command's targets deep inside Germany and, with a higher speed than our Beaufighters, we would have a better chance of catching the enemy night-fighters when we found them. With the news of two more squadrons being formed, all three with Mosquitos, and the whole Serrate operation being transplanted into a new radar-countermeasures Group (No. 100) being formed in Bomber Command itself, hopes were running high for the future.

> Michael Allen and Harry White remained together as a crew and, after a ground appointment, resumed flying with 141 Squadron. Both added two Bars to their DFCs and by the end of the war had been credited with destroying twelve enemy aircraft and damaging four others. Allen left the RAF in 1946 but Harry White served until 1977 when he retired as an air commodore having added a CBE and an AFC to his wartime decorations.

BIRTH OF THE STRIKE WINGS

David Ellis (left) and his navigator Eric Ramsbottom
of 236 Squadron. (David Ellis)

Coastal Command's campaign against enemy surface shipping during the early years of the war had met with limited success. The Blenheims, Hampdens and Beauforts rarely attacked as a coordinated force and, faced by a formidable threat, they suffered heavy losses for very modest results.

The availability of the Beaufighter brought about a dramatic change in the anti-shipping campaign and Coastal Command's Strike Wings were to change the course of the war in the coastal waters of German-occupied Europe.

The first of the Strike Wings was formed in November 1942 at North Coates on the Lincolnshire coast. Its task was to attack the important coastal convoys, heavily escorted by flak ships, transporting raw materials from Scandinavia to the Dutch port of Rotterdam. The wing consisted of two squadrons of the Beaufighter VIc, No. 236 armed with cannon, machine guns and bombs, and No. 254 armed with cannon and torpedoes.

The wing's first operation was mounted on 20 November 1942 when it was tasked with attacking a southbound convoy off the Hook of Holland.

The fighter escort failed to rendezvous with the Beaufighters and the force headed across the North Sea with only their own armament for self-defence. The formation had split up and 236 Squadron hit the Dutch coast to the south of the convoy and was unable to make an attack. Meanwhile, German fighters attacked the torpedo formation repeatedly.

This first operation by the Strike Wings was a tragic failure resulting in the loss of three crews, five aircraft and with others badly shot up. Amongst those lost were the CO of 236 Squadron, Wing Commander H. D. Fraser, and one of his flight commanders. Within days, Wing Commander Neil Wheeler arrived to take command.

Twenty-six-year-old Wheeler was a graduate of the RAF College, Cranwell and was one of the pioneer Spitfire photographic reconnaissance pilots, his exploits during fifty-six operations earning him the DFC. On arrival at North Coates he recognised the low morale on the squadrons and immediately reviewed and revised the tactics. To provide stronger support for the Torbeaus, 143 Squadron joined the wing in the New Year in the anti-flak role.

Wheeler recommended that the three squadrons should attack together and he established a period of intense training when everyone was expected to match his own high standards – during February some crews flew more than twenty sorties practising tactical formations and co-ordinated attacks. Wheeler was adamant that a fighter escort was essential and vowed that no matter how much pressure was put on him, he would refuse to lead a wing strike without an escort.

His firm views, natural leadership and example brought an enthusiastic response from his crews. He was soon recognised as a strict but fair man, a trait that would remain with him throughout his long RAF career. Finally, on 18 April 1943 his beliefs, intensive training and new tactics were put to the test.

David Ellis was a pilot flying in the anti-flak role on this first wing sortie under Wing Commander Wheeler and he continues the story.

After training on Blenheims and Beaufighters, my navigator Eric Ramsbottom and I were posted to 236 Squadron at North Coates where we joined 143 and 254 Squadrons to form a Beaufighter anti-shipping wing, a new concept in the air/sea war. However, each squadron had continued to operate individually and had only mounted a joint attack on one occasion, in November. This had been an attack on a large and well defended convoy off the Hook of Holland and it had proved a disaster. In return for minimal damage to the convoy we had suffered heavy casualties, including the loss of our CO and one of our flight commanders.

Our new CO, Wing Commander 'Nebby' Wheeler, had arrived and taken stock of the situation, including the low morale of his crews. He soon became convinced that the Strike Wing could be effective provided the right tactics were employed and that a fighter escort always protected us against enemy fighters. This had not been the case on the November operation.

So, a rigorous programme of training in formation attacks had taken place throughout the winter, in addition to our normal patrols. Now as we sat in the crew room on the morning of 18 April 1943, we knew that we were a force to be reckoned with.

All chatter stopped and crossword puzzles were discarded when the Tannoy crackled, hissed and announced, "All stand-by crew to operations immediately". The whole station was now aware of an impending operation.

A large heavily defended northbound convoy had been reported the previous evening and a Beaufighter had been sent from North Coates in the morning to plot its position, estimate its speed and take photographs. When it returned the photographs were immediately developed and the attack was planned. 254 Squadron was to attack the merchant vessels with nine Torbeaus while 143 and 236 Squadrons, with six aircraft each, would attack the escort vessels in order to engage their anti-aircraft fire and divert it from the Torbeaus. These aircraft were armed with four 20-mm cannon and two 250-lb bombs; one slung under each wing.

After briefing, activity on the station increased. Ground crews put the finishing touches to the aircraft, caterers provided rations and in due course our WAAF driver delivered us with all our equipment to our aircraft. Watches had been synchronised at briefing and, at the appointed time, forty-two Hercules engines roared into life. After warm-up and engine checks, twenty-one Beaufighters began to taxi to their take-off positions. Then, section-by-section, they followed the wing commander into the air. I was flying No. 2 to my flight commander, Squadron Leader 'Dusky' Denholm, and after retracting the undercarriage, I moved swiftly into formation with him as we climbed away. A few minutes later, all twenty-one Beaufighters were airborne and closing into formation as we set off down the Lincolnshire coast. Crossing the Wash we were soon overhead Coltishall where we could see our fighter escort taking off.

Crossing the Norfolk coast, the wing commander took the formation down to wave-top height, our normal height to avoid radar detection. It was even more exhilarating when flying as part of a large formation skimming the sea. Eric assured me that our fighter escort was in place – comforting knowledge!

Bob Irving, the wing commander's navigator, had set a good course and only one or two small course alterations were needed on the outward journey. Bob had been a promising young musician before the war. He was a Cambridge graduate, an organist and cellist and had taught music at Winchester School. A popular character at North Coates, he gave occasional piano recitals in the cinema and sometimes played the double bass in the station dance band.

Eric constantly checked wind drift and monitored our position. The formation maintained radio silence, and Eric and I spoke little to each other, so suppressing the tension we both felt. I saw Dusky take out his much-loved pipe and put it in his mouth. I'm not sure if he actually lit it!

After some forty minutes Eric said we should be nearing the Dutch coast at Den Helder. He moved forward to cock the four cannons and close the armoured doors, which divided our two cockpits. I peered ahead but the visibility was deteriorating. I locked my gun sight into position and turned off the safety catch on my firing button. Then I saw the wing commander turn to port and the formation turned with him. As soon as we started to climb we could hear the whine in our headphones, which meant that we were now being plotted by German radar. We levelled off at 1,500 feet. I suppose we all felt the tension at that stage, just before the attack – a mixture of excitement, fear and pumping adrenalin. There was no sign of Dusky's pipe now!

Then the convoy came into view, just off the island of Texel. Bob had done his work well. Eight merchant ships sailed in two lines of four protected by six escorting flak ships and with two minesweepers ahead. As I picked out the flak ship I was to attack, puffs of smoke appeared around us, indicating bursts of heavy flak. At last radio silence was broken as the wing commander called: "Attack! Attack! Attack!"

The formation turned to starboard, the Torbeaus remaining low over the sea and preparing to drop their torpedoes. The rest of us dived towards the flak ships and as I settled into the dive I brought my gun sight to bear on the target and saw cannon shell splashes in the sea move towards the ship. At the same time, tracer shells were rising to meet me. This was the crux of the attack when pilot and ship's gunner faced each other like duellists. The tracer appeared to come straight at us, but today we were lucky and the shells slipped past

Cannon strikes on the convoy attacked on 18 April 1943. (Air Historical Branch C 4381)

or above or below us. At the last moment with my sight still on the ship, I released my two small bombs and skimmed over it and weaved my way through the convoy. Then as we turned away Eric began taking photographs. The largest ship had smoke pouring from her. We learned later that she was the *Höegh Carrier*, which later sank leaving the balloon, carried by all the merchantmen, sticking forlornly out of the water. After the war, when German records were accessible, we were gratified to know that three flak ships were severely damaged and that two of them, one towing the other, had limped into the harbour at Den Helder for repairs.

The *Höegh Carrier* on fire before sinking. (David Ellis)

The release of tension was obvious on our return to North Coates and many of us, in high spirits, indulged in a low-level beat up of the airfield. As we landed, Eric and I could see that most of the station personnel seemed to have come out on the tarmac to meet us. As we taxied into dispersal the welcoming smile on the face of our WAAF driver brought extra warmth to our homecoming.

The debriefing confirmed the success of the strike. Wing Commander Wheeler's tactics had proved viable and his confidence in his crews justified. The element of surprise had been complete and the Germans had been caught off guard. The Luftwaffe had not had time to scramble its fighters and, best of all, the whole wing had come back without loss, only two aircraft having been slightly damaged.

No wonder the beer flowed that night. The wing was stood down but very few aircrews left the station to visit local pubs or girlfriends. We wanted to celebrate together, and we did!

So the future of Coastal Command's anti-shipping war had at last been established. More strikes followed with many successes. The bombs, with their rudimentary aiming techniques were later replaced with rocket projectiles, which proved much more effective and further Strike Wings were formed to operate on the same pattern in other waters. But there was a price to pay and we seldom again escaped without losses, and sometimes the losses were heavy.

Eric Ramsbottom and I completed our tour of operations, and later returned for a second tour together on the same squadron.

Flying on this operation in the torpedo section was navigator **Raymond Price** and he explains the role of 254 Squadron.

I had been on 254 Squadron since December 1941 when we flew the Blenheim. In early June 1942 the first of our Beaufighters arrived and I crewed up with Flying Officer 'Del' Wright. After moving to North Coates we learnt that our squadron would carry torpedoes when it was decided that we would bring up the rear of the formation in the hope that the heavy flak would be concentrated on the leading squadrons as they dived on the targets.

Our main problem was sighting the torpedoes to get a hit on the target ship. They had to be released at a height of 100 feet and a range of 1,000 yards. They had to be offset from the target depending on the speed of the target. This was a very difficult task for the pilots to carry out because there were no 'sights' provided in the aircraft for the attack. It just had to be estimated so we carried out a lot of training.

Del Wright and Raymond Price. (Mrs Wright)

Ground crew load an eighteen-inch Mk. XV torpedo, May 1943. (Air Historical Branch CH 9768)

On 18 April 1943 we took off to attack a convoy off the Dutch coast. As this was the wing's first real operation and, knowing we would be meeting the enemy face-to-face, we were all excited and apprehensive and, I suspect, a bit afraid. After an hour's flying we sighted the convoy of some eight ships, which was surrounded by a variety of flak ships. We closed up the formation and climbed to about 1,000 feet in order to view the convoy more clearly and started closing for the attack. Almost immediately the convoy saw us and fired at us with everything they had. My immediate reaction was one of awe at how pretty the trails of tracer bullets were coupled with the fact that at any time something could hit us in a vulnerable spot and down our aircraft. However, in spite of this, I had work to do and as we closed the convoy I had to assess the make-up of the convoy and escorts and take as many photographs as possible.

As we approached, Del decided on his target which was dead ahead and was a 5,000-ton cargo vessel. We then dropped down to 100 feet, adjusted our speed to the operational rate for dropping torpedoes, kept straight and level and offset our sighting by 'Mk. 1 Eyeball' before dropping our torpedo. This process took some two minutes in all during which we were most conscious of what sitting ducks we and the other torpedo-carrying aircraft were. We were lucky however, and were not hit by flak. As soon as the torpedo had been released we weaved up and down and approached the convoy, which was only a few hundred yards ahead of us. We were firing our four cannons all the time at the target and as we were about to fly over the convoy at mast height I managed to take a photograph of the ship's bows, which subsequently revealed its name. It was the *Höegh Carrier*, which the intelligence staffs back at base were absolutely delighted with as there was no doubt then what ship we had actually attacked. They were eventually able to establish what cargo she was carrying and from where.

Photograph taken from Del Wright's aircraft as he dropped the torpedo that struck the *Höegh Carrier*. (Mrs Wright)

The cream on the cake for Del and I was that we learnt later that we had scored a direct hit on the vessel with our torpedo. We considered this to be quite an achievement as it had been worked out that it required nine torpedoes to be dropped in order to guarantee one hit. All three squadrons had learnt quite a lot from this sortie. The main lesson learnt however was that the torpedo squadron should definitely be in the rear and Del and I heartily agreed.

> Neil Wheeler had a long and distinguished career in the RAF and retired in 1976 as Air Chief Marshal Sir Neil Wheeler GCB, CBE, DSO, DFC & Bar, AFC.
>
> At the end of his tour, David Ellis was awarded the DFC. He completed a second tour with 236 Squadron and left the RAF at the end of the war.
>
> After completing his tour on 254 Squadron, Ray Price later crewed up with New Zealander Wing Commander Bill Sise who took command of 248 Squadron flying the Mosquito as part of the Banff Strike Wing. Price was twice awarded the DFC and retired from the RAF as a group captain in 1973. His pilot Del Wright was awarded the DFC and remained in the RAF when he commanded a Canberra squadron and flew a Valiant on a bombing raid during the Suez crisis. He retired as a wing commander.

CHAPTER SIX

CONSPICUOUS GALLANTRY

Max 'Maurice' Guedj and Charles Corder. (Mrs Sue Rawcliffe)

Charles Corder completed his air observer training in September 1941 and was posted to 2 (Coastal) OTU based at RAF Catfoss near Hornsea in Yorkshire to convert to the Beaufighter. Here he was crewed up with Sous Lieutenant Max Guedj, an airman who had responded to General de Gaulle's exhortations and escaped from his native France to join the Free French Forces. It was the beginning of an outstanding flying team. At this point the authorities decided that to safeguard his Jewish family living in Vichy-held France, Guedj should adopt the alias 'Maurice', and for the rest of his service he was known by this name. The two men were to remain together until April 1943. Corder takes up their story.

Our last fight at Catfoss was in mid February 1942 and we joined 248 Squadron at the end of the month. We flew our first operation, a six-hour search for enemy shipping in the Skagerrak, on 1 April. For the next two months we operated out of Dyce and Sumburgh on convoy escorts, enemy shipping searches and line patrols. On one occasion we searched for a Dutch ship escaping to the UK.

Just after 1800 hours on 17 May we took off as part of an escort to Beauforts sent to attack the heavy-cruiser *Prinz Eugen*, which had an escort of four destroyers. We were allocated one of the destroyers as our target. The Beaus went in first to draw the fire and to allow the Beauforts to drop their torpedoes. Our Beaus were fitted with four 20-mm cannons and six machine guns. At that time the cannons were drum fed (later belt fed). To change the drums involved the navigator crawling along the catwalk between the pilot and navigator in semi-darkness, removing the empty drum and replacing it with a new heavy one. While carrying out this procedure I was unable to advise the pilot of any enemy aircraft approaching from the rear.

Maurice carried out three attacks on the destroyer before we returned to base where we were told that we should have made only one. By this time I began to realise that my pilot was dedicated to winning World War Two on his own as well as being an ace fighter pilot.

After the *Prinz Eugen* attack my logbook shows that we were stationed at Sumburgh in the Shetlands until early August 1942 when half the squadron was sent to Malta via

Beaufighter Ic formation of 248 Squadron. (Mrs Sue Rawcliffe)

Gibraltar to provide an escort for a large convoy of supplies and fuel for which Malta was in great need.

The convoy was named 'Pedestal'. We were to be the escort until it came into range of the Malta-based Spitfires. We saw the convoy just after it entered the Mediterranean and as we headed for Malta. On arrival at Takali we were tasked to attack airfields in Sardinia and we strafed aircraft at Decimomannu. We lost a Beaufighter on an early sortie and, at first light the next morning four us set off to search for the dinghy, which was found in roughly the right position and one aircraft was left to continue circling the dinghy. Late in the afternoon it was our turn to take over the patrol. We dropped rations near the dinghy and continued circling. After some time Maurice called, "I've lost it". I decided on a square search with frequent changes of course and soon Maurice called that he had it in sight again.

We continued circling waiting for the arrival of a Cant seaplane captured a few days before and now used by the RAF on Malta for rescue work only. After a while a flying boat arrived and started circling with us. Maurice contacted Malta and was told that there were no friendly aircraft in the area but "do not attack it unless it attacks you!" We continued circling with the flying boat for some twenty minutes when Malta signalled us to let the flying boat (a Dornier 24) rescue the occupants of the dinghy. Maurice twice had to fire shots into the sea close to the dinghy to help the rescue crew locate it in the failing light. The Dornier landed and we saw the occupants of the dinghy taken aboard. We then returned to Malta knowing they would become POWs rather than perish in the Mediterranean.

Twenty-nine years later I received a letter from a Generale Antonio Cumbat thanking me for helping to save his life in 1942! He had checked Allied and other records and contacted everyone remotely connected with that incident. He told me that on that day he and his colleague could not understand why Beaufighters were continually circling his dinghy and also that when they were taken on board the Dornier 24 the pilot said, "You should thank the Ju 88 for saving your life". Tonci replied, "That was a Beaufighter not a Ju 88!"

I started corresponding with Tonci and his wife, and my wife and I visited them. We met regularly and remained close friends for many years. We also became good friends with the Dornier co-pilot.

After the remains of 'Pedestal' arrived in Malta we left our Beaufighters in the Middle East and returned to Gibraltar where we boarded a ship for Gourock.

In September the squadron flew south to Talbenny in Pembrokeshire to bolster the long-range fighter force patrolling the Bay of Biscay in support of the increasing anti-U-boat patrols mounted by Coastal Command in the area. This increased activity seeking out the U-boats based in the Atlantic coast ports of France had drawn a response from the Luftwaffe who had based long-range Junkers 88 fighters at Mérignac, Bordeaux. On the 27th we were escorting a Whitley over the Bay when we encountered a Junkers 88, which we attacked and damaged.

For the next three months, we flew many patrols over the Biscay. The Beaufighters usually operated in formations of four sweeping the areas patrolled by Coastal Command's anti-submarine aircraft.

We moved to Predannack on the Lizard Peninsular in January 1943 and this gave us more time on patrol. On 10 March four of us took off on a line patrol into the Bay of Biscay when we sighted a Junkers 88. The leader attacked but his cannons jammed and, after the other two had attacked, Maurice closed in and we attacked from dead astern. Sitting in the back of our aircraft I could see the Ju 88 over Maurice's shoulder as he gave a long burst of fire as we got closer and closer and I began to feel that he was going to ram it. The port engine burst into flames and the fire quickly spread to the rest of the aircraft as it dived away. Unfortunately for us the Ju 88 had a belly gunner firing backwards and our aircraft sustained serious damage.

The port engine failed, the pilot's instruments were damaged and the starboard wing and aileron were also damaged. A big problem was the failure of the intercom and I couldn't speak to Maurice. We had over 150 miles to go over the sea before we could reach base. It seemed hopeless but I had every confidence in Maurice to whom I gave a course to Bishop's Rock. With only one engine he had great difficulty in keeping above the waves. He managed by flying up-and-down in a porpoise-like manner. After reaching base I discovered that Maurice had considered ditching and then the coast appeared.

> In this account, Corder makes virtually no mention of his role in this dramatic episode. The day after the event, his flight commander, Squadron Leader Burton DFC, asked **Maurice** to describe Corder's actions. This is what he submitted.

As requested, I have the honour of giving you the following information regarding Flight Sergeant Corder's behaviour during our last sortie in the Bay of Biscay.

As soon as the Junkers 88 went down in flames, the intercom was put out of order. Flight Sergeant Corder crawled through the cockpit and, standing behind the pilot worked out an accurate course home.

He then went back to his seat and tried to contact the other Beaufighters by Aldis lamp in order to get them to escort aircraft 'W' which seemed badly shot up. Finding that the Aldis lamp was out of order, he came once more to assist his pilot who was trying to pull back the pitch control lever on the port side; stuck in the fully fine position. Flight Sergeant Corder tried himself but the lever came off in his hand and nothing else could be done to it. He then endeavoured for ten minutes to turn the petrol cock on the port tank from the 'outers' position to the 'inners' position but unsuccessfully since the cable had been cut by the same bullet that jammed the pitch control lever. Apart from this damage, a quick check showed the following hits; a bullet strike on the windscreen just in front of the pilot's head, one bullet through the climb and descent instrument, one between the altimeter and the gyro artificial horizon, three big holes in the starboard wing, one-third of the starboard aileron missing and the starboard air intake shot away. The hydraulics were also out of order. It was found later that shells had hit both engines and that the pilot had sustained superficial wounds caused by very minor shrapnel in the head and the thighs.

In view of the apparent damage, Flight Sergeant Corder immediately went to his seat and advised group by W/T, receiving an answer in a few minutes. He then was able to re-join the intercom just in time to hear that the port engine had failed and been switched off.

As the port airscrew was still in fully fine pitch, the aircraft could not maintain height and came gradually down to 500 feet. Flight Sergeant Corder very calmly endeavoured to get QDM's from base. So accurate did he give the first course immediately after the combat, no alteration of course was necessary with both course and QDM, being 069 (no wind). By that time, the aircraft was flying at sea level in a semi-stalled condition at 125 knots. Instructed to get ready for ditching, Flight Sergeant Corder managed to send an SOS by W/T giving once more the position of the aircraft.

Soon after, the good starboard engine caught fire and oil started burning in the cockpit. Flight Sergeant Corder then sent another SOS, still remaining perfectly cool.

The crew then sighted land and Flight Sergeant Corder, still thinking that a ditching was imminent, for the aircraft was flying with one engine on fire, the other one in fully fine pitch and with one aileron damaged, seemed difficult to control, decided to fire some Verey cartridges in order to draw attention of people ashore, ships or aircraft that might have been flying in the vicinity. He thus fired every two minutes until no more cartridges were left.

As the aircraft could gain no more height, Flight Sergeant Corder directed it towards the lowest cliff on the Lizard so that the pilot could cross the coast, which was done with a clearance of a few feet.

Immediately afterwards, when he was told the aircraft was going to crash land straight ahead on the aerodrome, Flight Sergeant Corder calmly took the necessary actions.

After the crash landing, as the aircraft was on fire, he got out immediately and came to the front exit hatch to see if his pilot had been able to get out himself. As it was, the pilot was already out.

By his very accurate navigation, his resourcefulness as wireless operator and his coolness throughout, Flight Sergeant Corder undoubtedly saved the crew. He is the perfect observer. He is the better part of the crew.

> This remarkably modest account of a desperate situation not only reflects great credit on Corder but also the 'pilot', Maurice. Corder later wrote, 'I would never fly with anyone else. He is a wonderful pilot.'
>
> A month later it was announced that Flying Officer Maurice had been awarded the DSO, an award rarely made to such a junior officer. He was also the first Frenchman to be awarded both the DSO and the DFC (he would go on to earn a second DFC). Corder was recommended for the immediate award of the DFM but the air officer commanding-in-chief upgraded the award to the Conspicuous Gallantry Medal (CGM), second only to the Victoria Cross and one of only 110 awarded to airmen. The citation for Corder's award concluded, 'In the face of an appalling situation, this airman displayed skill and courage in keeping with the highest traditions of the Royal Air Force'.
>
> A special luncheon, with the menu written in French, was held at Predannack in honour of Maurice, attended by the AOC (Air Vice-Marshal G. Bromet) who presented him with the DSO and DFC. Corder received his CGM from HM King George VI at an investiture at Buckingham Palace. A few weeks later the French authorities awarded both men the Croix de Guerre avec Palme. **Charles Corder** continues.

Four more operations in April 1943 completed our tour – my logbook records seventy-five trips covering 294 hours. During our tour Maurice was awarded the DSO and the DFC. After a break he returned to our old squadron as a squadron leader and finally as CO of 143 Squadron. He was awarded a Bar to his DFC. He was shot down with I believe four others over Norway on 15 January 1945 when leading sixteen Mosquitos.

After our first tour I was sent on a squadron navigator officer course and was eventually posted to a Canadian squadron (No. 404) and flew with the CO, Wing Commander E.W. Pierce, first on Beaufighters and then Mosquitos in the Banff Wing. I have a letter from Maurice saying that he had tried to get me back with him but a squadron can only have one squadron navigation officer.

With just a few months before the end of the war, the quiet and thoughtful thirty-two-year-old Wing Commander Max Guedj ('Maurice') DSO, DFC and Bar, Officier de

Aircrew of 248 Squadron (CO Wing Commander Montague-Smith) in May 1943.
Corder is on the far left in the rear row with Maurice seated third from right. (Mrs Sue Rawcliffe)

la Legion d'Honneur, Croix de Guerre avec huit (eight) Palmes, Croix de la Liberation, Médaille de la Resistance avec Rosette, Norwegian War Medal, who had flown 150 operations, and the man many believe to be France's greatest wartime pilot in the RAF, was lost.

> In memory of his pilot, Corder and his wife christened their son Maurice. As soon as the war was over he flew to France to see Guedj's mother and wife. A lifetime family friendship was formed and he was present in 1977 at the French Air Force Academy, Salon to witness the graduation of the 1973 class of pilots who were given the name of Max Guedj. Corder was presented with a detailed scale model of their Beaufighter. He returned to France again in June 1995 when he was presented with the tie of the Free French Air Force to wear at a ceremony the following day when the French Air Force's pilot training school at Evreux was given the name Max Guedj, thus ensuring that his gallant memory will remain with today's and future generations of French pilots.

CHAPTER SEVEN

EARLY OPERATIONS OFF NORWAY

Des Curtis. (Des Curtis)

No. 235 Squadron was one of the first three Coastal Command squadrons to be equipped with the Beaufighter. At the end of 1942 the squadron moved to RAF Leuchars in Fife where it flew patrols and reconnaissance sorties along the Norwegian coast.

Des Curtis joined the squadron during 1942. He describes the role of the navigator on a reconnaissance sortie to Norway in early 1943.

The preparations for a single-aircraft reconnaissance flight from Scotland onto the Norwegian coast in a Bristol Beaufighter began with a briefing in the operations room. The essential features were; identify the part of the Norwegian coast to be covered, the time to commence the search, any reports on ship movements, and, from the met officer, a description of the likely weather en route and on patrol. The intelligence officer then issued a small escape 'purse', containing maps on silk, some Norwegian and Swedish money, a compass and some dry food. The signals officer listed the wireless frequencies to be used, then handed out a SYKO coding machine and the card of codes in use for that period, along with a Verey pistol with cartridges of the colours of the day. The crew were told which aircraft were assigned to patrol on either side of their flight. Pictures of lighthouses with the flashing/occulting sequences were important to verify landmarks.

The navigator then entered basic information onto the front page of the four A4-page flight log - the ETD (estimated time of departure), barometric pressure, the en route weather forecast, including wind speeds and directions. The Dalton computer was not a sophisticated device with microchips; it was a logarithmic chart, which was unrolled within a metal box, and covered by a Perspex disc, on which a triangle of velocities could quickly and easily be drawn. The track to be followed would be set on the outer ring, and by plotting the wind speed and direction, the course to steer was shown. He then plotted on a chart, about twenty inches by twelve inches, the tracks to be followed and the initial course to steer, and the ETA at the patrol area. The remaining pages of the log would be completed during the flight.

The next thing was to empty his green canvas 'nav bag' onto the table, and check every item as they were stowed back into the bag - pencils, sharpener, eraser, parallel ruler, dividers, protractor, Dalton computer, floating torch, the log clipped to a board, the chart clipped to a board, and the SYKO machine. All went into the bag, which measured about two feet square and as bulging as the contents made it.

He would make sure that a whistle was attached to his battledress collar, then stuff the escape pack into an inside pocket of his battledress jacket. Flying dress comprised long cotton underwear, a white oil-wool sweater, scarf, battledress and an Irving leather jacket. Fleece-lined leather flying boots, with a flat knife tucked inside, a pair of woollen gloves worn over a pair of silk gloves completed the dress.

On the way out to the squadron's flight office he would stop at stores to collect a handheld camera and a carrier pigeon in its cage.

From his locker in the flight office he would don the bulky Mae West life jacket and a parachute harness, pick up his leather helmet and a parachute pack. Weighted down with all this paraphernalia, he would climb into the truck to be taken to the aircraft. An armourer would be waiting to hand over a Vickers machine gun and two pans of .303-ins ammunition, for which he had to have a signature. Often, all this would be taking place in the dark or at first light.

The fuselage of the Beaufighter was just over 41 feet long, and at its highest, 19 feet. The navigator's position was halfway along the fuselage. Entry for both pilot and navigator was by way of trap doors; the pilot's door flap held a stowable ladder. The trap door for the navigator, facing forward when lowered, had a small toehold built in. The bottom of the fuselage was so near the ground that he had to bend right down before letting his head come up in the fuselage.

Standing nearly six feet tall, this was not easy for me. Once my head was through the trap door and I was standing upright, I would reach down for all my 'appendages', shoving them onto the metal floor on either side of the trap door. Finally, I would then haul myself into my tiny 'operations cabin', which would be home for the next four or five hours.

Standing astride the trap door, with my head bent low in the cupola, I would haul the door shut by way of a cable, then step down, both to ensure that the door was properly fastened and to give me a little bit of extra headroom that I needed.

The first stage of getting organised in the aircraft then began, often by the light of only a small lamp on a flexible mount. A swivel chair was bolted to the floor to the rear of the hatch well - this locked in the fore and aft positions. When the navigator was facing forward, mounted to his left was the wireless receiving and transmitting sets, below which was a Morse key. Below the sets was the aerial reel. The carrier pigeon, in its metal cage, would be placed on the floor below the wireless. On that same side was the rubber pee-bottle. That had to be checked to be sure it was empty. The golden rule was that if you used the bottle, you emptied it on leaving the aircraft. But I was to discover on one flight, not everyone was so thoughtful!

To the half right was a fold-down table, which would be the working surface. Below that the 'nav bag' would be propped up, at that stage still containing all the bits and pieces. During take-off, the machine gun and ammunition pans, bulky items, had to be stored on the floor in such a way that they would not slide away. Lastly, the parachute pack was hung on the fuselage wall in rubber straps.

Up front, the pilot would position his parachute and harness so that when he sat, the parachute filled the hollow seat, and he could pull the harness straps down and across his

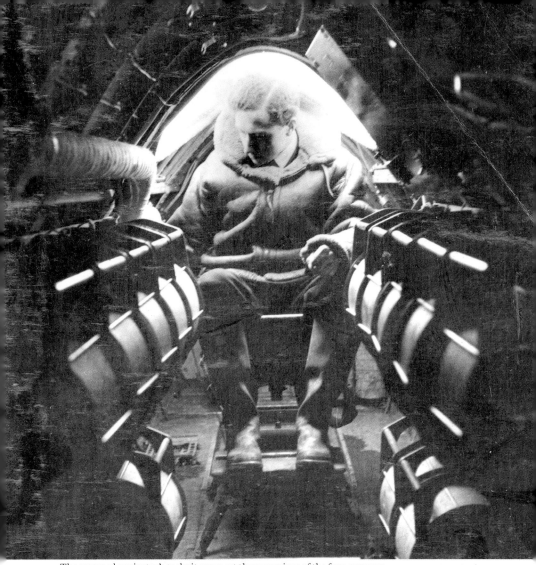

The cramped navigator's cockpit amongst the magazines of the four cannons.
(Air Historical Branch CH 17304)

body. Then he would complete his cockpit checks, starting the two big Hercules radial engines and preparing to taxi for take-off. I would switch on the wireless power, check that the intercom was working, and confirm that I was ready for take-off. Once airborne, I would confirm the course to steer and height to fly.

As soon as the aircraft had levelled off, I would note the take-off time and enter it into the log then work through the jobs in sequence. First, the trailing aerial had to be unwound. This aerial was 190 feet long with lead weights at the end to keep it stable. Wireless reception, with the T1154 and R1155 equipment, was virtually impossible until the aerial was extended. Before landing I had to remember to wind it in by hand on to its reel. Otherwise it could trail across power cables or catch in trees. It was not unknown for the aerial to be severed as the aircraft flew low level over a target ship.

Then it was time to look to our defences - setting up the machine gun. A hole had been cut at the rear of the cupola and just beyond the hole a spigot was welded to the fuselage. Putting the woollen gloves on, I would then climb down from the seat, pick up the gun and, with my left hand, push it through the hole until I could reach out and locate the swivel mount on to the spigot, finally locking it with a pin on a chain with my right hand. Then back down to pick up one of the ammunition pans and fix it on to the breech of the gun and check that the safety switch was set to ON. Further down the fuselage was a metal interrupter, which was there to prevent the navigator shooting off the tail fin as he swivelled the gun. The reserve ammunition pan would be strapped, with a rubber band, near the gun. Once the gun was mounted the trigger handles were only inches behind the navigator. If I swung round to the rear rapidly, the handles would hit my cheek with a painful whack. It was all very World War I stuff.

Then the wireless frequencies had to be checked – making sure that the 'click stops' locked on exactly to the frequencies we would use during the flight. The Morse key had to be locked off to prevent any accidental transmissions.

It was time to get down to work. The chart table would be let down and I could start to write up the centre pages of the log. The chart had to be put on the floor, as there was no space for both chart and log on the table. I could only take from the nav bag whatever was immediately needed.

The first log entries would state the time airborne, the actual time of setting course, the heading and height, then observations on cloud and sea conditions. For most of the outward flight we would be beyond the range of detection by German radar. Normally that part of the flight would be flown at 1,000 feet or at the cloud base, so there was plenty of time to do the chores. Part of a Coastal Command navigator's training was to be able to accurately assess the wind speed and direction by looking at the waves on the sea below. The longer the trail of spume as the wave broke, the stronger the wind. With a handheld compass it was easy to read off the wind direction. Each observation was recorded and small changes of course and ETA calculated.

My pilot, Doug Turner, was, like me, a heavy smoker. We would not be long into the flight before he would call up on the intercom; "How about a cigarette?" To give him a lighted cigarette meant undoing my harness, putting away all the navigation instrument and papers, folding back the table, then climbing forward – head well down – through the fuselage, over the main spar and through the armoured door, which was providing protection for the pilot. I would then stand in the well space behind the pilot, while lighting a couple of cigarettes. Dropping a lighted match or cigarette was not permitted – for our own safety!

Returning to my chart table I would confirm that all the guns were cocked before turning my attention again to the state of the sea. I would also resume listening out for any message for us.

About sixty miles from the Norwegian coast, Doug would bring the Beaufighter down to sea level, literally skimming over the waves and he would slowly increase speed. We would be getting within range of German radars and would be vulnerable to German fighters from the nearby airfields.

Navigation was set aside for the time being, apart from giving Doug a course to steer for the return leg in the event that I became a casualty. I would lock my seat so that I was facing backwards, turn off the safety catch on the machine gun and check that the camera was close at hand. My eyes would begin to scan the sky and sea looking for enemy activity of any kind.

Doug would then come up on the intercom to say that he could see land ahead. I would turn and start looking for landmarks. We would make our landfall at one of the islands that lie off the mainland and turn to make our reconnaissance along the leads that the ships used between the islands. Each fjord had to be checked carefully. The dark hull of a ship was not easily picked out against the grey background of the mountains. Doug would increase the speed to maximum cruising in straight and level flight.

The patrol was often along a fairly short stretch of coast – sometimes as little as thirty miles. The end of the patrol line was usually one of the many lighthouses when we turned out to sea, still at sea level and set course for home. This was not a time to relax as by then the Germans had sighted us and had time to send fighters in pursuit. We could breathe again when we were about sixty miles from Norway.

The task of the recce aircraft was to seek out, and report back and describe any likely target. We were not to attack any of the targets and would only fight in self-defence. There would be little purpose in exposing a recce aircraft to unnecessary risk, as the information would not get back to base.

Very often there was nothing worthy of note but if any shipping was sighted, we would approach close enough to take photographs and to note the type and size of each ship. I would plot the precise position of the ships and the time. As soon as it was safe to take my eyes off the sea and sky, I would compose a message to base giving all possible information, including weather, cloud base etc. Then I would take the SYKO machine and convert the message to code. Doug would, in the meantime, be climbing to a height of 6-7,000 feet to give a better signal strength. I would tap out the message on the Morse key and wait for an acknowledgement. Group HQ would then decide what action to mount against the targets that we had identified, without waiting for us to return to base.

Our pigeon was resting in its cage on the floor, possibly wondering if he would get the chance to practise his homing skills. If we had been hit and forced to ditch, I would have to make sure that I carried our friend out to the dinghy. Once in the dinghy, I would write on a tiny piece of paper our call sign and latitude and longitude of our position and time, roll up the paper and put it into the tube on the pigeon's leg before releasing it to fly home. That would give the RAF a chance to send a rescue craft to pick us up. The bird was only carried on a single-aircraft mission. In a formation of aircraft, the loss of one aircraft would be reported by one of the others.

The weather often played tricks on these flights. Coastal fog was fairly common in calm weather. It could be very dense but relatively shallow. In no circumstances was it wise to fly into fog since there was the danger of flying into what we called a 'stuffed cloud' – high ground obscured by the fog. So, the only solution was to climb above the fog, looking for breaks that might afford the chance to descend back to sea level to carry out the mission. This was a very dangerous time as an enemy fighter might suddenly appear in range. There was one occasion when our recce was the middle of three flights covering a long stretch of coast. We encountered the fog along almost the entire patrol area; the two outside aircraft flew in sunshine all the way.

The Germans were obviously more alert when a convoy of ships was in the area. If a convoy was sighted, the sensible thing to do was to quickly record its composition, location, course and speed, take some photographs and then get away from the coast as fast as possible. German fighters would arrive from airfields such as Stavanger and soon be able to engage us. That meant taking evasive action each time the fighter attacked whilst heading out to sea. My 'peashooter' Vickers gun had a totally ineffective gun sight but one in four rounds was tracer. My only hope was that by firing I might upset the fighter pilot's concentration. If the enemy aircraft crossed from port to starboard, my burst of fire would be interrupted as the muzzle of the Vickers came up to the interrupter. It would have been an entire fluke had I succeeded in doing any mortal damage.

The navigation back to Leuchars would have some approximations built in because any evasion could mean we were well off track. The important thing in such a situation was to use the wireless to get some bearings and work out a corrected course back to base.

Once R/T contact had been established with ground control, it was time to switch off the wireless set and to wind in the trailing aerial. Then I had to take the gun from its mountings, stow away all the instruments and charts into the nav bag, lock the seat into the forward-facing position and wait for my pilot to make an exhibition landing. The four or five hours of tension were behind us, and then, after debriefing by the intelligence officer, it was off to the mess for a hearty English 'aircrew' breakfast.

> Another important role for 235 Squadron during its time at Leuchars was to escort Hampden torpedo bombers on shipping strikes. As these activities increased in early 1943, the Luftwaffe reinforced its fighter squadrons operating from Stavanger and other airfields in southern Norway. **Aubrey 'Hilly' Hilliard** describes his encounter with a Focke-Wulf 190.

I was stationed at Leuchars as a sergeant pilot on 235 Squadron. My navigator was Sergeant Jim Hoyle. Our task on 3 March 1943 was to escort torpedo-carrying Hampdens of 455 Squadron RAAF to the Norwegian coast, arriving about thirty minutes before dusk. We were after enemy shipping and the sortie was carried out at low level, 500 feet or lower. We were flying in a Beaufighter Ic 'A' for Apple and it was our ninth operational sortie.

As the Beaufighters (about six) were faster than the six Hampdens we had to orbit them in a wide circle in line astern. The weather was good; broken cloud at 6-7,000 feet with a visibility of about ten miles. On an easterly heading nearing the south coast of Norway near Stavanger, my position was the rear aircraft (tail-end Charlie) of the formation, when Jim called, "enemy aircraft to starboard coming towards us".

He immediately realised the information he had given me was wrong as he was keeping watch facing backwards (he could swivel his seat to do so). The enemy aircraft on his right was actually on my left!

At the same time as Jim initiated the call I saw the enemy at the 9-10 o'clock position about 400 yards away closing, so I did a steep turn towards him to increase his deflection. He had already fired his guns and Jim recalled it was like someone 'banging a dustbin lid' as the shells hit us. The fighter pulled up and crossed our path from right to left and we recognised it as a FW 190 not more than 200 feet above.

At this stage, the formation had turned south along the coast but a long way off. The FW 190 continued in a port turn towards the north-east as I levelled out heading south-west. He came in again at four o'clock and fired at us at a range of 800 yards closing. I noticed he was using tracer so again I turned sharply to starboard in a steep turn towards him and in no time he pulled up crossing from right to left.

Aubrey 'Hilly' Hilliard.
(via Andrew Thomas)

Everything was happening so damned quickly, the 190 was extremely fast, the Beaufighter on the other hand was shuddering at 250 knots! As soon as he crossed over I continued the starboard turn and levelled out heading west.

During the combat when the fighter was attacking from behind, I carried out 'corkscrew evasive action' by diving to port then climbing and turning to starboard on top of the climb, then diving again, repeating the action as necessary. This action was being carried out from 0-700 feet and, as you can imagine, executing steep turns and 'skipping the waves' was hair-raising in itself, let alone being attacked by an enemy fighter at the same time. On one occasion when I was at very low level most of his tracer was going over the top of us.

Unfortunately, the Beaufighter I was flying was the only one on the squadron that had a white fuselage, which must have stood out clearly. Also, we did not have a rear gun. Some had the Vickers and others had the better Browning. Jim gave me good positions using the clock code, of where the 190 was when it was out of my sight, so I could take the appropriate action. More attacks took place and each time I took evasive action to avoid his fire and then turned west to get further away from the enemy coast.

The attacks lasted for about ten minutes and he had hit us several times in the starboard engine and wing. I saw the tracer go in, but I was unable to make an attack on him, as he was too manoeuvrable. To my advantage I was able to fly lower than he could. That was due to the excellent cockpit vision from the Beaufighter, compared with his restricted forward vision when very low. His last attack came from the rear with daylight fading and nearly dark. His tracer was high, as I was still very low, and then there was no enemy fire. On reflection, he would probably have done better by throttling back and attacking from 6 o'clock high.

At times I thought we would have to ditch and I glanced at the red release handle on my cockpit hood for just such an emergency, but it turned out not to be necessary – thank goodness.

After the engagement I climbed to 5,000 feet. It was now dark and the starboard engine had lost some oil pressure and was running rough so I reduced the revs to nurse it along. When we were some 200 miles from the Scottish coast, Jim got a QDM (course to steer) from Leuchars. After a few minutes he informed me that the wireless had been damaged.

By this time, Jim had got down to his navigation to make a reasonable landfall. He recalled he put a dot on the chart roughly in the middle of where we had been in combat then gave me a course to steer, which would take us north of Leuchars. He reasoned that a navigation error would be better made to the north of base rather than to the south with the possibility of getting mixed up in the Firth of Forth defence area. The starboard engine seemed to have settled down with the reduced revs, although I was apprehensive about the drop in oil pressure and whether the engine would last out.

Having checked his DR (dead reckoning) navigation Jim called me to look out for the flashing light at Rattray Head. We were now flying in and out of cloud and a little later I spotted an intermittent light at about 1 o'clock. "Keep it in sight," he called with some gusto, as it was indeed Rattray Head.

I descended to keep below the broken cloud. By this time the moon was up, which helped when we made landfall just south of Aberdeen having seen the flashing pundit at Dyce airfield. We then followed the coast south to head for Leuchars. On the way, however, I saw runway lights appearing just inland. They were set up for a westerly landing and all I had to do was make a ninety-degree turn to be on finals. So, after a quick re-think I told Jim I was going to land there.

Hilliard's damaged Beaufighter Ic T3295 after landing at Arbroath. (via Andrew Thomas)

I made a good approach and landing, as I couldn't afford to overshoot and go round again with a damaged starboard engine. Although I had to ground loop at the end of the runway, due to break failure, coming to rest in front of a large and sturdy post. The time was 2035 hours. We had been airborne for almost five hours and it was good to be safe on the ground again.

We had landed at the Fleet Air Arm station, HMS Condor at Arbroath. It was fortunate we did not head for Leuchars since a Beaufighter had crash-landed and blocked the runway. This led to others being diverted to Arbroath.

We inspected our aircraft in the morning to find cannon holes in the fuselage, starboard engine, wing and at the base of Jim's seat. The engine and wing were covered in oil and I don't think the Bristol Hercules engine, which had done its job, would have lasted much longer. Old faithful 'A' for Apple never flew again and was eventually replaced by a new Beaufighter VI.

> Des Curtis, 'Hilly' Hilliard and Jim Hoyle were founder members of 618 Squadron established with the Mosquito VI. The aircraft were to carry a modified version of Barnes Wallis' 'bouncing bomb' (Highball) to be used against enemy ships. Curtis was later posted to 248 Squadron and was awarded the DFC. Hilliard also received the DFC and went on along with Hoyle to survive the war.

CHAPTER EIGHT

DIARY OF A STRIKE WING PILOT

George Dowding DFC RCAF.
(Ian McIntosh)

George Dowding RCAF kept a diary of his operational sorties with 254 Squadron of the North Coates Wing.

This fascinating diary, which has been amplified by the official Coastal Command reports, provides a graphic illustration of the work of the Strike Wings in the period leading up to D-Day and the activities in the months that followed.

The diary indicates that crews were tasked only when there was a positive sighting or report of enemy activity and, even then, numerous sorties failed to find a target. Attacks made in force had spectacular results. Dowding's diary also highlights the variety of operations, both by day and by night. He makes little reference to the intense anti-aircraft fire encountered but the Command reports identify this constant and severe threat.

Another forceful feature is Dowding's press-on spirit continuing with sorties when many would have abandoned them.

4 January 1944   Anti-shipping sweep
                       Beau 'B' (JM 104) - Flying time 1.05 (day)

Just after take-off, ran into storm cloud, which prevented the wing from forming up properly over base. Managed to find one section of formation and proceeded with them to Coltishall to pick up fighter escort. As the weather was bad there too, the leader decided not to carry on operation and all aircraft returned to base.

7 January 1944   Anti-shipping sweep - Ijmuiden to Texel
                       Beau 'N' (JM 215) - Flying time 2.35 (day)

The sweep was carried out in the above area and no shipping was sighted.

28 January 1944   Anti-shipping sweep - Borkum to Terschelling
                       Beau 'M' (JL 954) - Flying time 3.50 (day)

Upon reaching the designated patrol area, the visibility was poor and a sharp turn was necessary to enable wing to carry out the patrol along the coastline without some aircraft being too close to the coast thereby presenting themselves as good targets for the enemy shore batteries. In the resulting confusion caused by the sharp turn, two Beaufighters are believed to have collided and crashed into the sea. The sweep was carried out without any shipping being sighted and the wing returned to base. Morale was pretty low after this trip due to the fact that two Beaufighters with crews (Sgt Yates [254 Sqn] and one crew of 236 Squadron) were lost without any damage being inflicted against the enemy.

29 January 1944   'Conebo' - off Dutch coast
                   Beau 'N' (JM 215) - Flying time 1.55 (1.25 D, 0.30 N)

A dusk anti-shipping sweep by six Beaufighters intended to catch any E-boats or other shipping that might come out of harbour at dusk to make their way by night. The patrol was carried out but no shipping was seen.

30 January 1944   Dart - Borkum to Terschelling
                   Beau 'Z' (JL 952) - Flying time 2.50 (day)

An individual reconnaissance flight sent out for the purpose of searching for shipping and if any was sighted, it would be reported to base, who would organise an attacking force to be sent out to attack it. Nothing was sighted on this patrol.

3 February 1944   Air-sea rescue - off Dutch coast
                   Beau 'V' (JM 395) - Flying time 3.20 (day)

A bomber crew was reported to have ditched in the sea just off the coast. Six Beaufighters were detailed to carry out a search in that area. Nothing was sighted on this patrol.

8 February 1944   'Gilbey' - off Dutch coast
                   Beau 'Q' (JL 828) - Flying time 2.10 (night)

A night trip in co-operation with a Wellington who would look for enemy shipping and, if any found, would drop flares over it so that four Beaufighters could make an attack. The Wellington reported no shipping after completing the patrol, so all aircraft returned to base.

11 February 1944   'Gilbey' - off Dutch coast
                   Beau 'T' (NE 225) - Flying time 1.50 (night)

Late in taking off due to original aircraft being unserviceable. Arrived in patrol area, but again no shipping was reported by the Wellington, so all aircraft returned to base.

29 February 1944   Anti-shipping sweep – Den Helder to Terschelling
                              Beau 'A' (LZ 436) – 2.50 (day)

Sweep carried out in above area and no shipping was sighted.

1 March 1944   Shipping strike – South of Den Helder
                              Beau 'X' (JM 394) – Flying time 2.20 (day)

Shipping attacked. Was flying in anti-flak section, armed with cannons only. Section led by Squadron Leader Gardiner.

Coastal Command Report: Force twenty-one Beaufighters.
Leader: Wing Commander Burns.
Aircraft on anti-shipping patrol escorted by Spitfires of A.D.G.B. sighted convoy comprising M/V of 5-6,000 tons being towed stern first by a large tug, one further tug to seaward and six or seven escort vessels. Four aircraft attacked the M/V with cannon and three with R/P, eight of which scored hits. Seven aircraft attacked leading tug with cannon scoring numerous hits and setting it on fire. The second tug was also hit by cannon fire from one aircraft. The remaining aircraft attacked the escort vessels with cannon fire, one being seriously damaged and possibly on fire, two more being damaged. Very little flak encountered and aircraft suffered no damage or casualties.
Claim: M/V damaged, Escort vessel seriously damaged. Two escort vessels and one tug damaged.

11 March 1944   Intended strike – off Dutch coast
                              Beau 'X' (JM 394) – Flying time 1.55 (day)

A reconnaissance aircraft reported enemy shipping and a force was sent out to attack it, but the weather and visibility were too poor and the leader decided, before the area was reached, to return the force to base.

21 March 1944   Intended strike – off Dutch coast
                              Beau 'U' (JM 338) – Flying time 2.45 (day)

Operating from Tain, Scotland, a force was sent out to attack enemy shipping reported off the Norwegian coast by reconnaissance aircraft. The anti-flak section was flying too fast to enable the torpedo-carrying Beaufighters to keep up with them and still maintain normal petrol consumption – an important item on such a long trip. A misunderstanding between leaders of sections ensued and the leader decided to return the force to base. Was flying in torpedo section, led by Flight Lieutenant Leaver-Power.

29 March 1944   Shipping strike - off Borkum
                   Beau 'G' (NE 216) - Flying time 3.10 (day)

Shipping attacked. Was flying in torpedo section led by Squadron Leader Gardiner. Attack carried out by torpedo on largest merchant vessel, which was sunk, the wreck being found later by reconnaissance aircraft. One Beaufighter of 236 Squadron missing. All other aircraft returned safely.

Coastal Command Report: Twenty-seven Beaufighters.
Leader: Squadron Leader Gardiner.
Aircraft on anti-shipping reconnaissance in force attacked a convoy of sixteen M/Vs in two lines, with five escort vessels, in face of considerable flak. The six aircraft of 254 Squadron all made torpedo attacks, while R/P and the anti-flak escort carried out cannon attacks. Torpedo hits were obtained on M/V 4,000 tons and cannon and R/P damaged a second M/V of 2-2,500 tons and at least three of the other M/Vs. One Beaufighter (of 236 Squadron) was lost as a result of action by two enemy S.E. fighters as the formation turned to attack.
Claim: Two M/Vs seriously damaged, three vessels damaged.

31 March 1944   Anti-shipping sweep - off Dutch coast
                   Beau 'M' (NE 428) - Flying time 1.15 (day)

Due to weather and visibility being poor over the sea, the leader decided to return the force to base before reaching the patrol area.

15 April 1944   Dart - off Norderney
                   Beau 'L' (NE 436) - Flying time 3.25 (2.00 D, 1.25 N)

Taking off at night, arrived in patrol area at dawn and reconnaissance patrol carried out, but no shipping was sighted.

20 April 1944   Shipping strike - off Borkum
                   Beau 'D' (NE 465) - Flying time 3.25 (day)

Shipping attacked. Was flying in torpedo section led by Flying Officer Oakley. One Beaufighter (236 Squadron) was seen to crash into sea during run in to target.

Coastal Command Report: Twenty-four Beaufighters.
Leader: Wing Commander Mitchell.
Aircraft on anti-shipping reconnaissance in force sighted one *Sperrbrecher* (flak ship) and four escort vessels on an easterly course. The torpedo aircraft all attacked the *Sperrbrecher* releasing torpedoes from 120-200

feet at a range of 700–1,000 yards. At least one torpedo hit was seen. R/P and cannon hits were also observed, after which the vessel was burning furiously and her back appeared to be broken. R/P and cannon attacks were carried out on the escort vessels, numerous hits being secured on all of them. As the aircraft left the area the *Sperrbrecher* was seen to blow up and three escorts were on fire, whilst smoke and steam was issuing from the fourth escort. One of the Beaufighters (236 Squadron) has failed to return from this attack.

Claim: One *Sperrbrecher* sunk and four escort vessels damaged.

Torpedo strike off the Frisian Islands in April 1944 and taken from the rear cockpit of a 254 Squadron Beaufighter. (Roy Nesbit)

26 April 1944   Shipping strike - off Terschelling
Beau 'X' (JM 394) - Flying time 4.45 (3.15 D, 1.30 N)

Shipping was attacked. Was flying in torpedo section led by Squadron Leader Gardiner. Just before releasing torpedo, aircraft was hit by light flak from one of the escort vessels. However, attack was carried out and returned to base. Before attempting to land, tried to lower undercarriage and flaps but discovered that hydraulic system had been damaged. As several aircraft had been hit, it was quite a job for control to get all the aircraft down safely. Had to circle for some time while the other aircraft landed, so there would be a clear area for a crash landing at Donna Nook. Eventually made a night landing with undercarriage retracted and without flaps, no damage being sustained by the crew of two, although both shaken up slightly. On arriving back at base, discovered that Flying Officer Kelshall was missing, no one seeing what happened to him during the attack.

Coastal Command Report: Twenty-four Beaufighters.

Leader:Flight Lieutenant Ivey.

Aircraft on anti-shipping patrol located a convoy consisting of two M/Vs of 1–1,500 tons followed by two M/Vs of 3–4,000 tons with a further two M/Vs of 2,000 tons astern, forming two columns, with four escort vessels, one leading the convoy, two to port and one to starboard and an unidentified escort vessel inshore at the rear. Attacks were carried out by the torpedo aircraft on the M/Vs but apart from a burst of smoke seen rising from the stern of one of the vessels attacked, no results were observed by these aircraft. However, other aircraft of the formation saw one torpedo hit on a M/V of 2,000 tons whilst a large explosion was also seen on another vessel towards the rear of the convoy. Other aircraft made cannon and R/P attacks and although no hits with R/P were seen, many cannon strikes were registered on the M/Vs and E/Vs. One of the E/Vs to port of the convoy was seen to burst into flames from stern to bridge and a number of explosions were seen on deck, whilst another E/V to the rear of the convoy was smoking furiously. Intense heavy and light flak was experienced, and seven of the aircraft sustained damage, whilst another (254 Squadron) failed to return. Photographs taken during the attack confirmed that a M/V of 2,000 tons was torpedoed and a M/V of 3–4,000 tons was damaged. An E/V was seen on fire and probably blew up.

27 April 1944   Air-sea rescue – off Dutch coast
                       Beau 'L' (NE 436) – Flying time 2.30 (day)

Led a formation of Beaufighters to carry out a search for Flying Officer Kelshall, who was reported missing from the attack on the previous evening. The search was carried out without anything being seen. Returned to base. Flying Officer Kelshall was later reported to be a prisoner of war.

9 May 1944   Dart – Spiekeroog to Borkum
                       Beau 'E' (LZ 223) – Flying time 3.20 (day)

Detailed to carry out a two aircraft armed reconnaissance with Flying Officer Florentsen with orders to attack any small shipping that might be encountered. The patrol was carried out without any shipping being seen.

14 May 1944   Intended strike – off Dutch coast
                       Beau 'A' (LZ 436) – Flying time 2.05 (day)

Force sent out to attack shipping, which had been sighted by a reconnaissance aircraft. As the force was sent out without a fighter escort, it was recalled to base by headquarters before reaching the target area, due to the report of enemy fighters being seen over the convoy.

18 May 1944   'Conebo' – off Dutch coast
                     Beau 'E' (LZ 223) – Flying time 1.55 (day)

Visibility being very bad over the sea, the leader decided to return the force to base before it reached the target area.

22 May 1944   'Conebo' – off Ijmuiden
                     Beau 'D' (NE 465) – Flying time 3.00 (day)

A dusk patrol was carried out in above area but no shipping was sighted.

6 June 1944 (D-Day)   'Percolate' – off Belgian coast
                     Beau 'E' (LZ 223) – Flying time 3.45 (night)

Four Beaufighters detailed to carry out patrol in co-operation with Wellington, with orders to attack any shipping found with bombs. No shipping was sighted by Wellington so all aircraft returned to base at end of patrol.

8 June 1944   'Percolate' – off Ostende
                     Beau 'E' (LZ 223) – Flying time 3.45 (night)

Four Beaufighters proceeded to patrol area. Messages received from Wellington concerning enemy shipping picked up. Proceeded to position given by Wellington, but the markers were not found by any of the Beaufighters. Spent some time in area, and then decided to return to base, not having heard anything further from Wellington.

13 June 1944   'Percolate' – off Ostende
                     Beau 'F' (NE 438) – Flying time 2.40 (night)

In the air within fifteen minutes of receiving message reporting seventeen E-boats in above area. Proceeded south from base to set course from a point further south in England. Before reaching position, was shot at by English gun batteries. This caused a slight delay in reaching position to set course. Proceeded to reported position of enemy shipping and located markers. Circled markers, awaiting the dropping of the flares over the shipping by the Wellington. After waiting some time, proceeded on vector given by Wellington towards position of some tracer fire. Stayed in area for some time, and as nothing further was heard from the Wellington, decided to drop a flare, but nothing was seen. Decided to return to base. Upon arriving back at base, was informed that the Wellington had not returned and was reported missing.

14 June 1944   Shipping strike – south of the Hook
                     Beau 'E' (LZ 223) – Flying time 3.20 (1.20 D, 2.00 N)

Rocket attack off the Dutch coast. (Author's collection)

Shipping was attacked with bombs. Led a sub-section of three, the whole force being led by Wing Commander Burns.

15 June 1944   Shipping strike - off Schiermonnikoog
                     Beau 'E' (LZ 223) - Flying time 2.55 (day)

Operating from Langham, a force was sent out. The shipping was attacked. Was in torpedo section led by Wing Commander Burns. Torpedo released at 8,000-ton merchant vessel.

Coastal Command Report: Forty-two Beaufighters.
Leader: Wing Commander Gadd.
Aircraft on anti-shipping recce in force attacked a convoy of one 8,000-ton M/V, one naval auxiliary of 4,000 tons and seventeen escorts. Nine torpedoes set at 10 feet were released at ranges of 1,200 to 800 yards and thirty-two R/Ps 25-lb A.P. heads were fired at ranges of 1,000 yards down to 400 yards while thirty-seven aircraft attacked with cannon. Two torpedo hits were obtained on the M/V, which was listing, down by the stern, and in a sinking condition. Two torpedo hits seen on the 4,000-ton auxiliary, also listing, down by the stern and sinking. One M-Class M/S blew up and sank, a torpedo hit another and five more were seen on fire. Strikes were also obtained on two more M/Ss and two R boats. Very little flak was experienced. Two aircraft crash-landed at

base – crew safe. Photographs taken at the time of the attack confirmed torpedo hits on the large M/V; the vessel was seen to be ablaze from stem to stern. The naval auxiliary is seen to be on fire and many cannon strikes on three others. Recce aircraft together with photographs taken by PRU aircraft confirm that the large vessel sank and that the naval auxiliary was beached and had broken up into three parts.

18 June 1944   Dart – off Norderney
                    Beau 'L' (NE 436) – Flying time 3.00 (2.00 D, 1.00 N)

Individual reconnaissance flight at dusk. Patrol was carried out but no shipping was sighted.

29 June 1944   Anti-shipping sweep – Ijmuiden to Terschelling
                    Beau 'M' (NE 428) – Flying time 2.45 (day)

Sweep carried out in above area but no shipping sighted.

30 June 1944   'Conebo' – Flushing to Ijmuiden
                    Beau 'E' (LZ 223) – Flying time 2.45 (2.00 D, 0.45 N)

Patrol carried out but no shipping was sighted.

5 July 1944   Special reconnaissance – Terschelling
                    Beau 'J' (LZ 221) – Flying time 2.40 (day)

Shipping was believed to have proceeded in behind Terschelling following a strike by Beaufighters earlier in the day. Was sent out on a special reconnaissance flight of that area to locate the shipping if any. No shipping was sighted in the area.

8 July 1944   Shipping strike – Near Heligoland
                    Beau 'E' (LZ 223) – Flying time 3.55 (day)

Shipping was attacked. Was in torpedo section led by Wing Commander Burns. Torpedo was released at large merchant vessel. After the attack, escorted damaged aircraft back to base.

Coastal Command Report: Thirty-nine Beaufighters.
Leader: Wing Commander Gadd.
Anti-shipping recce in force attacked a convoy of six M/Vs, 1,500 to 3,000 tons with ten E/Vs. Eleven torpedoes were expended with two hits seen on a M/V of 2,000 tons, one on a M/V of 1,500 tons and one on a third M/V. One M/V seen to heel over and there was a large explosion amidships of second M/V. As a result of R/P and cannon attacks, one E/V blew up. Several more E/Vs were severely damaged, in addition to hits on

the M/Vs. Several aircraft were damaged but there were no casualties.

14 July 1944   Intended anti-shipping sweep - off Dutch coast
                                 Beau 'E' (LZ 223) - Flying time 3.10 (day)

Due to bad weather in patrol area, the leader decided to return the force to base before carrying out the patrol.

16 July 1944   Anti-shipping sweep - Borkum to Heligoland
                                 Beau 'E' (LZ 223) - Flying time 3.30 (day)

Sweep carried out in above area but no shipping was sighted.

20 July 1944   Anti-shipping sweep - Lister (Norwegian coast)
                                 Beau 'E' (LZ 223) - Flying time 4.25 (day)

Proceeded to patrol area. Then leading formation was late turning on patrol, causing a general confusion. As the formation of the wing was upset, the leader decided to return to base rather than carry on with patrol under such circumstances.

22 July 1944   Shipping strike - off Langeoog
                                 Beau 'V' (NE 481) - Flying time 3.20 (day)

Beaufighter pilots attack at very low level. Note the two guns in the bow of this armed trawler. (Air Historical Branch C 4471)

Shipping was attacked. Led an anti-flak section of three. On first run in, there were two ships, but on second run in, there was only one ship left, the other one having been sunk, its balloon still floating on the surface. Attacked the remaining ship once again with cannon. After last attack, one Beaufighter (Flying Officer Banks - 236 Squadron) was seen with port engine on fire. The aircraft was pulled up to about 1,000 feet then one parachute was seen to open. The aircraft was then seen to fall into the sea, out of control. All other aircraft returned to base.

Coastal Command Report: Twenty-three Beaufighters.
Leader: Flying Officer Taylor.
Aircraft on shipping recce sighted two trawler-type auxiliaries and attacks were carried out with torpedoes, R/P and cannon. One TTA was seen to be hit by torpedo and was last seen ablaze from stem to stern. The vessel was listing badly to port and abandoned. Survivors and debris were seen in water. The second vessel blew up and sank.
'Z' of 236 Squadron (F/O) Banks) crashed in sea near target. One survivor seen in dinghy.

5 August 1944   'Purblind' - off Le Havre
                  Beau 'N' (JM 215) - Flying time 3.35 (night)

Operating from Thorney Island. Six aircraft sent out to carry out patrol at night, armed with bombs, in the above area. No shipping picked up by Wellington.

5 August 1944   Intended 'Conebo' - off French coast
                   Beau 'N' (JM 215) - Flying time 1.25 (day)

Operating from Thorney Island. As this patrol was to be made at dusk, and the visibility being very poor over the sea, the leader decided against carrying out the patrol and the force returned to base.

15 August 1944   'Gilbey' - off Juist
                  Beau 'L' (NE 436) - Flying time 3.55 (night)

Three Beaufighters proceeded to patrol area. Wellington sent message reporting that some shipping had been picked up. Proceeded to reported position and located markers. Circled markers until Wellington dropped flares over shipping. The Beaufighters manoeuvred into position to attack by the light of the flares but no shipping could be seen. Called the Wellington for more flares but no answer was received. As no more flares were dropped, it was decided to return to base. Ground fog over the airfield so diverted to Docking and landed there, returning to base later.

24 August 1944   Anti-shipping sweep - Egero to Stavanger (Norway)
                  Beau 'P' (LX 806) - Flying time 4.45 (day)

Force proceeded to area and carried out patrol. No shipping was sighted.

29 August 1944   Shipping strike - near Heligoland
                  Beau 'K' (NE 802) - Flying time 4.10 (day)

Shipping was attacked. Was in leading anti-flak section led by Wing Commander Burns. During actual attack, ran into stream of empty cannon shells falling from Wing Commander Burns' aircraft, which was above and in front during the attack. On returning to base, discovered several holes in the aircraft. Two Beaufighters and crews (Flight Sergeant Wood of 254 Squadron and one from 489 Squadron) were missing from this operation, one crew being seen in a dinghy.

Coastal Command Report: Forty-six Beaufighters.
Leader: Wing Commander Burns.
Aircraft on anti-shipping recce in force sighted a convoy consisting of two M/Vs of 5,000 tons and 2,000 tons with two escort vessels and an R boat. Six of the aircraft attacked with torpedoes and hits were seen on the leading E/V and both M/Vs. Eleven of the aircraft attacked with RP and hits were scored on both M/Vs and E/Vs. The remainder of the aircraft made a concentrated attack with cannon with numerous strikes seen on all vessels. After these attacks the larger M/V was blazing furiously from stem to stern. The smaller M/V was well on fire and both E/Vs were burning. Two of the Beaufighters, 'B' of 489 Squadron (seen to ditch) and 'Q' of 254 Squadron (Flight Sergeant Wood) have failed to return.

6 September 1944   Night strike - off Schiermonnikoog
                  Beau 'C' (NT 924) - Flying time 3.00 (night)

Proceeded to patrol area. Operation Gilbey carried out in co-operation with a Wellington, but no shipping was picked up. Having been detailed to continue on a rover patrol, looking for enemy shipping by moonlight, the Beaufighters continued the patrol along the enemy coast. Shipping was sighted and attacked. Upon leaving ship after making a torpedo attack, aircraft was hit by enemy fire from the ship, causing damage to rudder. Tried to contact the other three Beaufighters before returning but failed. Decided to return to base.

8 September 1944   Anti-shipping sweep - Egero to Stavanger (Norway)
                  Beau 'A' (LZ 436) - Flying time 4.40 (day)

Force proceeded to area and sweep carried out but no shipping was sighted.

10 September 1944   Anti-shipping sweep – Egero to Lindesnes (Norway)
                      Beau 'D' (LZ 267) – Flying time 4.45 (day)

On running up engines on the ground, one engine was vibrating considerably but decided to take off and try to clear vibration in the air. Unable to do so, so had to return and land. Rushed to another aircraft and took off in short order, hoping to catch up with the formation, which had set course over base some time previous. Was able to catch up on formation about an hour later, due to increased speed and accurate navigation. Took up position, leading a section of three anti-flak aircraft. Sweep was carried out but no shipping seen.

11 September 1944   Anti-shipping sweep – off Norwegian coast
                      Beau 'F' (NE 438) – Flying time 5.10 (day)

On take-off, could not get aircraft into the air in time to clear boundary. Starboard wheel hit fence, but managed to get into the air. Proceeded to target area with the force and enemy shipping attacked. Was in anti-flak section, led by Squadron Leader Simmonds. On returning to base, had to land on one wheel and a prayer. Landing very slow, the aircraft finally came to a halt after skidding considerably.

> This was the last operation flown by George Dowding who was awarded the DFC shortly afterwards. He returned to Canada.

CHAPTER NINE

THE ANZAC WING 1944

489 Squadron at Leuchars in April 1944. Peter Hughes (second from right in front row), Freddie Spink (sixth from right in second row) and Doug Young (second from right in third row) are all in the photograph. (Air Cdre Peter Hughes)

> Cranwell-trained Squadron Leader **Peter Hughes** was the flight com-
> mander on Coastal Command's 489 Squadron RNZAF when it was
> re-equipped with the Beaufighter.

After completing my fifteenth and last operational flight in Hampdens, the squadron was ordered to Leuchars in Fife to re-equip with Beaufighter Xs or, as they were
usually known, 'Torbeaus'. At Leuchars we joined our sister squadron, 455 Squadron
RAAF who were also re-equipping and we were to form the Anzac Strike Wing which,
together with the North Coates Wing, was to transform the battle to deny essential iron
ore to German industry. This eventually made a major contribution to the winning
of the war. We became operational with our new aircraft and tactics in January 1944.

No longer did we depend on cloud cover for an attack, nor were we any more pas-
sively vulnerable to the flak as we made our torpedo runs. We went over in force. The
leading Beaufighters attacked the flak ships with their four cannons to discourage the
anti-aircraft gunners so allowing the following torpedo-carrying aircraft a relatively
clear run in. We now rarely arrived on the Norwegian coast without seeing a target.
We assumed this was because of intelligence received from the Norwegian Resistance,
which may well have contributed in this way, but we now know that the cracking of
the Enigma code was mainly responsible.

I made my first attack in the anti-flak role on 14 January 1944 and learned the
hard way that if the cannons were fired with negative 'G' while pushing into the dive,
they all jammed! There was plenty of return fire from the convoy escorts, but one
5,000-ton ship sustained a torpedo hit.

On 25 February we reverted to the old tactics and I arrived off Stavanger at dawn to
see anchored ships and lined up on a 10,000-ton tanker and made a good drop without
any opposing fire before breaking away over Karmøy Island. I guess the torpedo is
still in the mud of Stavanger roads!

In addition to 455 Squadron, we shared Leuchars with 333 Squadron Royal

Norwegian Air Force operating with Mosquitos. The Norwegians hated the Germans so they took the war very seriously – even to the extent of getting up early and jogging around the perimeter track.

In mid-April 1944 the squadron moved again, this time to Langham in north Norfolk to be nearer to the action when the expected invasion of France took place. A further change in tactics resulted from this move; now we were usually escorted by fighters to keep us free from interference by the Luftwaffe. Spitfires when we attacked on the Dutch coast and Mustangs for the longer trips to Norway and Denmark. These squadrons, especially the Poles and the Americans, had no idea of radio silence for the creation of surprise and this worried us a lot. They wanted enemy fighters in the air on arrival at our targets; we did not!

On 6 May I led the Langham Wing on a strike to attack an Elbe-Ems convoy of eighteen ships, which had been detected off Borkum. I dropped my torpedo at a 3,500-ton merchant vessel and this was estimated a hit. Continuing my attack, I fired 600 rounds at two other ships. Too late, I saw that the last of these was flying a balloon and I struck its cable with the aircraft's wing root. The cable snapped and I returned with the imprint of its windings on the aircraft paint. A fortunate escape and, despite the considerable amount of flak we encountered, there was no damage.

Shortly after this attack I was awarded an immediate DFC. The citation for the award in the *London Gazette* read: 'This officer has completed very many sorties including several successful attacks on shipping. In May 1944, he flew the leading aircraft of a formation, which attacked a large and heavily defended convoy off the Dutch coast. In the fight, Squadron Leader Hughes pressed home his attack with great skill and obtained a hit on a medium-size vessel, which caught fire. His leadership was of a high order throughout and contributed materially to the success of this well executed operation. This officer has invariably set a fine example of courage and devotion to duty.'

Beaufighters of 455 and 489 Squadrons attack a convoy off Borkum. (Air Historical Branch C4986)

On 15 June, I took part in one of the classic strikes made by the Coastal Command Strike Wings. The Germans were moving an 8,000-ton merchant vessel (the *Amerskerk*) and a 5,000-ton E-boat (an MTB) depot ship (the *Nachtigall*) from Holland to Germany. I led 489 Squadron in the anti-flak role in company with 455 Squadron, also anti-flak, while 236 and 254 Squadrons from North Coates carried torpedoes. Wing Commander Tony Gadd led the strike. As we approached the Dutch coast, the sea fog cleared to reveal our targets off Schiermonnikoog, the two target vessels escorted by eighteen assorted flak ships. I shot up the leading armed minesweeper and an armed trawler. Both the main targets were sunk as well as four escorts with most of the others left on fire.

These operations were the highlights, although my logbook records many others before my final operation on 8 August, the thirty-eighth of this third tour.

Unlike Bomber Command, where a tour of thirty operations could be completed in two months, if one survived, we went to war only when intelligence indicated that a target was likely to be encountered. This meant that a tour could continue for a year or two and one normally had plenty of time to recover from a fright before setting off for the next one! Nevertheless, statistics show that of all the operational roles, the anti-shipping one suffered by far the most casualties. At one stage of the war the chances of surviving a tour were assessed at about 25% and of surviving two it was 3%. I was very fortunate to have been unscathed until that fateful day of 8 August 1944.

It was on 7 August that I was ordered to North Coates with a flight of 489 Squadron in preparation for a combined operation on the following day with the North Coates Wing. It appeared that HQ Coastal Command was concerned that Fighter and Bomber Commands were getting all the publicity so they had persuaded the press to visit North Coates to observe and report on a Strike Wing operation. It was not easy to select a suitable target and the Germans were unlikely to co-operate. However, we duly set out on the morning of the 8th led by Wing Commander R. E. Burns DFC of 236 Squadron.

Flying Officer Freddie Spink DFC was, as usual, my navigator as we took off in the lead of 489 Squadron in the anti-flak role. My port engine was misfiring and running roughly on take-off but settled down so any thoughts of aborting the trip were forgotten. We arrived off Egero Island to see a small convoy, which we proceeded to attack. I saw a Beaufighter go down in a pall of smoke away to my right as I raked a small flak ship with my cannons, breaking away over the land before heading back out to sea. I passed over the ships again and took the opportunity to fire more cannon shells into the same one before setting course for home at high speed and at low level.

Freddie called me on the intercom and told me there was smoke coming from the port engine. I looked and saw a furnace of red flame under the engine cowling. I closed the fuel cock and pressed the fire extinguisher but instantly the flame spread down the balance pipe to the cockpit. I ordered Freddie to bale out and tried to open my escape hatch behind and below me but this appeared to have been affected by the flames, which by now were coming up between my legs and burning my face. I jettisoned the starboard window beside me and leaned into the slipstream away from the flames and I was sucked clear of the aircraft. One was not supposed to leave by this route as one would hit the tailplane but with the port engine shut down and starboard one at full throttle, the aircraft rolled violently to port enabling me to pass below the tail unharmed.

We were at only about 300 feet but travelling fast so my parachute deployed rapidly and within seconds I was in the North Sea. I removed my harness and activated the gas bottle to the K-type dinghy and climbed on board. I could see no sign of Freddie but there was some spray and smoke where the Beau had plunged in. The sea was calm and warm. I could see the tops of the mountains of Norway and some smoke from the shattered convoy some ten miles to the east. It was about 1100 hours. The story of my operational career ended here and that of my time as a prisoner of war began.

Years later, I was told by Flying Officer Don Tunnicliffe from New Zealand that he had seen Freddie leave the aircraft before me. His death has always been a matter of the greatest regret to me ever since, but I am grateful to Don for relieving me of the fear that Freddie had died because of some fault of mine by leaving the aircraft before my crew.

A spectacular photograph captured by another Beaufighter as Peter Hughes parachutes into the sea (left centre) and his Beaufighter crashes close by. (Air Cdre Peter Hughes)

Peter Hughes was a prisoner for nine months, most of it in Stalag Luft III, the scene of the Great Escape. He remained in the RAF and retired in 1968 as Air Commodore Peter Hughes CBE, DFC. On 17 May 1989, Norway's National Day, Peter and his wife, together with three colleagues from his days on 489 Squadron, were flown by helicopter to drop a wreath on the spot where Freddie Spink died.

Doug Young. (Helen Evers)

Navigator **Douglas Young** and his New Zealand pilot Bertie Burrowes joined 489 Squadron at Leuchars as it was receiving its first Beaufighters. They flew on the strikes described by Peter Hughes and remained on the squadron until the end of November 1944 seeing a great deal more action. Doug describes some of the action around D-Day and also one of the Strike Wings' greatest successes.

There was much speculation about the approach of D-Day, when it was supposed that the invasion of Europe would at last begin. A more intensive programme of formation flying, practice torpedo attacks and bomb dropping heightened our expectation of this great event. We also began for the first time to make reconnaissance flights along the French Channel coast.

We were kept at a high state of readiness and during the early days of June, a mobile caravan had been parked near the end of the runway and, with our Beaufighters lined up nearby, we were prepared for instant take-off.

Early on the morning of 6 June a number of us were passing our time with a session of 'Shoot', a card game popular with the New Zealanders when, just after 0800 hours came the sudden order to scramble. We all flung down our cards, stubbed out our cigarettes, grabbed our flying gear and doubled to our aircraft. Within a few minutes we were airborne and, as we circled and got into formation, we were instructed by radio to set course for Manston in Kent. Although we didn't realise it, the great invasion of Europe had commenced.

Some forty-five minutes later we landed at Manston and found a spot to park our Beaufighters among a vast collection of all sorts and varieties of British and American aircraft; an amazing array of air power of that period.

Later that evening it became overcast and as darkness fell, Bertie and I were ordered to patrol off the Belgian coast from Flushing to Dunkirk, mainly to search for any German E-boats, which might be gathering for attacks against our invasion fleet. We took off at 2200 hours loaded with bombs and flew eastwards across the sea to make our landfall off Flushing. Conditions by now were not promising and we were finding patches of sea mist below us with thickening cloud above. We eventually got a clear view of the coastline ahead and we turned to follow the sweep of the coast to the south-west.

Soon afterwards, Bertie alerted me that he had spotted something ahead. Sure enough, in a clear patch in front of us there were the familiar shapes of four E-boats travelling at speed in line astern and close inshore. Bertie altered course a few degrees to bring us in position some way behind them as he started to lose height. They kept steadily on course and we began to think they had not yet spotted us. We were just on the point of getting into the correct position for a bombing attack when a bank of sea mist drifted below us. But by this time Bertie had already made up his mind to press home the attack and I could hear him counting the final seconds as he held our course rock steady. At the count of ten he pressed the release button and I felt a slight jolt as the bombs fell away. A few seconds later I could make out an orange glow reflected through the gloom below us as the bombs exploded. We made a wide circle to try and find out what had happened to our targets but by now the mist had thickened and nothing further could be seen. However, I felt reasonably sure that our bombs could not have been very far off target.

The following evening found us again on patrol along the Dutch and Belgian coasts from Ostende to Den Helder, but we were unlucky in finding no suitable targets to attack despite the excellent visibility. Within a week we were back attacking convoys off the Dutch coast.

A great day in the history of 489 Squadron was 21 July 1944. The day had dawned bright and sunny and a glance at the 'Mayfly' [daily flying programme] had shown that we were to be on standby. After a check of our aircraft and our personal equipment we sat outside and enjoyed the summer weather and all seemed peaceful for once.

As the day wore on however, an air of suppressed excitement gradually became apparent as more crews were assembled and even those nominally off duty were called in. Soon after lunch the rumour of something big taking place was reinforced by the sudden and noisy arrival of the two Beaufighter squadrons from North Coates. The crew room was soon crowded and alive with the boisterous greetings and good-natured banter. Speculation as to just what was afoot was to be laid to rest in the afternoon when we were all assembled in the operations room for a combined briefing.

It was at once made clear to us that intelligence reports of a considerable move-ment of shipping had just been received and that the vessels would probably be south of Heligoland within the next few hours. This was stirring news and we all listened with rapt attention as the various senior officers in charge of the organisation of this air strike gave careful and precise instructions. Finally, we were told that the met forecast for the southern part of the North Sea was favourable with good visibility, very little cloud and a gentle moderate breeze.

By 1940 hours we were airborne and circling as we settled into formation. We were soon tucked in on the left of the first wave of aircraft and as we crossed the Norfolk coast for the open sea we must have presented a warlike picture to any casual onlooker. Fifty fully armed Beaufighters in close formation at treetop height was certainly something rarely seen and perhaps never to be repeated. Especially as not only British airmen but also Canadians, Australians and New Zealanders were on their way to war from that quiet and still lovely corner of England. As the flat fields disappeared rapidly behind

A Mustang of 315 Squadron escorts the Beaufighter TF.X of Doug Young and his pilot Bertie Burrows as they head for a strike off Norway. (Helen Evers)

us, the profusion of red poppies growing amongst the wheat could clearly be picked out in the evening light.

Our first aiming point was an open position about fifty miles west of Heligoland. From there we were to alter course for a second sea position a mile or two to the south-west where we were to turn due south towards the German coast to approach the long narrow stretch of the East Frisian island of Spiekeroog.

After long hours spent flying at low level over the sea, we navigators had become very adept at judging the speed and direction of the wind by the appearance of the surface of the water. I estimated the wind to be from the north-east at fourteen knots and I corrected our position on my chart. Although we were flying in formation, it was always necessary for each navigator to know exactly where he was at all times. Sudden cloud cover or some emergency might cause the formation to disperse and I always worked as meticulously as if we were flying a lone mission.

At 2018 hours it was time to change the petrol feed to the outer tanks and I also set our forward-firing cannons to 'fire'. Forty minutes later a gaggle of fourteen small fishing boats was sighted ahead. These were not the sort of target we were looking for and our formation flew steadily on; we could only hope that they were not enemy controlled and already passing radio information to the enemy coastal authorities. Meantime, I noted their exact position on my chart as it might at least come in useful as a marker on our return journey.

We reached our first sea position and turned on to due east for Heligoland. There were now only small patches of altostratus cloud and visibility was excellent. Some ten minutes later the squat bulk of the island came into view and our leading formation of anti-flak Beaufighters began to climb for the attack. I hinged my chart table securely to one side and donned my metal 'flak helmet' over my leather flying one before checking my rear-firing Browning machine gun as well as my large handheld camera.

The whole formation was now turning to starboard to fly directly towards the German coast and within a very few minutes an amazing sight was spread before us. Over several square miles of sea, indeed as far as the eye could see, an ordered array of ships was proceeding like a great armada.

It seemed impossible to survey them all individually in the fleeting time available to us. As we steadily approached, the evening sun shed an even brighter light on the scene spread out below us. For a minute, perhaps two minutes, time seemed to stand still; the sea was blue, the toy-like ships kept rigidly on course in serried ranks, their creamy wakes making them look even more like models in some vast exhibition. It could even be imagined that they might have been lined up in precise order as for some long ago naval review.

Such fanciful ideas were soon swept brutally aside. As we got within range of their guns, rows of flashing bursts and puffs of grey and black smoke appeared above and around us. It all suddenly gave the impression that even a small bird could not have flown in safety anywhere within the vicinity of those vessels. Still we pressed on in steady formation.

All at once the expected command to attack was given crisply and clearly by our leader over the radio and we all immediately swooped down on that convoy like a flight of avenging angels.

Down we went and our four cannons burst into life with a shattering roar above the noise of our engines. Bertie had earmarked an escort vessel and this seemed to almost leap up out of the water at us as we pulled out of our dive only feet above its now smoking decks.

Clouds of steam and smoke, as well as streams of yellow flashes cascaded about us as we swept on just above the waves. A rapid exchange of words now took place with Bertie as to our best route of escape, and as we climbed and weaved our way clear I began to pump the handle that operated the shutter of my bulky camera. I hoped that I would have been able to record something of the results of our devastating attack; and so it proved. So much had occurred in such a short space of time that it would have been quite impossible for any one observer to have taken it all in.In the space of perhaps three or four minutes absolute havoc had been inflicted from the skies on that convoy. Almost every ship was belching thick clouds of oily smoke and some were already listing heavily and seemed to be turning in helpless circles. Those stricken ships were a dreadful and awe-inspiring sight that gradually faded into the distance as we departed.

We now flew steadily and settled down on the course I had given Bertie for the first leg home. We were at 500 feet and soon passed over the fishing fleet we had seen on

Beaufighters of 489 Squadron attack an armed trawler shortly after D-Day. (Air Historical Branch)

our outward journey. They had just passed out of sight when we noticed a Beaufighter some way ahead of us, which we rapidly overhauled. We made radio contact and it was soon apparent that it belonged to the North Coates Wing and had received hits in the starboard wing during the attack. We were asked to stand by in case an emergency developed. We slowed and kept close company with the aircraft during the rest of the flight back to base, which was reached without further incident.

With the number of Beaufighters already circling around Langham it was almost midnight before we finally landed safely on our Norfolk field.

A couple of days later we were able to 'read all about it' in the newspapers and the national press made a big splash of the event. Headlines such as:

BIGGEST GERMAN CONVOY OF WAR SMASHED BY RAF
40 Ships Put To Sea - Not One Escaped

Whilst our own losses were generally glossed over, I couldn't help feeling that, on the whole, the newspapers had been presented with a remarkable bargain. All the action photographs they were given were taken by RAF junior officers and NCOs whose pay, including flying pay, was a matter of a few shillings a day.

As an additional experiment a number of our aircraft had been fitted with a cine-camera in the nose and these pictures provided a close-up record of every movement made during the attack.

A few days later the aircrews that had taken part in the assault were ushered into the projection room and shown a re-run of these films. At first it seemed to be taken somewhat light heartedly, but as the pictures gradually and vividly recreated the atmosphere of the violent and headlong attack on the convoy, the atmosphere changed. When one saw again, at close quarters, the terrible impact of tracer cannon shells blasting their way into ship after ship and to re-live the dizzying effects of these vessels rushing towards you before dropping away with sickening speed, it became almost too much to take in unemotionally. Perhaps being crammed together in a pitch-dark room helped to dramatise the effect?

When, towards the end, one Beaufighter was shown attacking one vessel, climbing steeply away and then attacking a second, and then, with extraordinary courage not to say foolhardiness, actually diving on a third with all its guns blazing, the effect was electrifying. The sound of the almost hysterical burst of laughter that this singular feat of daring brought forth was perhaps the most chilling noise that I have heard in my life. To attack more than one well-armed ship at a time was always considered by pilots and navigators to be suicidal; but three?

The experiment of showing film playback of attacks on enemy shipping was never repeated.

> Douglas Young went on to complete a further fifteen operations before he left 489 Squadron to become a navigation instructor. He left the RAF in 1946 but remained in close touch with his New Zealand colleagues. Thanks to his tireless efforts he arranged for a brass plaque in memory of his fallen comrades to be installed in the Church of St. Andrew and St. Mary at Langham and it was dedicated on 3 October 1993.

Doug Young at Langham Church on 3 October 1993. (Helen Evers)

From the fields between this church and the sea, during the wartime summer of 1944, a small band of young men flew in defence of these islands. Most of these ardent volunteers had journeyed across half the globe to our aid in a time of desperate need. The many successful attacks on enemy shipping made by the pilots of 455 Royal Australian Air Force and 489 Royal New Zealand Air Force Torpedo Bomber Squadrons and their British navigators made a valuable contribution to the preservation of our freedom. Sadly many of these young men were destined never to return home again but to be lost somewhere across a waste of seas with their final resting place remaining unknown to this day. May their sacrifice never be forgotten.

CHAPTER TEN

BLACK FRIDAY

'Spike' Holly (left) and his pilot Percy Smith. (Spike Holly)

'Spike Holly' was on the last trip of his operational tour when he took off on 9 February 1945.

In October 1944 the Dallachy Strike Wing was formed consisting of four squadrons – 144 (RAF), 404 (RCAF), 455 (RAAF) and 489 (RNZAF). A similar wing of Mosquitos was set up at Banff just along the coast of the Moray Firth. The purpose of the two wings was to attack enemy shipping sailing along the Norwegian coast. Our activities caused the Germans to stop the movement of ships during the daytime when they concealed themselves in the more inaccessible fjords.

My squadron, No. 144, was torpedo trained. The other three Dallachy squadrons were armed with rockets. All the squadrons had four 20-mm cannons mounted in the fuselage. It was only south of Stavanger that there was open water where torpedoes could be dropped. Consequently, 144 Squadron usually flew in the anti-flak role in support of the other squadrons. Most of these operations took place between the Søgne and Nord Fjords.

On the morning of Friday, 9 February 1945, two recce aircraft from 489 Squadron found a variety of shipping, including five merchant ships at Nordgulen and a Narvik-class destroyer and other naval ships in Førde Fjord, about fifteen miles inland from the coast. Group HQ decided to leave the merchant ships and to mount an attack on the naval units. A force of thirty Beaufighters was prepared (eight from 144, and eleven each from 404 and 455 Squadrons). In addition, there were two 'outriders' from 144 and 489 Squadrons flying ahead of the main formation and it was their job to report any movement of the ships. Ten Mustangs from 65 Squadron at Peterhead provided fighter cover over the targets and two air-sea rescue Warwicks were airborne along the route.

This was the first operation that my pilot, Percy Smith, and I flew since we had both been commissioned, which had probably been awarded as a reward for surviving thirty-five operations. We were nearing the end of our eighteen-month tour and this operation was likely to be our last one.

The main formation set course at 1400 hours and we had an uneventful crossing at the usual fifty feet. When we arrived at the coast just south of Førde Fjord we climbed over the mountains. The outriders had reported that some of the ships had moved across the fjord and so there was likely to be some crossfire.

The strike leader led us over the moored ships to the north side of the steep fjord. The ships opened fire on us but there were no casualties. On the south side was a small bay where the other ships were moored. It was protected by high, steep cliffs, which cast shadows over the frozen water. The north side was not protected to the same extent but there were cliffs at the eastern end of the fjord, which made an east-to-west attack (towards the sea) extremely difficult. It was, of course, impossible to make an attack across the fjord since the cliffs and mountains were so steep and high and the fjord was very narrow.

When over the vessels on the north side, the leader took the formation in a wide circle to starboard, returning to virtually the same spot as before. Another part of the formation had made a wide circle to port and all this manoeuvring had taken about thirty minutes and we had lost the element of surprise. By the time the formation started to fly up the fjord it had become fragmented and, in view of the confines of the fjord, it had split up and crews made individual attacks.

Due to the terrain, we were flying much higher than usual and so we were in the dive longer during the attack. It seemed an age before the cannons opened up and filled the fuselage with their thundering racket, shuddering vibration and fumes. As we had started our dive there was another 'Beau' about 100 feet away on our port side. Suddenly, without warning it exploded into a ball of orange, red flames. One of the tailplanes broke off and fell away like an autumn leaf. I did not tell Smith.

We had made our attack on a ship in the south bay and so, when the firing finished, we had to turn to port to avoid the cliff ahead. We continued to dive until we were at 'nought feet' and flew further inland up the fjord. After a few miles the ground on the north side became less steep and opened into a wide valley, which had two branches. We turned to port into the valley on the left, which headed roughly westwards and to the sea. As we flew over a small village and past a white-painted church steeple, I put my handheld camera down on the deck and got a map out to try to pinpoint our position.

When I looked up I saw a fighter about 100 yards behind and slightly to port. My first reaction was, 'What is a Mustang doing here?' Then I saw the radial engine; it was a Focke-Wulf 190. I shouted to Smith and leaned over to release the restraining strap on my free-mounted Browning. The 190 fired its first burst of cannon fire. We were too low for Smith to take any evasive action as we were climbing over the rising ground of the wooded valley.

The first burst from the 190 raked our port side and knocked out the engine. One shell exploded in my cockpit, a few feet away, showering me with splinters. [Note: He was badly wounded in the legs and stomach and one bullet passed underneath his right armpit and through the back of his seat - Author.] It also put the intercom out of action. I fired the Browning - no deflection and almost at point-blank range - until it jammed where a shell splinter had damaged the belt of ammunition. The fighter

Beaufighters attack in the steep-sided Førde Fjord. (Air Historical Branch C 5274)

fired again and I wondered if I would be able to clear the stoppage before it made another attack. To my surprise, and relief, it suddenly climbed to about 2,000 feet and flew back down the valley.

Somehow, Smith managed to keep the aircraft climbing on one engine and I drifted in and out of consciousness. At one point a wing splintered the top of a tree, but still we flew on. By now we were over the worst of the high ground and descending slowly towards the next fjord. Then I saw water below us. When I next became conscious there was water in the bottom of the cockpit and I knew I had about ten seconds left to get out - the Beaufighter doesn't float! Fortunately, the top of the escape hatch was undamaged and opened without difficulty. I released my seat belt and the aircraft sank, leaving me floating in the icy water. I pulled the toggle on my Mae West but nothing happened. A shell splinter must have pierced it. The kapok pads on the front and round the neck of the jacket kept me afloat. I saw Smith a few yards away and he said he was not injured. There was no sign of the main dinghy, which was stowed in the port wing near the engine. We both tried to climb onto a floating wheel, without success. In the far distance I saw a rowing boat with two men in it. Had they seen us? Would they get to us in time? The next thing I remember was being pulled into the boat and, later, being carried up a path to a farmhouse.

After about six weeks in hospital in Norway, I eventually arrived at Stalag Luft I. By a strange coincidence, Smith and two other survivors from the raid, both from 455

Squadron, arrived the following day. By the time we were repatriated, 144 Squadron had already been disbanded. Nevertheless, we managed to make contact and report back. We then heard that Smith had been recommended for the DFC.

> This raid failed to inflict any significant damage on the enemy vessels and it proved to be a devastating loss for the Beaufighter crews. Altogether, nine were lost including Smith and Holly. Only five men survived to become prisoners and six of the aircraft lost were from the Canadian 404 Squadron. A Mustang was also lost. The remaining aircraft made their way back to Dallachy, but with many of them damaged, the airfield was soon littered with wrecked aircraft. It was the most costly anti-shipping strike of the war. The German fighters also suffered with five lost to the Beaufighter's guns.

Amongst the Beaufighters that 'littered' the airfield at Dallachy was the one flown by Flight Sergeants Stan Butler and 'Nick' Nicholl. **Stan Butler** describes their experience.

Stan Butler (left) and his navigator 'Nick' Nicholl at Dallachy in the spring of 1945. (Stan Butler)

This was our first shipping strike operation. After take-off we formed up and set course at low level in a loose formation of vics of three, led by Squadron Leader D. W. Rogers. As we approached the Norwegian coast everything was going according to plan. In these fjord attacks, it was usual to fly inland for a while after making a landfall, and then approach the fjord roughly at right angles. You would then turn down the fjord at a height that would allow you to both clear the high ground and dive to attack the target. The aircraft could then break away to seaward on completion of the attack and get a good start for the journey back to base. This type of attack could usually be completed with a minimum amount of time being spent over enemy territory and there would be a good chance you would be on your way home before any enemy fighters could intercept you.

But this time things were different. We made our landfall as normal and flew inland on the south side of the fjord. We turned north, with the intention of then turning west down the fjord and making our attack heading out to sea, but we suddenly found ourselves under fire from the ships that appeared almost under us!

The wing leader did a slow 270-degree turn to starboard to bring us back across the fjord and heading towards the sea on the south side parallel to the fjord. Wing

Commander C. G. Milsom DSO, DFC had probably decided that the way the ships were anchored under a steep cliff made a successful attack at right angles to the fjord almost impossible. We continued flying on the south side of the fjord back towards the sea for some time before turning north again, crossing the fjord for the third time. The wing was then ordered into echelon port before we dropped down into the fjord on our attack dive. Owing to our position on the extreme starboard side of the original vic formation, Nick and I had to be last over into echelon, making us the tail-enders. There was a further complication of which I was blissfully unaware; all this manoeuvring had taken a very long time, long enough for enemy fighters to appear on the scene.

We were flying close to a high flat area of ice and snow-covered rock on the north edge of the fjord when the attack order came over the radio from the wing leader. I began the attack procedure; lock the gun sight into position, flip the gun switches to fire, and adjust speed to maintain position, as we turned port into the fjord to make our dive. At first I couldn't see any ships but a few choice words from Nick put me right. I saw two targets and chose the easier one to get to. I settled into the dive, ready to start firing when I thought we were just out of range and I could 'hosepipe' my fire onto the target. Nick was now wide awake in his backwards-facing position. He wasn't very happy about the cotton-wool puffs of heavy anti-aircraft fire above us. I suppose they hoped the odd aircraft might fly into a shower of shrapnel. Agonisingly, to him, it seemed an eternity before I pressed the gun button. We got in quite a long burst, bang on target. Hypnotising for a first timer, so much so that there was a danger of not pulling out of the dive in time. We flattened out. Nick saw a ship's mast flash past and then, on our port side, a destroyer tucked in to the cliff. It seemed to be only yards away and was giving us a continuous broadside as we jinked along its length. Being last into the attack, and probably their only remaining target, we were getting plenty of unwelcome attention. It was a frightening moment.

Only as I pulled out of the dive did I, too, see the other ships. I opened up the throttles to take-off boost to get clear of the intense flak, but kept close to the water and ice, making no attempt to climb away and become more vulnerable to attack. In fact, we would not have been able to climb. Just before we cleared the destroyer there was a loud bang and a spurt of liquid gushed up from the floor of my cockpit. My jinking caused it to splash over the windscreen and over me seriously impairing my vision. Seconds later, Nick saw something that must have given him nightmares, the unmistakeable front silhouette of an FW 190 coming at us with little flashes sparkling along its wings. Nick's voice in my earphones almost blasted my head off: "Weave, for Christ's sake, weave, weave!" - not a textbook air force communication, and so shocking coming from one who benefitted from a Victorian church upbringing.

Meantime, I had gained a little height - it is too dodgy to fly low when you can't see properly - so I moved the gun sight to one side and wiped the windscreen with my glove to improve forward vision. We were now heading along the fjord, which, with a lowering cloud base, gave the impression of being in a large tunnel. Tracer was streaming from behind on our port side and I immediately began evading. Naturally, if you do this at a constant height, the enemy's shell stream passes through your flight path, but we were not flying at a constant height. I was pumping the control column backwards and forwards quite violently at random intervals and, when going down, getting quite close to the ice. This is relatively safe in a Beau, for it has excellent forward vision. Nick's blood pressure returned to normal at the sight of a saviour - one of our Mustangs appeared and he saw off the 190 after Nick had fired a red Verey cartridge.

The sides of the fjord disappeared into the lowering cloud above us, and the question now was how to get out and head back to the coast without hitting any high ground en route. Fortunately, there now appeared ahead in this somewhat menacing tunnel an area of snow and ice-covered shale and rock sloping gently into the water - a convenient opportunity to pull up sharply and continue climbing through the cloud, while maintaining a slow turn to port. I now had no idea of my direction because the instruments had toppled during the evasive action. I still resisted the temptation to push the throttles through the gate in order to climb quicker because I couldn't risk any engine troubles. I hardly expected the engines to have escaped damage and I still couldn't be certain that it was only hydraulic fluid that had leaked into the cockpit.

The cloud was thin and we were soon through it into a peaceful world, with just another thin layer of cloud above us. There was nothing else in sight and I just sat, stupefied, continuing the slow turn to port until we were heading due west by the sun. Amazingly we appeared to have got away with it. We were both uninjured, sitting in an apparently airworthy aircraft with our two sturdy Bristol Hercules engines performing faultlessly.

The compass settled down, so I could reset the gyro and set a course for Dallachy guessed by Nick, who also told me that a sizeable chunk of our starboard elevator was no longer with us. This surprised me, for it was having little or no effect on straight and level flight. I knew, though, that it could be a different story when slowing down to landing speed. We settled down to the return crossing at 3,000 feet, a good height should we need to put out a Mayday call before ditching.

We could relax a bit now and we eventually made contact with Dallachy Control to tell them that our hydraulics were u/s and we would be making a no-flap belly-landing. We were told to land on the grass as far down the field as possible as another aircraft would also be belly-landing behind us. I put my flak helmet on as we reduced height to cross the coast at low level in line with, and to one side of, the runway. I put the propellers into fine pitch and closed the throttles as we crossed the airfield boundary. All I had to concentrate on then was holding the aircraft straight and level a few feet off the ground. It was still handling well, but did require slightly more exaggerated movements of the control column to get a response as we lost speed. As we hit the deck I remember pressing hard on the brake, but I had no wheels! We came to rest just before the perimeter track, exactly as instructed, on the grass well down the airfield. Everything was quiet. I sat there dazed, automatically going through my cockpit drill, caging the gyro, all switches off, then collected my stuff together, opened the top hatch, nipped on to the wing and dropped on to terra firma.

Wing Commander J. S. Dinsdale DSO, DFC, a New Zealander who was wing commander flying at Dallachy, came rushing up in his utility truck, and then hurried off to another crew immediately he had ascertained that we were OK. One of our ground crew told me afterwards that a shell had hit us and pierced the fuselage on the port side at a point about six inches below and in front of the root of the leading edge. It had punctured the hydraulic system near the base of the control column. At least one bullet had gone into the self-sealing fuel tank and there were a few other holes in the wing. There was a two-foot-square hole in the starboard elevator.

It had been our very first shipping strike, and it was against a tough target; a German Narvik-class destroyer, two 'M'-class minesweepers and several flak ships. Although all the ships had been damaged, none had been sunk. It was a hairy experience, which served us well on a further eight shipping strikes before the end of the war in Europe and the disbanding of 144 Squadron.

> In 1979, Norwegian marine archaeologists located Holly's aircraft and salvaged a number of items including his seat and Browning machine gun. **Spike Holly** returned to the scene to meet the team.

After a visit to Norway in 1979, I returned with 'my' Beaufighter seat. There is a splinter hole in the back. If I had not been leaning over to release the Browning when the shell exploded, it is unlikely that I would be writing this. The seat is now on display in the museum at Fochabers, Moray.

Butler and Nicholl's aircraft after crash-landing at Dallachy on 9 February 1945. (Stan Butler)

In 1982 I learned that the pilot who shot us down was Oberleutnant Rudi Linz, a Luftwaffe ace credited with sixty-nine victories. After his encounter with us he had crashed and been killed. The first person to research the incident thought that I had shot him down but later investigators think that he had a subsequent meeting with a Mustang. In 1995 I placed some flowers on his grave in Bergen.

In 1997 I was presented with 'my' Browning, which had been salvaged and painstakingly restored. It is now on display in the museum at Frammarsvik, which overlooks the place on Førde Fjord where the action took place. In the same glass case is the gun from Rudi Linz's Focke-Wulf 190.

CHAPTER ELEVEN
OPERATIONAL TOUR IN MALTA

'Taffy' Bellis (left) and his pilot Denis Welfare photographed with their damaged Mosquito after joining 239 Squadron. (David Bellis)

David 'Taffy' Bellis trained as an observer in the USA and, after completing a short radio course at RAF Prestwick, converted to the Beaufighter and teamed up with Denis Welfare.

It was in May 1942 that Denis Welfare and I were posted to our first operational squadron, No. 141 at Tangmere in Sussex. The squadron had recently been equipped with the Beaufighter Mk. II for defensive night-fighting. They were armed with four cannons and six machine guns and, with the AI they carried were the most effective night-fighters in service. These Mk. IIs were powered by two Rolls-Royce Merlin engines and unfortunately had a bad reputation with the aircrew. Pilots, particularly those that had flown the sedate Blenheim previously, found them almost lethal on take-off and landing and few had a kind word to say about them.

The CO of the squadron was Wing Commander G. F. E. Heycock DFC and it was a tribute to his drive, energy and enthusiasm that confidence in the aircraft grew and that the newly joined aircrew, like us, settled in and quickly became part of the squadron.

Our first few weeks in the squadron were taken up by training – Denis to become accustomed to the Beaufighter and myself to the operation of the radar to achieve successful camera gun 'attacks' on target aircraft that were much faster and more manoeuvrable than the Blenheims on which we had trained at OTU.

By the late summer of 1942, German bomber activity over the UK was almost negligible and Denis and I were posted to the Middle East and to 272 Squadron at its home base Idku, near Alexandria. It was here that new arrivals were trained for long-range daylight fighting before transfer to the main squadron at its forward base in Malta.

We were introduced to the latest Beaufighter the Mk. VI, powered by Hercules engines, and soon found that the extra power transformed it from 'the b****y cow' into a friendly and exhilarating aircraft affectionately called 'The Beau' by all who flew it. Denis soon mastered the aircraft and became enthusiastic about it. I took a W/T course and we spent hours flying over the desert and the sea practising navigation with the minimum of visual and radio aids.

The chief instructor at Idku was Squadron Leader G. M. Coleman DFC, nicknamed 'Pop' because he must have been one of the oldest operational pilots in the RAF. He was a kind, shy and gentle man, but one of the most skilful and knowledgeable pilots I have ever known. Aircrew who completed their operational tours in Malta will know that their survival was in no small part due to what Pop had taught them. Pop returned to operational duties with 272 Squadron in 1943, but was forced to 'ditch' in the Mediterranean and was unable to fly operationally again.

A Beaufighter VIc (X8079) and a Mk. Ic (T5043) of 272 Squadron over Malta. (Air Historical Branch CM 5109)

By the end of 1942 Denis and I were ready for operations in Malta, but shortages of aircraft there meant that, first of all, we had to go to West Africa to pick up a new Beau. At that time the only feasible way to supply Beaus to Egypt or Malta was for them to be crated by sea to Takoradi, where they were assembled and flown across Africa. Thus, on 1 January 1943, Denis and I, together with about six other crews, were flown by Liberator to what is now Ghana. We arrived at Takoradi on the 5th, carried out an air test on our new Beau the next day and left that afternoon, finally arriving back at Idku on the 10th.

I shall never forget that flight – east from Takoradi along the 'slave' coast to Lagos, then north over the tropical forests of the Niger Delta to the grasslands of northern Nigeria. As we flew east the grasslands became sparser and were replaced by the desert of Sudan. We refuelled at Maiduguri and El Fasher – surely the hottest place on earth. Then ever eastwards with the desert below us, which was devoid of landmarks or life of any sort. We became mesmerised by the featureless horizon. We were hot and fighting sleep and were exasperated by mirages that appeared and disappeared. Then, in the distance we saw vegetation, which turned out not to be another mirage, but the Nile Valley.

I was overwhelmed by two emotions. First the relief that my navigation had been OK and secondly, to experience what was for me the most beautiful view I had ever seen before or since - the Nile Valley like a lush green ribbon stretching northwards through the desert as far as the eye could see from the confluence of the Blue and White Niles at Khartoum. After that it was easy to follow the Nile northwards, stay at Luxor then on to Idku with forty hours flying in our logbooks and 10,000 miles [sic] behind us.

A few days rest and we were off to Malta. No. 272 Squadron, like its sister squadron No. 252, was based at Takali, a grass airfield near Rabat in the centre of the island. We were introduced to the CO, Wing Commander J.M. 'Buck' Buchanan DSO, DFC & Bar. Buck had been a Wellington pilot operating over Europe during the first year of the war, when he was awarded the DFC. He then saw action in Eritrea before moving to Egypt in 1941. He flew Blenheim IV bombers in the early desert campaigns and by 1942 had completed over 200 operations and been awarded a Bar to his DFC. He took command of 272 Squadron in Malta in November 1942, flying fighters for the first time.

Buck's exploits in the Middle East were legendary and were talked about over and over again during our period in Egypt. We heard how he had shot down about ten enemy aircraft during his first six weeks with 272 Squadron and awarded a DSO, how he appeared indestructible even when attacking destroyers with cannon fire, how he escaped from an operation over the Western Desert with half a squadron of Italian fighters on his tail and how a blonde female correspondent from an American news magazine had stood behind him in the cockpit during an operation.

The charismatic Wing Commander J. M. Buchanan DSO, DFC & Bar. (Air Historical Branch CM 4523)

To my surprise, Buck was quite different to the mental picture I had of him. He turned out to be a small, slight man with long blonde hair and a trim moustache who walked with short, mincing steps and he was very quietly spoken. We soon found out that looks were deceptive and it did not take many ops for us to realise that he was one of the bravest men I ever knew. He became one of the top-scoring Beaufighter pilots of the war. Sadly, Buck's aircraft was hit by light flak over the island of Kos towards the end of the Mediterranean war. He was forced to 'ditch' but died from exposure in his dinghy.

Our operations fell into several categories:

• Patrolling the German and Italian supply routes between Sicily and North Africa and attacking any aircraft or shipping we found.
• Escorting Beaufort torpedo bombers attacking convoys and 'drawing' the fire from escorting destroyers to give the Beauforts a chance.
• Escorting Allied convoys heading for Malta and protecting them from enemy bombers.

Life expectancy on such daytime operations was not high. Anti-aircraft fire from Italian destroyers was intense, while single-engine fighters based in Sicily were lurking nearby. The Beau, for all its plusses, was not a match in speed or manoeuvrability for the Messerschmitt Bf 109; indeed, it was suicide to try and take them on.

Many of my close colleagues were shot down. I particularly remember a group of Canadians who came out with us to Egypt, back to Takoradi and on to 272 Squadron. I spent hours with them playing poker and bridge. Amongst them were Frazee and Steele, and Cozette and Fletcher, who were shot down on 8 May 1943 by Bf 109s off Sicily. The fight they put up helped Buck and us to escape back to Malta. Another Canadian crew, Grimes and Dawson, disappeared after a dawn operation and we spent four hours searching for a dinghy, but no luck. Dawson was a massive young man – a lumberjack at home – while his pilot Grimes had married a WAAF in the UK, to whom he wrote a letter every day and always ended it with a poem that he composed on the spot.

Another operation I should mention had a happy and memorable ending. Buck, ourselves and two other crews went night intruding over Sicily to shoot up anything that moved. Three of us landed safely but by the time Buck returned, sea fog covered Takali.

He was advised to try and land at Luqa, but Buck was not the type to take the easy way out. The whole squadron came out to watch him doing a circuit with almost ninety-degrees of bank at about fifty feet, before he landed safely with only a few yards to spare. The story of that landing was told many times afterwards in the mess bar and each time the fog got thicker. The last time I heard it, Buck said, "the fog was so thick when I landed, even the birds were walking".

Our last nine days on our tour were memorable. On 14 May we shot down a Dornier 24 in the Bay of Naples and set an Italian 'F' Boat on fire near Sicily. On the 16th, four of us were on patrol when we intercepted two Junkers Ju 52 transports off Sicily and shot them both down. On the 18th we escorted a convoy into Malta and the following day we flew a Beau to Cairo for a service and flew back with a new one on the 20th. On the 21st, I spoke to Dolores for the first and only time and on the 22nd was nearly killed. Dolores was a legend. She was an attractive, vivacious Maltese brunette who lived not far from our mess. Aircrew went to any lengths to meet her and take her out - especially as she liked aircrew. However, there was one major snag. It was said that anyone who dated her was killed on ops soon afterwards. By May she apparently had six 'victims' to her credit, mostly new aircrew who did not take the advice of the old hands. Whether this was true or just a coincidence, I do not know, but what I do know is that I was shot up on the day after my brief conversation with her.

The op on the 22nd was our thirty-sixth and last on 272 Squadron. Four crews, including Buck, two new Australian crews, and us set off from Takali to patrol between Sicily and Tunis. We spotted a Dornier 26 flying boat heading towards North Africa and went in to attack it. Unfortunately, we did not spot the six escorting Bf 109s. The two Australian crews were shot down. Two Bf 109s attacked us and we managed to damage one (apparently it crash-landed on its return). The other riddled us with machine-gun fire and badly damaged our Beau. I had a bullet through my shoulder and waited for the next burst, which would have finished us off. I remember my last split-second thoughts – not fear but sadness – sad that my life was going to end, sad for my fiancée waiting for me in Wales and sad for the children we would never have. But, miraculously, the final burst never came. Perhaps the Bf 109 had run out of ammo or, more likely, we were flying too low for the comfort of the enemy pilot. No pilot likes flying at 300 mph at about ten feet and looking into a gun sight at the same time.

Buck, as usual, escaped unscathed, but Denis and I crash-landed at Ariana near Carthage and our aircraft was a write-off. We had survived due to Denis' skill as a pilot and because the Beaufighter VI was a tough, dependable aircraft with a design that allowed it to be flown at wave height with perfect safety. There was another reason – perhaps the most important of all – the expertise and dedication of the ground crew at Takali and back in Egypt who maintained the Beaus in tip-top condition.

Some called the Beau an ugly and unglamorous aircraft, but they were not to the aircrew that had flown one. To Denis Welfare and myself it was a friend that never let us down. It carried us safely over the jungles of Nigeria, over the deserts of Sudan and over the hostile skies and seas around Italy and Sicily. Finally, Beau 646, which we had picked up only four days earlier in Egypt, had enough resilience, in spite of being terminally damaged, to take us to safety at an obscure airfield in Tunisia, where it ended its days.

> David Bellis spent three weeks in hospitals in Malta and Egypt before being evacuated to England where he spent another three months recovering. He teamed up with Denis Welfare again and they converted to the Mosquito before joining 239 Squadron. Together, they were credited with shooting down seven enemy aircraft and sharing another. Both were awarded the DFC and Bar.

CHAPTER TWELVE
NIGHT-FIGHTER NAVIGATOR ACE

Leslie Stephenson (left) and Arthur Hall in North Africa.
(Arthur Hall)

Arthur Hall joined the RAF in May 1941 and trained as a navigator before converting to the Beaufighter night-fighter. Initially he was based in the north of England with 141 Squadron. With the decrease in Luftwaffe night raids, and an increasing need for night-fighter crews after the landings in North Africa, he left for Algiers. He recounts his experiences.

Towards the end of 1942, the Allies, including the British First Army, landed in North Africa with the intention of driving eastwards against the Afrika Corps, which was already being driven west in Libya by the British Eighth Army. In January 1943, my pilot, Leslie Stephenson (Steve), and I were informed that we had been posted to North Africa with three other crews.

The first step we took towards joining our new squadron was to go to the Bristol aircraft works at Filton to collect a brand new Beaufighter, which we had to fly out to North Africa. We took over the aircraft and left for Lyneham where we were briefed on all the arrangements for the journey. We also carried out a fuel consumption test to ensure that with full tanks we could safely complete the first stage to Gibraltar, which was expected to take about six hours. In order to achieve this sort of range the aircraft had to be stripped of all non-essential equipment and in particular we would carry no armament.

The flight plan was to depart Portreath on the southerly tip of Cornwall and cross the Bay of Biscay to a point about five miles off the north-west corner of Spain and from there we would take a course parallel with the west coasts of Spain and Portugal before turning east towards Gibraltar. After refuelling and an overnight stay the final stage of the journey would be to Setif in Algeria, which was a receiving centre for aircraft travelling from the UK to North Africa.

On 16 February we flew to Portreath in readiness for the big adventure. On arrival the ground crew discovered an oil leak and our departure was delayed. The following day we took off to carry out a test flight to ensure the aircraft was fully serviceable before our long trip. The airfield at Portreath is right on the coast and the main runway takes you over the edge of a cliff and out to sea. We were just airborne when we ran into a flock of seagulls and one smashed into our starboard wing. When we landed, we discovered a large bird embedded in the wing. It took three weeks to repair the damage.

By 11 March the repair was complete and we tested our Beaufighter again in preparation for an early morning take-off the following day. Soon after 0500 hours we were taken to dispersal and two hours later we were airborne.

I gave Steve a course roughly south-west and we flew at low level across the Bay of Biscay because we were aware the Germans had the long-range Ju 88s operating there and we were conscious that our only armament was two revolvers. It must have been about two-and-a-half hours before we saw the coast of Spain and only a slight change of course was necessary to take us down the west coast of Spain and Portugal about five miles out so as to avoid infringing the neutrality of those two countries. Two hours later we were off Cape St. Vincent and turning in an easterly direction towards Gibraltar where we landed almost six hours after leaving Cornwall.

The next day we left Gibraltar at about 1000 hours with a flight of three hours ahead of us to Setif. Both Steve and I had imagined that North Africa was relatively flat and we were astonished to find that we had to cross mountains almost 10,000 feet high.

The conditions at Setif were chaotic. There were very few buildings but hundreds of tents of all shapes and sizes. Aircraft were scattered all over the place and there were thousands of jerry cans from which aircraft were refuelling direct. We were directed to an area where security was non-existent and the native Arabs wandered around at will.

A Beaufighter VIf of 153 Squadron at Setif, Algeria. The censor has erased the AI aerials. (Air Historical Branch CAN 369)

After what seemed ages we were transported to the officers' mess (a large tent) and there we met the station commander, one of the characters of the service by the name of Group Captain 'Batchy' Atcherley.

Happily our stay at Setif was only two days and we then left to join 153 Squadron at Maison Blanche, the former civil airport for Algiers where the facilities were a vast improvement. We were billeted in what had been a very large house and the sleeping arrangements were quite simply that you put your sleeping bag in any space you could find on the floor. The officers' mess was a French-style café where we could buy unlimited amounts of cheap wine. The food was boring but wholesome and there was a plentiful supply of gorgeous oranges.

Operationally it was anticipated that the Luftwaffe would attack Algiers and Oran where supply ships were arriving in great numbers to reinforce and supply the First Army and the Americans who were already driving east towards Tunis. The bulk of these attacks were expected at night and our squadron was there to deal with them.

For the first few weeks there was surprisingly little enemy activity but things began to hot up as the army advanced eastwards and within range of the enemy airfields in Italy. Moreover, the supply lines to the army were shortened by using smaller ports further east such as Bône, which were less well defended by anti-aircraft guns and therefore an easier target for the enemy. These increasing attacks were countered by sending a detachment of two aircraft from our squadron to a small airstrip at Bône. It was there on 17 April that we had our first taste of real action.

We were airborne at 1730 hours on a dusk patrol when ground control advised us that bandits (enemy aircraft) were approaching from the east at 5,000 feet. We were given a steer but were soon told that the aircraft were friendly. We turned to a westerly course and almost immediately saw ten aircraft some 3,000 feet on the starboard side, which we took to be the 'friendlies', reported by control. However, on closing, we realised they were Junkers 88s and they scattered as soon as they saw us. We closed on one and it began to take violent evasive action, which I followed on the radar. Several short bursts of fire set the starboard engine of the enemy aircraft on fire. We experienced some return fire but Steve gave it a final burst when we were only 100 feet above the sea. The port engine and wing caught fire and the Ju 88 crashed into the sea.

We returned to base highly elated by our first success and our ground crew took great pleasure in painting a swastika on the nose of our Beaufighter.

As the army advanced eastwards our squadron detachments moved up behind them and we started to use small airstrips, which had been constructed by the Royal Engineers. One was at Taher. Unfortunately, this was not equipped with full night-flying facilities and, although we could take off in the dark, we could not land there. This meant that once we were scrambled at night we had to go all the way back to Maison Blanche when we had completed our mission. It was at Taher that we encountered our next real action on 11 May.

We were scrambled at 1945 hours under 'Funless' Control and given a vector of 060 degrees but no height. We climbed to 2,000 feet and after a few minutes we met twelve Ju 88s head on and slightly above. After a 180-degree turn I picked up the bandits on the radar and we closed in until Steve got a visual on one of them. From a range of about 300 yards a short burst from our cannons hit the enemy aircraft and its starboard engine and wing burst into flames with pieces breaking off, one of which hit our windscreen. The enemy then dived steeply into the sea completely enveloped in flames. We were near Bône, probably the enemy's target, and as we turned out to sea, we saw a second Ju 88. We lost visual on it but I got a radar contact and we closed in as the enemy started evasive action. We followed it to very low over the sea but I held it on radar for several minutes until Steve was visual. By this time the Ju 88 was flying straight and level at 200 feet. A two-second burst set its starboard engine on fire and it crashed into the sea.

We landed back at Maison Blanche at 2330 hours after a flight of almost four hours feeling tired but happy and we received a marvellous welcome from the CO, our flight commander and our friends because this was the first time a crew of 153 Squadron had destroyed two enemy aircraft on one sortie.

Wing Commander W. G. Moseby addresses the crews of 153 Squadron. Stephenson is standing second from right and Hall is kneeling third from right. (Arthur Hall)

During the month of May there was a marked increase in enemy action as they attempted to impede the advance of the allied armies eastwards and the aircraft of our squadron were constantly in action. Our own next involvement was on 24 May when, once again, we were on detachment at Taher.

We were scrambled at 0045 hours and told two bandits were approaching from the north-east and to climb to 2,000 feet. We were vectored onto a westerly heading north of Djidjelli. I got a radar contact at a range of 1,200 yards and 2,000 feet above crossing from starboard to port. We followed until the enemy levelled off at 10,000 feet when we increased speed. At 500 yards Steve was visual and soon identified it as a Ju 88. He gave it a two-second burst and it caught fire and dived vertically into the sea just off the coast.

We were immediately given an easterly vector to pursue a bandit leaving the area. We were at 5,000 feet and saw an aircraft in the moon's reflection on the sea flying just above the surface. We dived and I got a radar contact at two miles and vectored Steve to visual range when he identified another Ju 88. A two-second burst resulted in its port engine catching fire and it crashed into the sea.

We climbed to 3,000 feet and were immediately vectored onto another target. It was at 10,000 feet and we closed in to visual range. It was about to dive on the target area when Steve opened fire and scored some hits. It immediately started to climb and we hit it again and it was soon enveloped in flame. It crashed into the sea ten miles off the coast. We then headed back to Maison Blanche.

News of our triple success had reached base via control and although it was five o'clock in the morning we had a marvellous reception from those members of the squadron who were on duty and the pride shown by our ground crew was the most heartening of all. The following night we had a whale of a party in the mess, not only in celebration of the fact that this was the first time a crew had destroyed three enemy aircraft in one night-time sortie but also that the squadron's tally was thirteen destroyed in thirteen days.

With the Afrika Corps now driven into a small pocket in the north-east of Tunisia, enemy air activity on the coast of North Africa became greatly diminished. Our squadron began to send a detachment even further east to an airfield at Sebala, which was not very many miles from Tunis itself.

We were operating from there on 9 June when we were instructed to fly to the island of Pantellaria, after reports that the enemy was evacuating it. Control requested that we fly round this small island at 400 feet to see if we attracted any ground fire. This we did and reported no enemy action. We were then asked to repeat this at 200 feet and we saw no activity and reported accordingly. The following day, the army landed on the island without any opposition and we always maintained (tongue-in-cheek) that we really captured the island of Pantellaria.

A quite remarkable incident occurred whilst Steve and I were on detachment at Sebala with an NCO crew of Flight Sergeants Downing and Lyons. Control required a dusk patrol and a dawn patrol and being officer crew we 'pulled rank' and chose the dusk patrol because experience had shown that this was when it was more likely to see some action. In the event, we spent three hours patrolling up and down the coast with not a trace of enemy air activity and we landed back at Sebala and went to bed.

We rose early next morning in order to be at dispersal when the two flight sergeants returned from their patrol and we asked them if there had been 'anything doing'. When Downing replied that at first light they had shot down five Junkers 52s full of German troops we really thought this was his idea of a joke and told him to stop mucking about and tell us if anything had really happened. At this point, the telephone rang and when Steve answered it he was told the AOC wished to speak to the crew who had shot down five German transport aircraft evacuating troops from Tunisia – he had been given the news by the controller. We then realised that our two colleagues were telling the truth and that we had missed an easy chance to add five to our tally. Downing and Lyons were later awarded the Distinguished Flying Medal and for the rest of his RAF career, Downing was known as 'Ace'. This was in fact quite a unique achievement because so far as I am aware this was the only occasion at that time when an Allied pilot on one sortie shot down five aircraft.

Flight Sergeant 'Ace' Downing and his radar operator John Lyons after their epic night when they claimed five enemy aircraft. (Air Historical Branch CAN 827)

The next momentous event so far as Steve and I were concerned happened on 19 June when we were both summoned to the CO's office and were each handed a personal message from the air office commanding North Africa which read, "My heartiest congratulations on your well-deserved immediate award of the Distinguished Flying Cross". These were the first decorations awarded to the squadron in North Africa and, not surprisingly, were celebrated with a great party.

The following afternoon we flew to Taher on detachment feeling in great spirits and really hoping for a night of action. Little did we realise the disaster that lay ahead. We were scrambled at dusk and everything seemed quite normal as we completed our final cockpit drill and Steve gave both engines the usual run-up with the brakes on. We then started the take-off run and just as we reached flying speed and were a few feet off the ground, the starboard engine gave a great bang and stopped. This was the situation dreaded by all airmen because we did not have sufficient speed to climb and control the aircraft on one engine and with only a few yards of the runway left there was no chance of aborting the take-off.

Steve did the only thing possible and closed the throttles and did a belly-landing straight ahead. Fortunately, straight ahead was woodland and we crashed into the trees at a speed of about 130 mph. Both wings were ripped off and the tailplane broke off two or three feet behind my seat. The remainder of the fuselage with us in it hurtled through the trees before coming to a halt. Everything went dark for a few seconds and

I really thought I was dead until I looked up the front of the wreckage and saw Steve's legs disappearing through the top hatch. I realised this was no time to be hanging about and I too made a rapid exit through my hatch. By this time the surrounding woodland was on fire and the ammunition was exploding so we beat a hasty retreat and then fell flat on the ground until the fireworks finished.

It took some time for the fire tender and the 'blood wagon' to reach us and they were quite amazed to find us quite unscathed apart from a few cuts and bruises as they could not imagine how anyone could have survived such a horrific crash. We realised afterwards that we owed our lives to the Beaufighter being built like a tank and also to the wings, which contained the fuel tanks, shearing off at impact.

It was the next morning before an aircraft could be sent from Maison Blanche to collect us. We had not slept well as we relived our experience and wondered how we had survived. I did not enjoy the take-off of our 'rescue aircraft' particularly as we just got airborne and in my imagination I could hear again the starboard engine blowing up. We had a very sympathetic reception back at base and we appreciated the seven days off given to us by the CO.

In July the Allies landed in Sicily and our primary task was to provide cover for the invasion fleet usually at dusk and at dawn. We were always a bit peeved when we arrived over a convoy for the sole purpose of giving it protection only to be greeted by a hail of anti-aircraft fire from the escorting warships. On reflection, however, we did not really blame them for their 'shoot first and ask questions afterwards' attitude and we would probably have done the same in their vulnerable position. What I did not realise until after the war was that at about this time my younger brother and I must on occasions have been only about a mile apart because he was with the army in Sicily and I was some 5,000 feet above him.

At the end of July, we received the news we had been longing to hear. Our first operational tour was at an end and we would be returning to England for a 'rest' as instructors at an operational training unit. Our friends gave us a great send-off and we left the squadron in the middle of August. I was glad to be leaving North Africa and I made a mental note never to return.

Arthur Hall and his pilot Leslie 'Steve' Stephenson returned to operations in March 1944 when they joined 219 Squadron flying the Mosquito. By the end of the war they had shot down three more enemy aircraft and each had received a Bar to the DFC.

CHAPTER THIRTEEN

MEDITERRANEAN STRIKE PILOT

Tom Freer (left) and his navigator Paddy Holman.
(Mrs Miranda Freer)

Immediately after finishing his schooling at Eton College in June 1940, **Tom Freer** joined the RAF. He trained as a pilot in South Africa under the British Commonwealth Air Training Plan. At the end of 1941 he returned to England and converted to the Beaufighter.

It was at the Beaufighter OTU at Catfoss that I met my navigator Paddy Holman. We got on very well together so we decided to become a crew. I could not have made a better choice. In a Beaufighter, the pilot is helped by the illusion that he has his fate in his own hands, whereas the navigator is a passenger, and in an air battle he has nothing to do except try not to let his fears get the better of him. I had the greatest respect for Paddy and during the next two years he displayed an impressively calm courage, in addition to his great technical skill at his job.

Teaching us to fly Beaufighters was clearly rather a strain for the instructors, and a great deal had to be packed into a short space of time. I never understood why we did not get enough practice aiming the guns, and single-engine landings were considered too dangerous to teach. My instructor told me that if I lost an engine "do your best to get it down!"

When we finished the course we were posted to the Middle East but the question was how to get there. We were sent to Takoradi in West Africa by sea to pick up a Beaufighter. They had been shipped 'in boxes' and assembled at Takoradi before we flew one across Africa to Egypt. It was while we were at Takoradi that I experienced an event that altered my perception of what it is to be a pilot. We were allocated an aircraft to fly to Egypt and were told to take it up and test everything to ensure that all was in order. We flew around for about an hour then suddenly one of the engines stopped. I was therefore faced with having to make a landing with only one engine; the very thing my instructor had said was too dangerous to teach.

I returned to the airfield but lowered the undercarriage too early on the approach and with insufficient speed. The aircraft lost height rapidly and we were going to undershoot the runway. I dived to almost ground level to gain enough speed to overshoot to make a second attempt. I made a much steeper approach before lowering the undercarriage but the 'round out' was difficult to judge and we made a very heavy landing. Later, after we joined a squadron, I persuaded all pilots to practise single-engine landings.

After the aircraft was repaired, we set off the next day for Egypt. The long flight across the continent took several days in stages. On arrival in Egypt we were sent to Malta to join 227 Squadron. Our job was going to be a varied one, protecting our own shipping from being attacked or attacking enemy shipping that was carrying German reinforcements and supplies to North Africa.

Our first operational flight on 14 October 1942 was nearly our last one. We were sent as a formation of three to try and sink an enemy ship nearing the German-held port of Tripoli on the North African coast 200 miles south of Malta. The target was the Italian merchant ship *Trapani* escorted by the torpedo boat **Medici**. We were carrying bombs for a low-level attack.

Freer's Beaufighter at Takali, Malta.
(Mrs Miranda Freer)

Our flight commander, Squadron Leader Peter Underwood DFC, led the attack but he misjudged his pull-up and hit the mast of the *Trapani* and crashed into the sea. He and his navigator were lost. The anti-aircraft guns shot down the number two and I heard later that the crew were rescued from their dinghy and taken prisoner. Then it was our turn and to my dismay the bombs did not drop. I then made a foolish decision and decided to make a second attack; in fact, it did not occur to me to do otherwise. Of course, the anti-aircraft gunners had plenty of time to see us coming in and we were nearly shot down. But our aircraft kept going in spite of being hit and this time the bombs released. I would like to say that we sank the ship, but we did not. We flew back to Malta with punctured hydraulics and no airspeed indicator and had to make a belly-landing, which was a success (if you can use such a description) and we were uninjured.

We made a number of such attacks on enemy shipping and I think our activities caused them a lot of trouble, but I never felt that our results were as good as they should have been. We were very professional at flying and navigating, but when it came to anything that required accurate aiming, we were amateurs.

On one of these flights to attack a ship off Pantelleria I made the mistake of misjudging the pull-up. I left it a fraction of a second too late and, as we passed over the ship, one of our propellers hit the top of the funnel. The damaged propeller caused the engine to shake rather badly, but we got back to Malta quite easily.

A few sorties later we ended up in the sea. It was not because of enemy action but due to engine problems. We almost got back to Malta, but not quite and we had to ditch. It was frightening but we got out all right and were rescued by a fishing boat. Paddy wrote in his logbook that he thought our survival was attributable to my having handled the situation with great skill. I don't agree with that; if I had handled it differently, we might have reached Malta. The cause of the trouble was an oil leak and we were unable to 'feather' the propeller so the engine had to be allowed to continue running and I was worried what would happen when all the oil was lost so I decided to make use of the engine while I could but it might have been better to throttle it back and nurse it along.

Two flights that were out of the ordinary were to carry the AOC, AM Keith Park, famous as a commander in the Battle of Britain. He was an independent-minded New Zealander, a born leader, and we all liked him immensely. I was very proud to be chosen as his pilot when he went to conferences in Algiers and Egypt. He preferred to travel in a Beaufighter rather than in a slow transport aircraft. There was no seat for him but there was adequate space to stand behind the pilot.

On our return flight from Algiers, he rather naughtily asked me to fly him over Bizerta harbour, near Tunis, so that he could see the German shipping. I thought it was a very bad idea and said so. He then said, "What will you do if I order you to do it?" I replied that my CO had warned me before the flight that the AVM might try it on and had told me to ignore it as I was in charge and he was my passenger. (The bit about the CO was my invention but I knew he would back me up.) The AVM loved it and used to recount the story afterwards with great amusement.

In addition to attacks on shipping, we were also occasionally engaged in the Beaufighter's fighter role. Our real fear was the Messerschmitt Bf 109 and, in a dog-fight with one, there was no way that we could win. The Beaufighter was much less manoeuvrable and a Bf 109 was sure to get behind us. Fortunately, we rarely saw them.

On 12 December we were flying in a mixed formation led by the flight commander of 272 Squadron, Squadron Leader R. Rankin, when we encountered a Junkers 88 and we shared in its destruction. [Note: Tom Freer fails to mention that a week later he shared in the destruction of a Heinkel III. Return fire damaged his aircraft but he managed to get back to Malta when the undercarriage collapsed. Nor does he men-

227 Squadron aircrew at Malta. (Mrs Miranda Freer)

tion that he was awarded the DFC on 5 January 1943 for his 'high skill, outstanding determination and courage'. Author]

As General Montgomery advanced westwards after the Battle of Alamein, our squadron left Malta for North Africa and as the battle moved westwards we moved from one airfield to another in support.

On one of our flights, Paddy and I ended up being interned in Turkey. We were attacking a small vessel in the Aegean Sea, near the island of Melos north of Crete when one of our engines was put out of action by a single bullet. I doubted that we could get back to North Africa on one engine so we headed for Turkey knowing we would be interned. It was a nervous time because we were very vulnerable if we met any enemy fighters. We flew from one island to another – the Aegean is full of islands – and, as we passed one, we wondered if we would reach the next but all went well and we landed at the Turkish airfield at Smyrna (now called Izmir).

Our internment was a very mild affair. International law required us to be interned since we had arrived in a neutral country in uniform. We were placed in a lodging house in the outskirts of the capital, Ankara. It was just like being on leave. At night, a Turkish soldier was placed in the front hall to prevent us walking out of the place. During the day we gave our parole and were free to go where we wished. We drew our pay once a week at the British embassy, ate in the best restaurants and had a good time.

However, our real intention was to return to our squadron, so we discussed at the embassy how we might escape. The air attaché made plans for our route; all we had to do was to escape from our house. The method we chose was to slide down a rope from the balcony into the street below. We did it in the middle of the night.

We walked through the streets of Ankara to an address we had been given. It was full of British engineers in civilian clothes who were building airfields for the Turks. They arranged our journey across Turkey to the west coast where we boarded a sailing schooner the size of a large fishing boat. The schooner was in the service of the British Foreign Office making clandestine voyages under the noses of the Germans taking supplies to British agents on remote islands in the Aegean. We knew very little about its activities and we did not enquire too closely.

We arrived in Cyprus and then re-joined our squadron at Derna in North Africa on 26 June. We arrived back in time to see the preparations for the invasion of Sicily and flew patrols over the fleets. Towards the end of our time with the squadron, Paddy was awarded the DFC. It was well deserved. His loyalty and dedication, and most of all his self-control and cool courage, were always an astonishment to me.

For our final months on the squadron we were based in Cyprus and, compared to the deserts of North Africa, it was paradise. In the autumn of 1943, we left the squadron and Paddy and I were sent to Shallufa in Egypt as instructors. Beaufighters were being equipped with rocket projectiles (RPs) with each aircraft carrying eight. My job was to teach pilots how to fire these weapons (I first had to learn myself).

We spent about a year as instructors and then it was time to re-join a squadron. We were sent to Italy in October 1944 to join 272 Squadron at Foggia. Our first patrol was on the 21st when we carried out a rocket attack against a large barge. Two days later we

Ground crews servicing Beaufighter VI of 227 Squadron, using a Coles Crane probably in Cyprus. (Air Historical Branch CM 5381)

were leading a pair near Trieste when we suddenly came upon a large naval ship. I think it was a German cruiser [Note: It was the old Italian battleship *Conti di Cavour* damaged by the Fleet Air Arm at Taranto and now used as a block ship.] I decided to attack it with our rockets.

I hoped we had not been seen, but that was a forlorn hope. Before we got near the ship they started firing at us and our aircraft was soon damaged. I realised that to attack such a formidable ship as a pair was suicidal so I turned away. A fire started in the port engine so I shut it down. While I was doing this and flying on one engine, anti-aircraft guns on the nearby shore hit us again. There was a terrific bang and Paddy let out a cry but before I had time to ask him where the damage was, or whether he was injured, we hit the sea. I escaped as quickly as I could and as I did, the aircraft sank. Paddy never got out. I swam about the wreckage but there was no sign of him. I shall never know exactly what happened to him. Our two cockpits in the Beaufighter were a long way apart, with a bulkhead of armoured doors in between, so I had no opportunity to help him.

The Germans came out in a rowing boat and picked me up. They were Luftwaffe personnel and very kind. I was eventually taken to Germany by train. I was grateful to be in the hands of the Luftwaffe for the next six months and not the German SS.

The shock of Paddy's death affected me profoundly, as it still does sixty years later.

Tom Freer left the RAF and began a long career in civil aviation. He flew during the Berlin Air Lift before joining British European Airways retiring in 1971.

CHAPTER FOURTEEN
SHIPPING STRIKE OFF ITALY

Jack Howe (right) and Bill Shepherd. (Jack Howe)

Jack Howe trained as a pilot in Canada and on his return to the UK, he began his conversion to the Beaufighter.

After flying the Blenheim and the Beaufighter II at 132 (Coastal) OTU at East Fortune, I went to Crosby-on-Eden near Carlisle to fly the Hercules-engined Beaufighter VI and where I teamed up with Bill Shepherd. We then had a spell with 2 Torpedo Training Unit at Castle Kennedy near Stranraer where we practised attacking ships in nearby Luce Bay.

We joined 144 Squadron at Leuchars, which had earlier been equipped with the Hampden. After an abortive foray to Russia it had returned and re-equipped with the Beaufighter VIc. We soon moved to a frozen Tain airfield on the Cromarty Firth where we flew to the Norwegian coast looking for shipping taking iron ore down the coast to the Frisian Islands and on to Rotterdam for the great industrial factories in the Ruhr.

We did six sorties and never saw a ship and hardly ever saw Norway. This was partly due to the very bad weather but also because the Germans realised it was better to sail at night and hide in the fjords during the day.

In May 1943 the squadron was sent to North Africa. The TF Mk. X had replaced the Mk. VI and sixteen set off for Algeria. Being the junior crew, we sailed with the ground party to Algiers and then on to Blida. We then went by road to Tunis and on to one of the complexes of nearby airfields at Protville just to the south. The onward journey should have been by rail but the wagons had recently been used to transport donkeys and the RAF said, "thank you, but no". We arrived ahead of the aircraft but fourteen soon arrived, two having been lost en route.

We became operational in June just before the Allied invasion of Sicily. Operations were of two types. 'Rovers' were patrols looking for ships to attack and 'Strikes' were pre-planned on specific targets. Formations were normally eight aircraft with four attacking the escorts with cannons and the other four armed with torpedoes.

Opposite: Jack Howe's office in a Beaufighter VI. (Air Historical Branch CH 17305)

On a typical 'Rover' we took off and coasted out at Cap Bizerta and then headed up the east coast of Sardinia and Corsica before turning east for Elba and then south down the Italian coast to Sicily and back to base. Most of the flying was at very low level, which kept us below enemy radar cover but, unlike the choppy North Sea, the Mediterranean was often very flat like glass making it very difficult to judge the height above the sea.

The squadron's first operation was a disaster. The leader, Flying Officer Eric Muller-Rowland was flying at very low level when I think his propellers clipped the sea. He suddenly pulled up before crashing into the water. He escaped, got into his dinghy but did not survive. His navigator did not manage to escape. The other seven aircraft milled around and some tried to drop more dinghies to Muller-Rowland. Two of the aircraft managed to collide but were able to limp back to base.

Bill and I attempted our first Mediterranean operation on 26 June but we had a hydraulic failure on take-off and had to return. Two more sorties followed when we carried a torpedo but we failed to find a target, but matters changed on 13 July. Again, we had a torpedo and flew as number two to the CO, Wing Commander J. McLaughlin DFC, after intelligence had identified a convoy. Attacking from the north, the CO launched his torpedo against an escorting destroyer but it went directly under the target. We soon discovered that the escorts drew less water and our torpedoes were set at a depth suitable for the merchantmen. We dropped ours and it hit a 7,000-ton merchant ship amidships and we learned later that it had sunk.

On the next operation on 20 July we failed to find the main target but shot up some barges escorted by a Siebel ferry. These converted flat-bottomed barges were a nest of flak and one of the formation was shot down and had to ditch. We orbited and dropped Bill's dinghy to the pilot (the navigator was lost) and he survived to become a prisoner. Losses were high on these strikes, which were many miles from friendly territory.

On 23 July, eight Beaufighters were tasked to attack a convoy near the coast of Italy north of Rome. Four carried torpedoes and we were in the anti-flak section. Two destroyers, three flak ships and two flying boats escorted the vessels. We found the target near Civitavecchia but saw only one of the destroyers. The torpedo Beaufighters climbed to 150 feet for their drop and the anti-flak team climbed to 500 feet. Flight Sergeant Hamer shot down one of the flying boats and we tackled the destroyer, which appeared to be in the lead.

We dived steeply and aimed at the destroyer's stern where the depth charges were likely to be positioned. We hoped for a lucky strike with the cannon, which would cause an explosion. Intense flak was encountered, which we hoped meant that we had distracted attention from those attacking with torpedoes. In fact, it seemed that we had attracted too much because there was the proverbial large bang and we took a hit in the nose of the aircraft, which was badly damaged. I was hit in the legs but we managed to complete our attack.

We headed for base, some 400 miles away and the remainder of the formation provided an escort. After crash-landing I was taken to hospital and it was the end of my time on Beaufighters.

The author meets Jack Howe (left) in Vancouver in 2000. (Author)

The author met the very modest Jack Howe in 2000 when he visited Vancouver where Jack was the chairman of the local branch of the Aircrew Association. When questioned about the details of his final attack, Jack made light of his experience but the fact that he had been awarded the Conspicuous Gallantry Medal - one of only 120 awarded to airmen - made it clear that this was no 'normal sortie'. Jack's Canadian friend, **Jack Meadows**, also a Beaufighter pilot, provides the details of Jack's final flight.

Jack had been severely wounded in the leg and in the face. The flight to base involved ninety minutes of flying, all over the sea. Jack's main fear was if he lost too much blood and passed out, it would not only be the end of him, but also for his navigator. Even if Bill Shepherd had known how to fly the aircraft, he would have had the greatest difficulty in getting Jack backwards out of the narrow pilot's seat, even if the aircraft had been serviceable and flying normally. He would then have had to climb into the seat himself. Jack got Shepherd to tear his shirt into bandages to wrap around his leg above the wound and was relieved when the blood flow was less severe.

The aircraft's instruments were severely damaged and the pitch control levers had been jammed in fine, so the engines were over-revving badly and overheating, another great cause for concern. If both failed he would have had to ditch. On one engine he could probably have got home, unless it was the starboard as his damaged leg would never have kept the aircraft flying straight, despite full rudder trim. In the circumstances a diversion to the nearest land, hostile Corsica or Sardinia, or even Sicily where the Allies had a bare foothold would have been understandable, but Jack was determined to keep going. The engines lasted well enough to get back to Protville. As his hydraulics had also been shot away, he had to do a fast belly-landing. He dimly remembers his CO fanning with his hat at a fire in the exhaust of one engine as he was pulled out through the top hatch of the cockpit. The overheating of the engine had led to the inevitable fire. He got home only just in time.

Jack was taken to hospital in Carthage, once a monastery. As he lay in bed one day there was a flurry as lots of top brass on a special visit approached him. His AOC, Air Vice-Marshal Hugh Pughe Lloyd, told him that he had been awarded the Conspicuous Gallantry Medal. The AOC apologised that, since the medal was so rare, he had been unable to find any ribbon anywhere in North Africa or the Middle East for Jack to wear.

The squadron soon returned to the UK where Bill Shepherd flew with another pilot. They had to ditch in the North Sea, and he was picked up from his dinghy but his pilot was lost.

Jack Howe spent four months in hospital before returning to England. Within days his wound re-opened and he was hospitalised for a further four months during which time he celebrated his twenty-first birthday. Eventually, in March 1944, he returned to fly with No. 4 Delivery Flight and later with No. 2 Ferry Pool at Aston Down. He was commissioned in late 1944 and left the service in July 1947.

Remembering his time in Canada, Howe emigrated to Vancouver where he spent the rest of his life.

CHAPTER FIFTEEN
COMBAT OVER SICILY

Northern Irishman **Desmond Hughes** was a well-established night-fighter 'ace' having flown Defiants and Beaufighter IIs when he left for North Africa in January 1943 to join 600 Squadron. Further success came before the invasion of Sicily by which time he had been credited with destroying ten enemy aircraft with another shared and a probable.

Wing Commander Des Hughes DFC & Two Bars. (Air Historical Branch CH 14226)

When I heard in January 1943 that I was to depart the UK for Algeria and join 600 Squadron, I invited Pilot Officer Laurie Dixon to join me as my nav/rad (navigator/radio). He had recently served on 600 and jumped at the chance to re-join his friends in Algeria and thus we started a long and productive association. We enjoyed some success in the months leading up to the defeat of German forces in the desert and their attempted evacuation from Tunisia in May.

On 25 June, 600 Squadron moved to Malta. We reached there in an exhilarating wave-top flight of about two hours, skirting Hammamet and Linosa on the way. There wasn't a cloud in the sky and nothing to be seen on the empty sea until the yellow-ochre smudge of the Maltese cliffs showed up on the horizon. A gentle climb up to circuit height and we dropped down on Luqa, each aircraft being marshalled into its individual blast pen of soft yellow sandstone blocks and rubble-filled petrol cans.

The island was choc-a-bloc with ships, aircraft, equipment and men. The Luqa mess was full so we found ourselves most comfortably billeted in the Meadowbank Hotel in Sliema – a welcome improvement on our tented camps in Africa, especially the grotty one at Bône. Everyone seemed to be still celebrating the end of the long siege. Good food and drink were plentiful and, to us newcomers at least, the fare and the service at the Union Club (lobster thermidor, no less!) were remarkably luxurious for wartime. We were glad, too, to be able to buy decent bush-jacket uniforms and suede boots – we must have been a pretty scruffy-looking lot on arrival.

Luqa was commanded by Group Captain 'Willie' (later ACM Sir Walter) Merton who personally welcomed us on arrival; our month's stay was to be a very happy one. The AOC, Air Marshal Sir Keith Park, driving his scarlet MG sports car, was one of our first visitors. The airfield, considering the pounding it had received from the Luftwaffe and the Regia Aeronautica, was in astonishingly good nick, though the sheer drop off the end of the main runway into a sandstone quarry gave one food for thought.

The radar coverage towards Sicily was superb and the fighter controllers were a formidable lot - the splendid Group Captain 'Woody' Woodhall, from my Duxford days, in overall charge in the operations room; the former 601 Auxiliary, Roger Frankland, leading the resident team and 'Brownie' and Bill Pratley due to go ashore in Sicily with their mobile GCIs soon after H-Hour. All these people really knew their stuff and had our complete confidence.

During the run-up to the invasion, code-named 'Husky', the Axis scarcely ever tried approaching the island, let alone attacking it; this was so by night as well as by day. At this time Malta's night-fighter force comprised, in addition to us, 108 Squadron with Beaufighters commanded by Wing Commander Jasper Read and a flight of Mosquitos of 256 Squadron under Squadron Leader Ian Allen; they were not part of the Desert Air Force and the Mosquitos were not allowed to fly over enemy-held territory lest their Mk. VIII AI should fall into enemy hands.

During the night of 10 July Sicily was invaded, the Americans on the left and the British on the right, and 600's 'purple patch' began. After a quiet start, which suggested they had been taken by surprise, the Axis bombers showed up in agreeable numbers over the beachheads and as our GCIs got ashore and deployed - which they did with quite remarkable speed - we inflicted grievous losses on them. No. 600 knocked down twenty-five in the first week; the most successful crews were Paddy Green and Reg Gillies with seven, including four in one patrol, and Johnny Turnbull with Sergeant Fowler who notched up six. I was content enough with two in ten days.

The morale of the squadron hit a new high and the competition between the crews to be allocated the most favourable slots in the night-flying programme became intense. Over 1,000 hours were flown in a month, a high figure for defensive night-fighters. Incidentally, the night after Paddy Green got his four bombers, Ian Allen of 256 Squadron in his Mosquito shot down five on one patrol. Enemy losses at night were appalling, but they kept coming.

The Allied armies made steady progress, the Eighth going up the east coast and the Americans sweeping through the west of Sicily towards Palermo. Enough airfields had been captured for us to follow the Spitfires into the island so, a fortnight after the initial assault, we flew into Cassibile, just south of Syracuse. We were to stay there for two months. The airstrip was magnificent - long and smooth and cut clean through a very large plantation of olive and orange trees. There we found a complete Italian flare-path outfit, including a mercury-vapour floodlight and searchlight to act as a homing beacon if required. We also acquired a cooking-trailer, which we adapted to act as a mobile operations room.

There was only one drawback to Cassibile - it was altogether too close to the Syracuse anchorage and our dusk patrols were fired on by the assembled shipping every night as we took off and climbed away. We protested vigorously to the navy by telephone but they swore blind that they were attacking Ju 88s. It was not until one aircraft, flown by Flight Lieutenant Hilken, was hit by a 20-mm Oerlikon shell (fortuitously, not an HE one) that

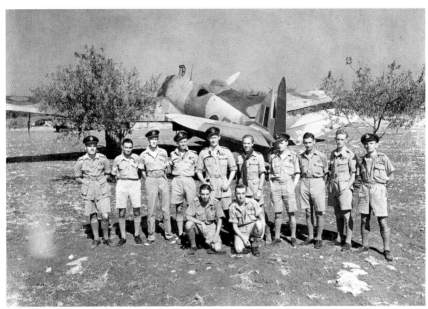

600 Squadron aircrew at Cassibile, Sicily. Des Hughes pictured with scarf and Wing Commander 'Paddy' Green on his right. (Air Historical Branch CNA 1181)

the navy believed us – and then only because we were able to plonk the offending missile on the local captain's desk. Faced with this powerful evidence, he immediately offered Paddy Green and I a large pink gin and a hot shower, which we were very glad to accept. *Mirabile dictum,* we were not shot at after this.

It was now the very height of the Mediterranean summer and midday temperatures were horribly high. We had to rig makeshift sunshades to shield the cockpits; this made them just about inhabitable as we strapped in to fly but, even so, the temperatures ran way above 120 degrees by the time we started up and taxied to the end of the runway. The ground crews also had their problems in this searing heat. They had to be very careful not to touch the flat surfaces of the wings and fuselage with their bodies as they worked stripped to their shorts. It was only too easy to lose a large expanse of tender skin from inside the forearms.

For me, one side effect of the scorching heat was sheer fatigue. I would be up all night supervising the programme and taking my turn to fly patrols of three or four hours. What worried me particularly was that I was beginning to feel tired in the air and on one occasion, when required to fly a second sortie one night, I asked Peter Scurlock, our doctor, to give me something to keep me awake. He said: "I have just the thing – some caffeine tablets." Despite taking these just before I flew, I had the greatest difficulty keeping my eyes open as I returned from a patrol. I had turned the Beau on to the approach path when I was many miles out to sea, for I could see the flare-path from an altitude of 4,000 feet. I dropped the wheels, set the flaps and trimmed for a powered approach. All seemed to be going nicely but I clearly nodded off because I was rudely awakened by urgent shouts from Laurie. He was just in time for we had sunk well below the glide-path and would have hit the sea about a mile from the runway. Poor Peter was very upset when I hinted that he had got his tablets mixed up and given me sleeping pills!

I soon forgot about this little bit of excitement for a week later I was on patrol north-east of Catania when a determined attack was mounted on a clutch of Spitfire airstrips at Lentini. These were liberally scattered with incendiary and fragmentation bombs. Bill Pratley at the GCI put us into contact with a Ju 88, which never saw us and was smartly sent down in flames. Pratley then put us on to another Ju 88, which did see us and tried to evade. Three of my cannons jammed but I was lucky enough to knock it down with a one-second burst from the fourth cannon and the machine guns, using a lot of deflection. We saw this crash and then Laurie re-cocked the cannons. He had no sooner got back on his radar tubes when he picked up a third Ju 88 without help from GCI. This one was happily wending its way home after dropping its bombs, Laurie produced another copy-book interception; I hit the Hun in the starboard engine but it refused to burn. The top gunner sprayed tracer around us hitting the starboard wing and engine air-intake as he dived away. I pushed the nose hard down (propelling Laurie sharply up into his Perspex dome!) and gave a very long burst, hitting him hard. He crashed into the sea this being witnessed by Paddy Green who had arrived to join the fray. Pratley then put me on to a fourth target and I was closing on AI radar when it flew into the 3.7 AA barrage defending the airfield. I immediately received all the unpleasantness aimed at the Hun. When I began to hear the shell bursts as well as see them and could hear splinters tickling the belly of the Beau, I decided that discretion was very much the better part of valour and broke away before getting into visual range. On landing I found that my aircraft was not seriously damaged but did require quite a bit of patching up. Paddy Green got another Ju 88 and Flying Officer Ripley a fifth and one damaged, so it was a very expensive raid for the Luftwaffe. However, whether they knew it or not, they killed twelve men

Beaufighter VIf of 600 Squadron parked amongst the olive trees at Cassibile, Sicily. (Air Historical Branch CNA 1185)

and put out of action some twenty fighters on the Lentini strips - which they might have considered a fair exchange.

Just a week later, I was returning at dawn from the last patrol of the night. It had been totally uneventful and I was quietly gliding down towards Cassibile when the controller came up: "I have something for you - coming north of Syracuse, quite low." He then skilfully vectored me so that the target would be silhouetted against the dawn glow to the east. There was no need to use the AI as a Ju 87 Stuka was clearly visible a couple of miles away at low level. Turning gently to port, I was swinging in nicely behind him when, at a range of about half a mile, he spotted me. He immediately pulled into a violent left-hand turn. I hauled the Beau around after him, thinking this was going to be one helluva dogfight, and fired a two-second burst with all guns. I saw no results at all from this but perhaps the awesome sight of the flames from the Beau's gun ports made

Wing Commander Green of 600 Squadron (wearing a flying officer's jacket) in the cockpit of Beaufighter VIf (V8762). The AI Mk. IV radar aerial is prominent. (Air Historical Branch CH 15214)

some impression for he eased the turn. The gunner fired some tracer well over the top of us but I now had an easier shot and the next burst hit him firmly in the crank of the port wing. The Stuka turned on its back and went into the sea with an enormous splash. I still can't understand why that Stuka crew allowed itself to run out of darkness, its only real protection against fighters. Half an hour earlier and it would have got home for our AI would probably not have coped at that low altitude.

Enemy activity had now started to taper off quite markedly, the only raid of significance being a massed Stuka attack on Augusta just after dark. This was difficult to deal with because the targets were so slow that the Beaufighters tended to overshoot and, secondly, they were so concentrated that both GCI and AI pictures were very confused. Even John Turnbull couldn't cope, which is saying something! Much later that night, I was on patrol and was put on to a bandit flying south towards Malta at 20,000 feet. Laurie was bringing me in beautifully when, at a range of 1,000 yards, the AI died. Cursing our luck, I pressed on hoping that I might still get a 'visual' but to no avail and I had to turn away. As we were descending towards Cassibile, Laurie reported an aircraft to the south going down in flames. This proved to have been the one we missed, a Cant 1007 destroyed by Ian Allen of 256 Squadron. Much grinding of teeth!

The Axis troops had been thrown out of Sicily by mid-August as we were beginning to plan to cover the invasion of Italy. I flew to the north of the island to choose a forward landing ground in the Milazzo area and settled on the San Antonio strip. The idea was to refuel there to give us plenty of time over distant landing beaches.

The Eighth Army went across the Straits of Messina on the night of 2 September and we expected a violent reaction from the Luftwaffe, but nothing turned up.

The only excitement in the next few days occurred when the least bright of our sergeant pilots carried out a forced-landing into the forest near our runway (see p.103 for full account). It turned out that he had mishandled the fuel cocks during his pre-landing cockpit drill and turned off the fuel supply to both engines. In consequence, just as he was flying downwind with his wheels down, there was a deathly hush as both engines packed up. That they survived at all was a tribute to the strength of the Beaufighter. In contrast, a couple of weeks earlier, a Mosquito of 23 Squadron went into the same forest and disintegrated into matchwood, killing the crew instantly. This night was also memorable because I received a second Bar to my DFC and Laurie got his Bar - this crash interrupted the celebration.

Operation Avalanche, the invasion of the beaches at Salerno, broke on Italian soil during the night of 8 September. Shortly after we heard that Marshal Badoglio's government had accepted unconditional surrender. During the night, John Turnbull got a Ju 88 and 'Ace' Downing two more, which brought 600's score past the century since the beginning of the war. Since the squadron's total had been only seventeen when it flew out to Algeria it was obvious that before long we would clock up the century overseas. However, we were far too busy to have a celebratory party as we were keeping a standing patrol of at least one aircraft, and often more, over the beaches from dusk to dawn. As the flight to the operational area took about an hour, we were often in the air for more than four hours. We flew due north from San Antonio to Licosa Point, lit on our way by the permanent beacon of the active volcano on Stromboli. Even when Licosa was cloud covered, we knew we had arrived because we were invariably welcomed by bursts of anti-aircraft fire from the US Army. At first we were controlled by naval ships but after a while a GCI got ashore, which much improved the handling capacity of the ground control organisation. Laurie and I were not lucky at this time. We made no contact with the enemy, we were hit by US flak and on one patrol we intercepted five Dakotas, a B-25 Mitchell and two Beaufighters!

However, things were generally on the move. Our advance party (or 'Spearhead' as they liked to call themselves) had got ashore quite early on but found themselves in the middle of the battle for the beachhead with our 25-pounders behind them and Tiger tanks making forays around them in the night. They were due to go to the airfield at Monte Corvino but for more than two weeks they were unable to get there. Flight Lieutenant Raleigh Hilken made a splendid job of commanding them and, despite at times being in dire straits, finally brought them to the airfield without a single casualty.

On 25 September, Paddy Green ordered me to fly into Monte Corvino and be ready to accept the rest of our aircraft next day. Laurie and I packed all our kit, including a tent, into our aircraft and we set off in the afternoon. The weather was perfect and we had a marvellous trip via Taormina, Reggio di Calabria and the west coast to Licosa Point. Here the whole vista of Salerno Bay opened up, with hundreds of ships lying off the beach, the umbrella of day fighters overhead and bright flashes of artillery fire in the mountains towards Naples. Being the first Beaufighter into the Salerno area by day, I took no chances and approached Monte Corvino for about five miles with my wheels down. I believe I can claim to have been the first pilot to land a Beaufighter on mainland Europe!

I spent the next day visiting the navy and army operations centres to make sure that they knew we were going to fly into Monte Corvino by night. I must have said the right things because the boys flew in before dark without trouble and operated from there without difficulty – apart from the atrocious weather which then set in. Talk about 'Sunny Italy'! I have never experienced such violent thunderstorms and downpours anywhere; vast black-based cumulonimbi, shattering thunder, lightning bolts snaking to earth and torrents of rain, which turned our camp into a quagmire. On 7 October I had my last flight with 600 Squadron and the following day I went down with a second bout of jaundice.

Eventually, I was passed fit to travel and after a gentle farewell party I left for home on 8 December and finally arrived on the 22nd, weary after three-and-a-half years of continuous operations.

Des Hughes had two further successes later in the war when flying the Mosquito to bring his wartime total to eighteen destroyed with one shared. He remained in the RAF post-war and filled a number of senior appointments including AOC 18 Group, commandant, RAF College Cranwell and SASO, Near East Air Force. He retired in June 1974 as Air Vice-Marshal F.D. Hughes CB, CBE, DSO, DFC & Two Bars, AFC.

CHAPTER SIXTEEN

THE WESTERN MEDITERRANEAN

Neil Cox enlisted in the RAFVR just before his eighteenth birthday. He trained as a pilot in the USA before being posted in May 1943 to a Blenheim squadron in North Africa. He soon volunteered to join a Beaufighter unit.

Flying Officer Neil Cox of 39 Squadron. (Neil Cox)

Before joining 39 Squadron in September 1943, I was flying Blenheim Vs with 614 Squadron based in Algeria. I teamed up with Bill Spearey and he turned out to be a first-class navigator - entirely reliable and cool.

In early September the Italians surrendered and shortly after this the Germans started evacuating their troops by air from Corsica. On 23 September at a sudden briefing we learned that our squadron had been given the task of intercepting the German aircraft carrying out this evacuation. During the late afternoon two Beaufighter TF.X took off from our airfield at Protville, Tunisia, and I was the pilot of one of the aircraft.

I was number two to my leader and we flew low level, to the east coast of Corsica reaching it after about two-and-a-quarter hours. We spotted five Junkers 52 transport aircraft just leaving Corsica flying low on a north-easterly course.

I throttled back so that the leader could go in first and attack. To my considerable surprise the Ju 52s were armed and returned a very concentrated fire - machine guns firing from every porthole manned by the German troops being evacuated. Almost immediately my leader was brought down and ditched in the sea (later I discovered he was picked up and became a POW). Then I started my attack. Using the four 20-mm cannons in the nose I shot down a Ju 52 on the starboard side of the formation and closed in on the leader of the formation and also shot him down.

I turned round to head back south to North Africa. It was always my policy to have ample fuel in case of an emergency when returning to base - including getting lost! Soon we were attacked by two Bf 110s (twin-engine aircraft). To begin with they had a speed advantage having dived from a higher altitude. They scored several hits on us before running out of steam and abandoning the chase.

Cox approaches a formation of seven Junkers 52s off Corsica. (Air Historical Branch C 3853)

The Beaufighters of 39 Squadron were equipped for daylight operations (not being the night-fighter version). By the time we crossed the North African coast it was dark and this was my first experience of flying a Beaufighter at night. Whilst Bill was engaged in navigation calculations, suddenly I noticed a red glow alongside the starboard engine and momentarily thought that the engine was on fire. Immediately I called Bill and told him to stand by for a bale out. I gazed with concern at the engine and I was puzzled that the glow remained constant and did not spread. Then I realised that it must be some sort of exhaust pipe, which in daylight did not show up. With embarrassment I explained the misunderstanding to Bill.

Our base at Protville was a desert airfield with no runways and no night-flying facilities. To my relief as we approached the airfield I could see a ready-made flare path for our landing and I lowered the undercarriage. The cockpit indicator lights showed that the port wheel had locked down in position but the starboard wheel was neither down nor up. I tried to retract the undercarriage so that I could select the lever again in the down position - but there was no response (I assumed due to the attack by the two Bf 110s). When landing, if it is not possible to get both wheels to lock down, it is considered better to retract both and do a belly-landing. With only one wheel locked down there is the likelihood of some sort of crash. To bale out was an alternative - but at night-time this had no appeal for me! - so I told Bill to prepare for a crash-landing and informed the base accordingly.

There were two advantages in our favour - the airfield was wide and with a base of packed sand there was less risk of the Beaufighter catching fire.

My objective was to make a 'wheelie'-type landing and let the aircraft run on the port wheel as long as possible and then, when at a slow speed, collapse on to the starboard wing. Fortunately, this was achieved and when the speed reduced the starboard wing hit the ground and we spun to the right – rather like a sharp Christie when skiing. Both of us got out very swiftly in case the aircraft caught fire. After a couple of minutes, Bill ran back to the aircraft, despite my shouts, to recover his peaked cap.

Trucks rushed out and then leisurely took us back to the squadron. Our medical officer checked us over and confirmed no injuries. We were both feeling rather exuberant at having got safely back from our first operation.

At breakfast next morning we both decided that we must have some photos of the crashed Beaufighter. In the truck going out to the airfield with our cameras, a pilot warned us not to take photos of our crashed aircraft telling us that it was believed to be unlucky. We dismissed this superstition (unwisely?) and took photos.

The following afternoon, six of us took off for the same area off Corsica to intercept more enemy aircraft evacuating troops from the island. Orders were given that our attacks should be head on against the Ju 52s so as to reduce/eliminate the effectiveness of the machine guns being fired by the soldiers from the open port holes of the aircraft.

At about 1630 hours off the east coast of Corsica near Bastia we came across a formation of fifteen Ju 52s flying low over the sea. Our leader manoeuvred the formation to carry out a low-level head-on attack.

The contact being head on was very brief. One moment we were firing our cannons at the oncoming enemy aircraft and the next instant we whizzed past their formation. Afterwards, I made a wide right-hand circuit and spotted three more Ju 52s in formation heading south-west. I climbed up to 1,000 feet on their port side and turned in to make a stern attack on the leader. At approximately 450 yards I opened fire and saw hits and broke off my attack at 200 yards in order to make a slight turn to the left to engage the port aircraft. I fired one long steady burst at him, closing in to about fifty yards, when he exploded in flames. Pulling back on the stick I just managed to climb over them. Very shortly afterwards Bill saw this aircraft and the leader's aircraft, whose starboard engine was pouring out black smoke, crash into the sea.

Cox's victim hits the sea. (Air Historical Branch C3859)

Seeing that the rest of the Beaufighters were heading south I turned on to a south-east heading in an endeavour to catch them up. Almost immediately a Bf 109 was on our tail and soon after another joined in. This was at low level over the sea. Fortunately I managed to shake off one of them but the other stayed with us. On his first attack my elevators were hit so, to prevent the nose coming up, I needed to keep forward pressure, using both hands and my knee on the stick.

He continued making a series of attacks. Over the intercom Bill constantly gave his position - reminding me of a Wimbledon umpire on Centre Court. Bill was very calm. The attacks generally started from the five o'clock or seven o'clock positions and each time I weaved across the direction of the attack. Then suddenly Bill told me a Bf 109 was coming in very close behind our tail. Numerous hits were scored on our aircraft. The armour-plated door between us had swung open and one bullet passed just to the right of my head. I realised Bill must have been wounded as he was no longer using the intercom.

I had been heading out in an easterly direction away from Corsica but immediately after our aircraft was damaged. I turned back west towards the coast of Corsica to fly south as soon as reaching the land and try and evade the Bf 109 by very low flying. (In Arizona on Harvards an instructor named Beeman had taught me the art of low flying round the tall cactus trees. As time went by I came to regard low flying - really low - as a sport and enjoying it so much I developed quite a flair for this activity.) As soon as I reached the coast I swung on to a southerly course. However, my low flying ability was rather handicapped because of the problem with the elevators.

After just avoiding a head-on collision with an aircraft that had apparently just taken off, I realised that I was rapidly approaching an airfield and soon I spotted Ghisonaccia. Immediately to the south of the airfield there was a range of hills. Then I saw the Bf 109 again at seven o'clock at about 500 feet and he was starting to dive on us. With my reduced manoeuvrability the situation was getting very tricky. There seemed to be one last chance for me and that was to position my aircraft between the Bf 109 and the airfield, so that if he opened fire he would probably hit personnel or aircraft on the airfield. Just in time I managed to achieve this and the Bf 109 did not fire. Perhaps he had no intention of firing at all, but was trying to force me to land. Another possibility is that he had used up all his ammunition.

Flying very low immediately past the east side of the airfield I flew into a valley and without regard to any particular direction remained very low along the valleys and over the hills. It did seem as though I had at last shaken off the enemy fighter.

Looking round I was very shocked to find Bill slumped in his seat, covered with blood. I gazed for a while hoping to observe any movement - but there was none. Was he dead or unconscious?

At low level to have allowed my attention to stray even for a brief moment was incredibly careless - yet I was upset by what I had seen. As I looked forward to my horror the aircraft was flying in to the top of a low peak. With a lightning release of the forward pressure on the stick the nose soared up just in time. By mistake I pressed the gun button for the cannons and the burst of fire gave me an incredible surprise! I resumed control of the aircraft. I had lost all sense of direction in the effort to shake off the Bf 109. I was somewhere in the hills of Corsica. I set a southerly course but realised there was very little chance I would get back to base with the damaged elevators.

The necessary forward pressure on the stick and general instability of the aircraft absorbed my concentration. Climbing up and baling out was not an option because there was no way of knowing if Bill was dead or alive. So in these circumstances I decided to fly low and if the elevators started to fail I could put the aircraft down quickly obviously not on hills but somehow ditching on the sea – but where and when?

Whilst I began to form some outline of a plan something on the starboard side caught my eye. I turned my head and to my astonishment there was the Bf 109 in tight formation with me and tucked behind my starboard wing. The pilot and I took a long look at each other and then I saw him wave and I, astounded, raised my arm in reply and then he broke formation and I never saw him again.

Flying at about 1,000 feet in a southerly direction, yet lost over the rugged mountains of Corsica, I reached the coastline much to my relief. The elevator problem began to worsen and I decided to fly at 200 feet above the sea so that if necessary I could very rapidly ditch the aircraft. I thought (subsequently correctly) that I was on course to North Sardinia and crossing the straits of Bonifacio.

Soon I could see land and I decided to ditch in the sea very close to the shore. The feel of the elevators (still forward pressure was necessary) seemed to be changing; perhaps it was because the response to the movement of the stick gave the impression of slackness.

It was about 1730 hours and the weather was perfect with late afternoon sunshine and a cloudless blue sky. No wind and a very calm sea, in fact the smoothness of the sea was a hindrance in judging height.

Flying instinct warned me that it would be too risky to try to reach the shoreline and that it was imperative to ditch the aircraft very soon whilst I still had sufficient elevator control. I began to throttle back – the sea looked deceptively friendly. I overlooked swivelling back the gun sight, which was very near my face. I eased the throttle back gradually but the aircraft seemed reluctant to settle down and appeared to want to glide on indefinitely above the sea.

All the time I was reducing the necessary forward pressure of the stick instead of pulling it back in the normal way and thus gently raising the nose of the aircraft. We touched the water smoothly then there seemed to be a huge jolt. My cheek (right side) hit the gun sight and for a brief moment dazed me or knocked me out. Yet without thinking, immediately I was climbing out of the cockpit on to the port wing. With the aircraft nose slightly down and tail up, I was relieved to see the aircraft dingy inflating beside the port wing tip. It seemed like a miracle – Bill was gradually stirring. He was attempting to open his Perspex canopy but without success. I assumed that it would not open because he was too weak. But no, the canopy had jammed. Standing on the edge of the trailing edge of the wing, leaning sideways I could see that the Perspex looked like a sieve riddled with bullet holes.

Often I flew wearing leather gauntlets, and I was wearing them on this occasion.

I brought my fists down on the Perspex but nothing happened. Very gradually the aircraft was starting to sink so there was little time left. I gave the swiftest of prayers for strength to smash the Perspex and then resumed crashing my fists down. Within seconds I had broken through the Perspex in several places and Bill began to pull the pieces away. I think seawater was around Bill's feet. Leaning forward and sideways, and with Bill gripping my shoulders, our joint efforts got the cork out of the bottle.

In an instant we were both in the water but close to the now fully inflated dinghy and then alongside it. Bill's leg was broken and was swinging in the water and he was in great pain. Later I learned that he had a bullet through a finger and two bullets one on each side high up on his back. I climbed into the dinghy and leaning on the side tried to pull him up and over but with no success and the dinghy began to topple over. Quickly I abandoned this attempt and got back into the sea. Luck changed. Whilst Bill somehow held on to the sides, I managed to exert pressure from underneath him and together with his determined efforts push him up and over. He collapsed flat out on the floor of the dinghy. Meanwhile the aircraft was starting to slide under the sea.

I found one of the dinghy paddles. The dinghy seemed relatively large but unfortunately and most important it was round. In the calm sea I began to paddle but of course with only one person paddling the dinghy went slowly round in a circle. I tried forward and then some backward movements of the paddle. No progress was being made towards the shore. This was probably about a mile away and somehow I had to get to the land before it was too late for Bill. I had a bright idea – I would get back into the sea and holding the roped ladder with one arm tow the dinghy. Some progress through the water was made but it was slow. Another idea came to me and this was to put the end rung of the ladder over my head so that it rested just above my chin. This was the answer and with both legs and arms free for the breaststroke I knew we would get to the land. With the sea warm and calm, swimming was easy and would have been relaxing but Bill was silent and I was worried again (though I am a slow swimmer distance was not a problem for me provided the temperature was warm enough).

As I swam away I think only the tail of the aircraft was above the surface, so in the circumstances, having regard to the elevator problem, the ditching was very successful. I would guess that to land an aircraft by reducing forward pressure on the stick instead of pulling back on the stick is an exceptional experience.

After what seemed a long time, I reached the beach and dragged the dinghy on to the sands. Not far away on the cliffs and beside a track I could see a group of people standing. As I strode across the beach in their direction, I realised they were soldiers (also there were some villagers) and as I got much nearer I could see an officer in charge. I shouted, pointing to the dinghy and waved my arms as a signal to come and help. They remained motionless and did not shout back. I tried a mixture of English and French but still there was no response. The officer carried a holster and the soldiers were armed. I found it incredible that they would not come and help. Then I tried my mixture of English, French and Italian indicating that it would be "splendido and magnifico" if they would come and "aidez-moi". The response came at last – laughter!

They came hurrying down and immediately rushed across to the dinghy, carried it up a steep track and put the dinghy and Bill inside the truck. This was Sardinia and perhaps we were the first of the Allies to invade by sea! Establishing a good rapport with the officer and the soldiers we were taken to a convent in Castel Sardo about two miles away. There was an air of serenity and the nuns showed great kindness to us. I got the officer to arrange for an ambulance from the nearest hospital – this was at Sassari. The road to Sassari was very bumpy and gave Bill so much pain that at times it was necessary to drive at a walking pace. He was very brave.

On reaching the hospital, Bill was immediately taken to the operating theatre and I was shown to a small chapel. I went in and stayed for a few moments praying that Bill would survive. I was taken to the senior surgeon – a small and lively person who immediately gave me confidence and reassured me about the prospects for Bill. His assistant was also most likeable. The surgeon insisted on tending to the minor cut on my cheek before operating on Bill.

Next morning I woke up in a dormitory ward full of Italian soldiers and they were amazed to find an Englishman there. Moved to a private ward I was given luxury treatment and being fit was able to use it as a hotel room. When I walked along the hospital corridors the soldiers would make way and salute me! The senior surgeon used to invite me to his house to hear superb opera records.

After about four days a message from an English secret agent was passed to me with instructions for me to go to Alghero airfield to be flown to North Africa by an American aircraft. It did not arrive, so I hitched a ride to Decimomannu in the south of Sardinia. That night Brigadier-General Roosevelt arrived with his staff. On hearing what had happened to my navigator he told me that he would go to Sassari and see Bill on his way back to headquarters next morning.

On 29 September a USAAF B-25 flew me to Tunis near our airfield at Protville. On reaching the squadron I was greeted with amazement as we had been posted as 'missing'.

Sometime later, Norman Baker my WOP/AG on Blenheims, heard that I needed another navigator. He got himself posted from his squadron (Marauders) to 39 Squadron and became my new man in the back.

Throughout the early months of 1944 the squadron was engaged on daylight operations. Then it was decided to start individual anti-shipping patrols by night and in practice this involved flying in good weather conditions on moonlit nights. The squadron's role was predominantly anti-shipping rather than as a night-fighter squadron. From March, we began training with the 25-lb rocket projectiles and we carried eight in addition to the four cannons. The start of this new venture of night-intruder sorties began on 1 June when three Beaufighters took off early one evening from our base at Alghero in Corsica to patrol the coastal area covered from the Gulf of Genoa and west along the coast of the South of France. I was on this operation and my sector was the most westerly.

Our CO was away and, as my navigator was sick, I was allocated his navigator, Flight Lieutenant Harry Wheeler. He was probably the most experienced navigator

A 39 Squadron Beaufighter attacks a convoy off the coast of Sicily. (Air Historical Branch CAN 4169)

on the squadron. An Australian, he was quietly spoken and a calm philosophical type. He seemed rather old, probably at least thirty-eight, and this was about the time of my twenty-first birthday!

Our route was to fly north from Corsica and, as we approached the French coast, to set course in a westerly direction. We flew about one mile off the coastline and our altitude was about 500 feet. The weather was perfect and the moon was out. When off Monte Carlo I recalled playing as a junior in a mixed-doubles tennis tournament there partnered by my mother who had been a Wimbledon competitor!

Proceeding along the coast, and somewhere between St Tropez and Toulon, I spotted a ship about half a mile off the coast and it presented a broadside-on target. I climbed up to gain a few hundred extra feet, levelled out and then put the nose down to dive at the ship. I fired the two outer rockets as a 'sighter' and once in range I fired the remaining six. Just as I flew very low over the ship (much lower than intended) there was a huge explosion. Presumably the cargo was munitions or explosives. Instantly a very light spray of water swept my face! Then the shore batteries opened up. I continued flying parallel with the coast and jinking so as to present a difficult deflection target. When out of range, I turned south-east setting course for Corsica.

About fifteen minutes later, Harry Wheeler was on the intercom warning me that he had seen two night-fighters in the distance. I took vigorous evasive action and eventually they abandoned the chase.

As we approached the Corsican coast the weather began to deteriorate and so, in poor visibility, we turned south before getting too close to the land. Eventually we arrived over Alghero to find low cloud. The airfield night-landing facilities were rather basic so it was a relief to land.

Next morning I walked out to inspect the aircraft and to see my ground crew. I was directed to inspect the under surface of the fuselage and was shown a large hole about the size of a football a few feet behind the pilot's seat. Was this the explanation for the light spray of water that swept my face?

Apparently on that same morning at the daily headquarters conference attended by my CO, our result was greeted with considerable interest as it was, I think, the first successful night anti-shipping attack with rockets.

Within a few days the CO returned to Alghero followed soon after by AVM Sir Hugh Pughe Lloyd the commander of Mediterranean Allied Coastal Air Force as he wished to have a demonstration of a night-rocket attack. This was to be carried out in the bay near Alghero opposite the Lido (beside the beach where we had our quarters) and a flare was to be dropped as a target. The members of our squadron, with our CO and AVM Lloyd, were to be the spectators and I was required to give the demonstration. So I was rather anxious!

I took off from Alghero on a clear night. The flare was dropped in the bay and then I circled and dived on the target and fired the rockets. Luckily I scored a direct hit!

Soon after this I finished my tour on Beaufighters and my first job (about July 1944) was to be the manager of the Allied Officers Club at Alghero.

> Neil Cox fails to mention that after his flight off Sardinia and the rescue of his navigator he was awarded an immediate DFC. Soon after finishing his tour on 39 Squadron he received a Bar to his DFC. Bill Spearey made a remarkable recovery from his wounds. He stayed in the RAF after the war and became a squadron leader.
>
> **Cox** adds a very interesting postscript to his time on 39 Squadron.

Whilst collecting German aircraft from Schlesweg to bring back to Farnborough in 1945 I asked for some information about the handling of a FW 190 single-engine fighter that I was to fly. The German CO of the maintenance unit came to meet me to provide the required information. When he mentioned that the RAF had shot him down off Corsica, I discovered that he was the leader of the Ju 52s and it was me that had shot him down. He leapt to attention clicked his heels and shook me warmly by the hand! He then gave me a photo of himself wearing the Iron Cross.

ACTION OVER THE AEGEAN

Bob Milne DFM (left) and his navigator Larry Loman. (John Milne)

After the surrender of Italy on 8 September 1943, Hitler decided to hold on to and reinforce the occupied islands in the Aegean when the German forces and remaining Italian Fascists were supplied from the Greek mainland. The supply lines were short and could be protected by fighters and some powerful naval escorts.

Prime Minister Winston Churchill was keen to mount an offensive in the Aegean and in the Dodecanese Islands, and it was decided to invade the islands of Cos, Leros and Samos in September 1943 – it was a costly failure. Protection of the Allied invasion forces by RAF Beaufighters based in Cyprus was inadequate since they were operating at extreme range and were no match for the German single-engine fighters.

On 3 October, the Germans invaded Cos and quickly overran the island. By 18 November, they had recaptured all the occupied islands. The enterprise had ended in disaster, by which time the Beaufighters had lost half their numbers. Nevertheless, the Germans lost about a quarter of their shipping in the region.

Three squadrons of Beaufighters (Nos. 227, 252 and 603) had borne the brunt of operations in the Aegean when the crews of 47 Squadron with their Beaufighter TF.X aircraft moved from Tunisia on 22 October 1943 to El Adem and then to Gambut where it remained for the next five months. It was soon ready to strike at the Germans as they reacted to the British occupation of the islands.

On 5 November, the squadron lost its CO when Wing Commander J. Lee-Evans DFC was forced to ditch. Over the next fourteen days, eight crews were lost. One of the survivors of these costly operations was **Sergeant Bob Milne** who summarises events over this difficult period.

After the loss of the CO, Wing Commander Jimmy Lee-Evans and then Squadron Leader C. A. Ogilvie the following day, we took off on our next operation on the 8th when six of our aircraft were joined by six from 603 Squadron to attack a convoy west of Cos. Three of our squadron aircraft were carrying torpedoes, of which I was one, and my navigator, Larry Loman, and I were certainly rather fearful that we would be shot down. We were expecting to lose some, if not all, of our Torbeaus. I remember the ground crew waving us off - i.e. waving good-bye!

On reaching the target we encountered a terrible storm, at times the waves seemed higher than the four low-flying aircraft and it was the first time I had seen St. Elmo's fire. Then, suddenly, as we were coming out of the storm, we sighted the ships. We attacked and a hit was observed on the leading ship. An Arado Ar 196 fighter was also shot down. Clearly they were not expecting Beaufighters to come out of a storm at sea. In the event, all the Beaufighters returned to base although most of our aircraft had been damaged by flak.

On 11 November we were briefed to attack shipping off Kalymnos and Cos but Messerschmitt Bf 109 fighters from Cos intercepted us before we could locate the target. The engagement lasted twenty-two minutes. On similar operations on 12 and 13 November we lost three more Beaufighters including Squadron Leader S. Muller-Rowland who had joined a few days earlier. He and his navigator were seen to get into their dinghies and were eventually picked up having been wounded. [Note: He returned to operations in 1944 and was lost off the Dutch coast on 3 October 1944.]

Then, on 16 November, a Siebel ferry carrying troops with an escort of two ships and fighter cover was located west of Kalymnos by a reconnaissance aircraft. It was vital to prevent these forces reaching Leros. The squadron had only five aircraft left serviceable plus one used for training. Only five crews of 47 Squadron were available to fly so Squadron Leader G. Powell, who had recently left the squadron as 'tour expired', happened to be available and he asked to return and lead the strike and bring up to six the number of crews available for 47 Squadron. Two Beaus of 603 Squadron were added to the strike force. I flew the training aircraft 'E' for Edward.

On approaching the target we could see enemy aircraft circling the ships. There were at least four Ju 88s, seven Arados and six Bf 109s. We managed to get to the target before the enemy saw us. We attacked with cannon and machine guns blowing up the ferry and damaging some barges. The Bf 109s dived on us and three of our aircraft were shot down. Only one man survived, Sergeant Alfred Cottle, who was awarded the MM for his exploits in evading capture. Powell received the DSO and his navigator, Flying Officer C. Adams an immediate DFC. Sergeant Vic Borrowdale and I received the DFM.

Leros fell that evening and this phase of the Aegean campaign came to an end. No. 47 Squadron had no serviceable aircraft and with two pilots off sick Borrowdale and I were the only pilots immediately available.

Summarising the Aegean/Leros campaign as far as 47 Squadron was concerned, it lasted eighteen days during which time the sixteen crews were reduced to just five. All these losses occurred in the twelve days from 5 to 16 November. The squadron re-

A Beaufighter attacks German F-boats off Leros. (Roy Nesbit)

covered quickly with an influx of new crews and aircraft, together with a new CO, Wing Commander D. L. Filson-Young DFC, who was to be a much-admired leader. The Aegean campaign would continue with Leros another enemy-occupied island. When we were up to strength, we moved to the nearby airfield at Gambut III. We continued operations in the Aegean for another three months before going to the Far East to take on the Japanese.

Life in the desert was not all gloom. We were fortunate to have visits from the NAAFI at El Adem, so we could supplement our rations of 'Bully Beef' and 'Soya Links' (sausages made of soya beans) which we couldn't eat. We were able to buy such things as tinned meat, puddings and vegetables. These needed to be cooked so we bought primus stoves that required paraffin. In the desert the only source of this commodity was the flare path where goose-neck flares were fuelled with paraffin. The aircrews on flare path duty had to economise by only lighting the flares when needed and reducing the number set out. Have you ever landed with only three flares?!

American units flying Mitchells provided entertainment. They had a projector, and films flown over from Hollywood. The screen was put against the side of a lorry and we took our own petrol cans to sit on. Betty Grable was very popular.

One of the replacement crews in November was **Bob Willis** and his navigator Tommy Thompson. After completing their conversion to the Beaufighter, they were posted to the Middle East and on 26 October 1943 they left Portreath to fly a Beaufighter to Cairo via Rabat, Castel Benito and El Adem in Libya arriving in Cairo five days after departing England. They joined 47 Squadron towards the end of November.

We arrived at Gambut where all the talk in the sergeants' mess was full of details of the destruction of the Siebel ferry and the loss of three crews. We flew three training sorties, and then on 26 November, we took off on our first operational mission, carrying a torpedo, in the company of three other torpedo Beaufighters from the squadron and three B-25 Mitchells of 310 Bombardment Group USAAF. To our disappointment, tinged with relief, no sightings of our target were made.

Tactics changed in December as we largely discarded our torpedoes. For the next few months most operational flying by the squadron consisted of attacking small cargo ships and caiques in the ports and harbours of the Cyclades and Dodecanese Islands. When we found any caiques of cargo-carrying size, which were usually holed up during the day in well-defended harbours, the Beaufighters attacked with cannon fire, supplemented by 500-lb bombs in the target area. These operations could be hazardous, demanding an element of surprise through low-flying tactics, although pretty intense and accurate return fire from the ground was the usual experience. Additionally, light or heavy anti-aircraft fire was also to be expected from Crete, Rhodes, Cos and Leros

Bob Willis (right) with his navigator Tommy Thompson. (Bob Willis)

if one flew too close. Other tasks could be escort duty for destroyers of the Royal Navy, or convoy escort. However, the main objective was to disrupt the supply chain from Greece to the German garrisons on Crete and the other major islands they occupied in the eastern Mediterranean.

After another abortive sweep, the long-awaited action came on 4 December when our formation of four Beaufighters sighted four Arado Ar 196 single-engine floatplanes circling at about 500 feet over the sea near the island of Kinaros to the west of Leros. With a crew of two and armament fore and aft the Arado was quite a manoeuvrable aircraft and very useful in island waters as an escort for transport aircraft or small ships plying between the islands.

With the Arados in sight it was maximum concentration, safety catch off and gun sight in place, all rather exhilarating. The first Arado I attacked was stationary on the water. It had apparently landed on the sea with engine failure with its three companions circling overhead. I strafed the aircraft on the water with cannon. Arthur Unwin, as leader of the formation, was concerned that Bf 109s would jump us. He circled above ready to give warning if the dreaded 109s appeared. Arthur explained at the debriefing that he thought the Arado on the sea might be a decoy designed to get us into difficulty and here was I having a go! The Arado on the sea was an easy target. Through the gun sight I could see the 'plane breaking up with one of the crew clambering onto a float as it sank.

After this first success I set to attack another Arado still circling overhead. Climbing at full throttle I made a quarter attack and shot off the support of one of the floats. It was left hanging down making the aircraft un-flyable. It went down and hit the sea. As it was going down the rear gunner was still firing at us, well wide of the mark, but we did admire his courage. So, I was credited with those two aircraft.

After another uneventful sweep on 10 December north of Crete we had better luck on 14 December with another formation of four aircraft. South of Stampalia we sighted a Heinkel 115 flying low over the sea escorted by four Arado 196s. The Heinkel 115 was a large twin-engine float-plane with a crew of three, similar in size to the Handley Page Hampden. It was used as a troop carrier or supply aircraft to the various German garrisons on the islands. Whilst two Beaufighters of our formation were paying attention to the escorting Arados, I attacked this large floatplane in formation with another Beaufighter, flown by Sergeant Ken Thomas. I could see my cannon fire hit the wings of the Heinkel and about twenty feet of the port wing fell off. Concentrating too hard in my eagerness to finish the job, I came too close to the enemy aircraft, forcing me to fly over to avoid a mid-air collision. We presented the Heinkel rear gunner with an easy target and his hits set us on fire. Turning and looking out I saw the Heinkel splash into the sea, as confirmed by other members of the formation. The downed Heinkel was credited to my score.

Cannon attack on a Greek caique. (Roy Nesbit)

With our aircraft full of smoke thoughts were quickly concentrated on survival. The Heinkel rear gunner had shot off the tip of our starboard wing and also ignited the Verey cartridges stored in the rear of the aircraft. These contained magnesium powder, which gave off a tremendous cloud of white smoke and the whole aircraft filled with this choking smoke. The magnesium deposit blotted out the instrument panel. Through the smoke I could not even see the horizon or any of the instruments. It appeared impossible to fly the aircraft. Tommy had evacuated his position at the rear where all his navigation equipment and charts were burnt out, but he had very courageously beaten out the flames, despite the heat, preventing any further damage to the aircraft. My immediate reaction was to jettison the cockpit hatch with a view to baling out. This brought in an immediate rush of air completely clearing the cockpit of smoke.

The aircraft was still more or less straight and level with both engines functioning normally. I cleared the instruments and windscreen of the magnesium dust and, thanks to Tommy, the fire had not spread and had slowly burnt out. Without our cockpit roof the noise of inrushing air made communication on the intercom impossible. By hand signals I indicated we would fly south until the coast of North Africa was sighted. Approximately two hours later the coast came into view. Tommy indicated our location on a map and we followed the coast to Gambut. I had become aware that the elevator was partially damaged due to its lack of response from the controls. With the wheels and flaps in good order, I was able to land without any real problem, helped by Gambut having a very long landing strip. We had been in the air for over five hours.

As we climbed out, the leader of our formation was waiting at the foot of the exit hatch. All he said to me was; "Oh, we thought you had bought it!" That was a typical greeting as we went off to be debriefed. The rest of the formation had already reported our possible demise as they had seen us disappear over the horizon with smoke pouring from our aircraft. We soon discovered that shooting down the Heinkel, or the Arados ten days earlier, attracted little comment. It was taken as part of the day's work. Later that same day, Tommy and I examined our damaged Beaufighter. The heat from the fire had been so intense that the aluminium stringers in the rear section that make up the aircraft frame had partially melted and run into each other.

From 2 to 17 January 1944 Tommy and I were despatched on a refresher course to 5 Middle East Torpedo School at Shallufa. The course provided more training on torpedo tactics against enemy shipping, with a particular emphasis on night operations. During those sixteen days we made seven practice attacks at night and three attacks by day. Eleven ships of the Royal Navy in the Suez area were involved. Practice night attacks were made in moonlight but on moonless nights a Wellington illuminated the target with flares.

My last night exercise on 15 January was with Squadron Leader Stanley Muller-Rowland flying the aircraft and I stood behind him in the aircraft well. The plan on these exercises was for a formation of four Beaufighters to mount a simulated torpedo strike against the 1st Battle Squadron exercising in the Gulf of Suez. As the torpedo Beaufighters approached the capital ships, flares dropped behind the ships by two Wellingtons illuminated the target. The flares, as they hovered in the sky, allowed us to see the silhouettes of the ships enabling us to position ourselves to launch a dummy runner torpedo against the best positioned target ship. Torbeaus carried a F.24 camera to assess results and to assist in deciding the best tactics to use against capital ships. In view of the intense AA fire expected, night attacks were deemed at the time to have the most chance of success. Either way it would be a hazardous mission.

After returning to Gambut our first operation was on 23 January as part of a formation of six Beaufighters led by Flying Officer Arthur Unwin for a daylight attack on Rhodes harbour. The old crusader fort adjoining the harbour housed the German garrison. Each aircraft carried two bombs. The fear for interception by Bf 109s based on the airfields on Rhodes decided a strategy of approaching the island at sea level from Turkish waters. Group gave permission to fly over Turkish territory for a short while despite Turkey's status as a non-combatant. We did succeed in achieving surprise by climbing off the sea and over the cliffs to 1,000 feet for the bombing run on the old fort. The whole operation was quite futile. Our bombs made little impact on the thick walls. The attack on Rhodes was followed by a strafing run on the caiques and stores in Cos harbour. There was intense light and heavy flak from both Rhodes and Cos. On the latter, caiques moored against the harbour jetty were hit and damaged. Tommy had his handheld F.24 camera and took photographs of the harbours.

Operational flying was not the only hazard we faced. On 29 January I took off to carry out practice bombing on a wrecked freighter beached on the coast west of Tobruk. I took LAC Johnny Bull with me for some air experience. Just after completing a second

run there was a loud bang and the port engine seized. I was only at 400 feet and the port propeller failed to feather. Pushing the starboard throttle through the 'gate' I managed to stop the aircraft losing more height. The only sensible option was to make a wheels-up landing on the escarpment. With an un-feathered propeller and maximum power on the other, making the aircraft difficult to control due to the severe torque, I cleared the escarpment with two hundred feet to spare. I found a clear area and we touched down and slid to a halt. A very relieved airman and I climbed out and viewed the scene. We were in the middle of a deserted and barren landscape.

Bob Willis after crash-landing his Beaufighter T5171 in the Libyan desert. (Bob Willis)

Just before dark a squadron aircraft flew over and we fired a red Verey cartridge. We slept by the aircraft and the following morning a group of Senussi Arabs appeared and gave us hard-boiled eggs to eat. Late that afternoon the rescue party arrived. It was quickly established that the main crankshaft had fractured. The guns were taken out with all the ammunition together with the radio and any loose equipment and loaded on to the truck. The fuel tanks were drained leaving the aircraft abandoned to the desert. Much to my surprise following this rather minor incident, I was given a commendatory endorsement in my logbook for 'executing with skill' the forced landing.

On 7 February we struck Khios harbour when we bombed and strafed a merchant vessel and caiques moored against the jetty. Later reconnaissance reported that at least six had been sunk.

Locating ships used by the enemy to supply the islands of the Eastern Mediterranean was far from easy. Apart from accurate flak the Bf 109s were a major threat as our operations were far removed from any possible single-engine fighter support. We aircrew, as just a small part of the extensive operational activity of 201 Group, found it difficult to appreciate the full strategic plan and tactics applied in this theatre of war. The Germans now occupied all the islands in the Aegean. For them it was to become a wasting asset as we relentlessly harried their supply routes. Over these months, four Beaufighter squadrons, supplemented by Mitchells, Marauders, Baltimores and Venturas based near Gambut, were deployed against the Germans on Crete, Rhodes and the Dodecanese Islands. Two of the Beaufighter squadrons, 227 and 252 were based at Berka in Libya and in Cyprus with the other two, 47 and 603 at Gambut. 47 Squadron was the only squadron equipped with torpedoes but by the beginning of 1944 there were very few targets remaining, which could be attacked using torpedoes.

As March 1944 came in the squadron continued to fly an assortment of missions against defended harbours in the Dodecanese targeting the supply caiques supporting the German garrisons, or to the less dangerous convoy escort duties and naval co-operation patrols. Usually formations of four or six aircraft were involved. Invariably attacks on defended harbours took place in daylight when the cannon fire of the Beaufighter was accurate and effective.

March was our final month at Gambut and our first sortie was on the 4th when, with a formation of four Beaufighters, we had a good look at Leros and its harbours. For our pains we drew much ack-ack, but found no target. We had better luck on the 6th when with a formation of six aircraft we strafed four Arado Ar 196 floatplanes drawn up on the beach at Scarpanto, north-east of Crete. One of the Arados caught fire but seeing two unidentified aircraft overhead we beat a hasty retreat. Having destroyed three enemy aircraft, and participated in damaging three others, I was not anxious to meet any Bf 109s.

Our last sortie over the Mediterranean was on 12 March with a formation of four Beaufighters led by Flying Officer Bill Bailey. This sortie was a sweep at maximum range to the harbour at Naxos where we attacked with cannon two large caiques and a 300-ton schooner when we inflicted much damage. Despite some intense ground fire, all aircraft returned safely. On 13 March, the squadron stood down to prepare to move to India.

Four months in the Libyan desert was now coming to an end. At least we had survived. Pilots and navigators soon learnt how to reduce the risks, but luck also had to be on your side. Careful pre-flight preparation and constant practice in air-to-ground firing, bombing, evasion tactics and low flying over the sea in formation certainly improved one's chances. The glare of the sun on a calm sea made it quite difficult to judge height when flying at low level to avoid radar detection. More than one accident, with the inevitable fatal consequences, happened as a result of a misjudgement. Wing Commander Filson-Young took every opportunity to maintain a continuous training programme, all designed to raise the standard of our operational activities.

Bob Milne, who was awarded an immediate DFM after the attack on the Siebel ferry on 16 November 1943, Bob Willis and 'Tommy' Thompson continued to serve with 47 Squadron in Burma, initially on the Beaufighter before the squadron converted to the Mosquito. They were commissioned and Bob Willis and Tommy Thompson were awarded the DFC.

CHAPTER EIGHTEEN
AEGEAN OPERATIONS – 1944

Bernard Slydel outlines 252 Squadron's activities in the Aegean.

When the Spartan mothers sent their sons into battle they exhorted them to acquit themselves nobly in fight, and to "return with your shields or on them". No more fitting motto could have been carried on the crest of 252 Beaufighter Squadron whose harassing of German shipping and garrisons in the Aegean earned them the additional soubriquet of the 'Scourge of the Islands'.

From the beginning of 1944 to early 1945, the squadron concentrated on, sought and harassed enemy shipping along the coasts, in the harbours and on the waters of the Ionian and Aegean Seas. In 1944, 252 Squadron made 700 sorties and flew over 3,000 operational hours.

252 Squadron in the Western Desert 1944. Wing Commander Meharg is in the centre of the second row and Ernest Thompson is fourth from left in the front row. (via Mike Napier)

In May it struck a serious blow to the German shuttle service between the many Aegean islands when it destroyed a 200-ton lighter, a 100-ton caique, two eighty-foot armed launches, numerous barges, assault craft and smaller caiques.

Not only was June a profitable month but its first day marked the beginning of the end for the Nazis in the Aegean. It was known that the enemy forces on Crete were extremely short of supplies and that a convoy was loaded and ready to sail from Salamis. During the early hours of 1 June, a Wellington of 38 Squadron on patrol spotted the convoy on the move. An attack for just such a move had been planned weeks before and at dawn, two strike forces of rocket-firing and torpedo-carrying Beaufighters left Western Desert bases. One formation, led by the CO, Wing Commander B.G. Meharg

AFC, approached from the west and located the convoy twenty-five miles north of Candia (on the north coast of Crete) steaming south at approximately eight knots. It comprised the merchantmen, *Gertrud*, *Sabine* and *Tanais*.

Squadron Leader I. Butler, a flight commander on 252 Squadron, attacked the *Sabine* with rockets and his and a following attack by a 603 Squadron Beaufighter produced direct hits on the stern of the vessel, which was completely blown away. 252 Squadron aircraft also hit the *Gertrud* and, although she and a destroyer made Candia, both were sunk the following day when they were moored in the harbour. Wing Commander Meharg failed to return from this operation.

Rocket attack on the MV *Gertrud*. (Roy Nesbit)

On the night of 2/3 July the German merchantmen *Anita* and *Agathe* - 1,200 and 1,000 tons respectively - left Rhodes for Portolago on Leros. *Agathe* was one of the Germans' largest vessels in the Aegean. Beaufighters of 252 Squadron were alerted and took off as pairs at ten-minute intervals. Wing Commander D.O. Butler, now the CO following the loss of Wing Commander Meharg, saw the convoy and decided that his No. 2, Flight Lieutenant C.A. Whyatt, should fly near the ships to act as a decoy and draw their fire while he approached from the south-west. Unfortunately, only two guns engaged Whyatt while Butler flew into the face of the remaining flak. He decided to try another plan and Whyatt made four dummy runs before launching his eight rockets against the *Agathe*, which was hit amidships.

Whyatt's aircraft was damaged and he was forced to carry out a belly-landing back at base. He commented, "The rockets started quite a healthy fire, but the other boys were a bit sore because when they arrived, the *Agathe* was a total write-off". Shortly afterwards AOC Eastern Mediterranean, AVM T. A. Langord-Sainsbury, signalled his congratulations.

September was 252 Squadron's 'finest month'. They destroyed the *Drache* (2,400 tons), the *Orion* (1,000 tons), three coasters, two armed caiques totalling 4,690 tons. They also damaged merchantmen, coasters and a minesweeper.

When the *Drache* was destroyed, war material and armaments piled up on the jetty of Vathi harbour were also destroyed. The squadron led an attack against Naxos when the garrison refused to surrender in November. They did eventually surrender after the Royal Navy asked for help and 252 Squadron attacked with rockets. It was later learnt

Attack against the SS *Drache* moored at the port of Vathi on the island of Samos on 22 September 1944. (Roy Nesbit)

that the German commander from Leros was visiting the island to boost morale when the attack was made. He was 'badly shaken'. No doubt the morale of the troops was also similarly so.

> **Stuart Legat** was a pilot on 252 Squadron at the time and he recalls some of the major attacks made by the squadron.

We made a very successful attack on an ammunition ship on 17 May. Four Beaufighters led by Squadron Leader C. Foxley-Norris (later Air Chief Marshal Sir Christopher) took off on an offensive sweep.

The aim was to search for and attack any random targets. A small convoy of five ships, apparently unescorted, was sighted north of Symi near Cos. Unseen, the four aircraft approached the target over the peaks of some hills about four miles south and in line astern - I was number three. The largest ship, about 1,000 tons, was selected as the primary target. The last man in, number four, saw heavy smoke already starting to develop. Of my own rockets, about four went astern of the ship but the remainder secured hits on the stern. The leader decided to make a further attack and this was to be made with our cannons - all our rockets had been used. By this time, we were fairly well spaced out.

Closing fast, the leader was extremely fortunate to survive, for just as he was sighting his cannons there was an enormous explosion. From about a range of three miles the shock waves were felt in my cockpit. As number three I had a grandstand view of the flash with a quickly developing column of smoke and large lumps of steaming ironmongery flowering out of it and the additional sight of the leader and his number two pulling hard to port to escape the flying debris. The smoke and steam cloud developed to a few thousand feet and the foaming surface of the sea revealed no sign of the ship. Our attention was turned to the three remaining vessels, probably of about 500 tons each. With cannon fire we could only cause damage with no further sinkings. On return to base we enjoyed an extra - though rationed - beer or two!

The convoy strike on 1 June was in the evening at about 1900 hours. The tactic involved in this operation was to approach the target out of a low sun thus impairing the vision of the convoy's defences.

603 Squadron Beaufighters prepare to taxi at Gambut. (Air Historical Branch CM 5575)

Elements of 603 Squadron's Beaufighters with cannons were tasked as anti-flak escorts to keep the anti-aircraft gunners' heads down. In addition to the escorting destroyers, Bf 109s from Maleme in Crete provided air cover. The aircraft of 252 Squadron's leader of the strike force, Wing Commander Meharg, was hit in the starboard wing as he closed on the target. The aircraft immediately caught fire but he managed to fire his eight rockets before passing over the convoy and crashing into the sea two miles east of the target. I was following close behind the leader as his number three and saw the whole event apart from the ditching. After firing my rockets, I was engaged by a Bf 109 and the following few minutes seemed a lifetime as I concentrated on evading at sea level before the enemy fighter disengaged. We lost two aircraft and others were damaged.

> Initially it was thought that Wing Commander Meharg and his navigator Flying Officer Ernest Thompson had been killed. On 9 August, Meharg's wife received a telegram informing her that he was a prisoner of war.
> **Ernest Thompson** recounts their survival.

I was wondering vaguely, in my confused mind, why everything was so still and peaceful, and slowly I became conscious of the fact that my body was in water, which was steadily coming up to my head. Suddenly I realised fully everything that had happened and knew that I must get out quickly, before the aircraft sank.

Two mistakes in the next few seconds might have cost my life there and then. I tried to throw myself out of the hatch, but I had not released the seat strap harness, which had held me so securely at the moment of the terrific impact with the sea. Frantically the straps were undone and I dived through the hatch, to be pulled up short with a sudden jolt, which seemed to almost break my neck. The lead from my headphones to the intercom socket was still plugged in, but fortunately the strain jerked the earphones from the helmet.

As I came up to the surface my eye caught sight of the yellow rubber dinghy not more that ten yards away. I struck out for it immediately, only to find that the enemy fire had accounted for this as well - it was holed and useless. However, this shattering blow was temporarily forgotten when I turned to look back towards what was left of the aircraft. There was the nose and the pilot's cockpit still above the water, and I was so relieved to see this that I found myself shouting, "Willie, Willie!" and trying to swim my fastest at the same time. I was about halfway there when I saw the skipper already in the sea, hanging on to a small piece of floating wood. I called out "You OK Willie?" and he replied that he was all right and asked if I was OK. Yes, I thought for the first time, how am I? I glanced down at my right arm and it looked horrible, a piece of raw flesh with streamers of skin trailing in the water like the white of an egg. But there was no pain - yet. We were both holding on to the plank when what was left of the aircraft went down, nearly taking us with it.

We turned our attention towards the distant object of our attack of a few minutes before and now, possibly, of our salvation. There was one large vessel burning furiously at the stern with four escorts nearby. The fire was growing larger every minute but all this was some five miles away, although there were circling German aircraft between the convoy and us. Our only hope was for the crew of one of these aircraft to see us - just two tiny specks in the water miles away in an ever-fading light.

The situation was hopeless. By now, we were both bitterly cold and my left leg had begun to give me hell. I wondered what the night, and the future, held in store. Often during the past six months, like most aircrew types, I had given this sort of situation serious thought. Willie thought it was only a matter of time before one of the aircraft spotted us. However, darkness seemed to be coming on fast and my left arm and leg were now terribly painful. Willie's teeth were chattering and altogether our prospects for the night seemed very, very bleak.

Then looking away from the convoy, we simultaneously sighted a small yellow object about forty yards away and recognised it as a dinghy pack. Willie kicked off his shoes and swam towards it. He brought it back and together we opened it thinking of the precious Verey pistol and three cartridges in the survival pack in the now inflated dinghy. It was our only hope.

The pistol was quickly assembled and now we settled to wait for the circling aircraft to be in the most favourable position to see us. Three cartridges meant three chances. Willie held the pistol aloft and, at what he thought was the right moment, fired a cartridge. A red star sped 100 feet skywards and then descended leaving a trail of smoke. We waited in anticipation, but it was soon obvious that our God-sent chance to claim attention had gone unobserved. The pistol was reloaded and again we waited. A few minutes later, two Arado 196s made a very wide orbit and were approaching close to us.

Again, the little red distress star sailed skywards and this time our prayers were answered. Almost immediately they turned and came in our direction. One of them did a tight turn directly over us and I watched its gunner closely but his guns did not move. It was obvious he had no intention of shooting at us. A few minutes later the second aircraft arrived very low and dropped a smoke float and our position was now obvious.

Then we saw the Arados land and taxi towards us. Willie hastily threw the pistol away and our saviours came alongside. Willie made for one machine and I went to the other, where the gunner was standing on the float. "Climb on the float," he ordered, surprising me with his very good English. But I found it impossible to obey. My leg seemed paralysed and my arm and hand were so tender that I couldn't bear to touch anything. Somehow he managed to haul me out of the sea and into the aircraft, and I took his seat at the rear, chilled to the bone. The air was now at my burns and it was incredibly painful.

The engine of the aircraft roared and I looked round to see it take off. We were turning into wind when the gunner told me to sit on the floor. I did so and he began to unwrap a first-aid dressing, but the aircraft began to leap forward and, after a succession of bumps, it suddenly became smooth. Never was I so glad to be airborne.

The gunner kept a sharp lookout for about ten minutes – no doubt he thought another attack might happen but I knew differently. The idea of being shot down by my friends was not exactly attractive. Now the gunner turned his attention to my burns and began dressing them. The powdered bandage brought some relief, but the cold, soaked clothes made everything seem miserable, the more so since I now realised I was a prisoner of war. All the good things in life were gone 'for the duration of the war'.

About thirty minutes later my rescuer – to whom I felt I owed my life – said in perfect English, "We are about to land at Suda Bay. Can I have your Mae West as a souvenir?" He could have had all I possessed.

Beaufighters of 252 Squadron over the Aegean. (via Chris Goss)

Losses at this stage of the air offensive in the Aegean were high. Within days of the Meharg/Thompson crew finding themselves in captivity, another pilot was to suffer a similar fate.

Harold Yorke of 603 Squadron, also based at Gambut, often flew in company with 252 Squadron. On 19 July, he and his navigator, Jack Shaw, were briefed with three other crews to fly a sweep among the western Greek islands.

The first misfortune that occurred was the failure of my number two to become airborne due to an engine malfunction. Only three aircraft took off on our sortie towards the enemy coast, flying just above the sea at zero feet and maintaining strict radio silence. We kept fairly close together and constantly checked course and drift to ensure a correct landfall. There was a sea haze, giving both an advantage and a disadvantage, and as our ETA came up, grey shapes of the islands of Zakinthos and Cephalonia loomed before us. The gaps between all Greek islands were known by all aircrews as 'The Gates of Hell', for it was said that they could be heard to clang shut once all attacking aircraft had gone through.

The sweep was to be up the east coast of Cephalonia with the island of Ithaca to our starboard. As we passed the first harbour of Sami there was an eerie stillness, with nobody to be seen. It was mid-afternoon, a time for resting in southern Greece in July, but we knew the wary enemy would be very much awake and quickly assessing our route through the islands and warning garrisons and AA batteries ahead.

We still maintained very low level and with nothing worthy of an attack around Sami we continued up the coast where a small caique was seen in the cove. The fearfully steep cliff faces presented the greatest difficulty in getting into the bay and banking the aircraft almost vertically to get out again so preventing any chance of an attack, although one of the formation did try.

The attack at Fiskardo immediately before York's aircraft was hit and he was forced to ditch. (Air Historical Branch C 3822)

Side slipping out of the cove he skilfully re-joined our little force as we raced round the point towards Fiskardo. As the harbour entrance loomed up, there was a burst of fire from the end of the harbour wall. I saw the shell splashes on the water and started to take evasive action but the next burst hit the aircraft behind the wings and a fire broke out inside the fuselage directly in front of the navigator's position. In seconds the smoke and flames became intense and I shuddered at the thought of the four boxes still full of HE and incendiary 20-mm cannon shells between the nav's position and myself - just where the fire had started. Smoke and flame started to engulf me and my first impulse was to turn to port straight into the cliff face and a quick end, for my calls on the intercom to Jack brought no response and a quick glance told me that he must be dead. In any case, at ten to fifteen feet above the sea at 250 mph in an aircraft with the controls becoming unmanageable, my own chance of survival was pretty slim but somehow I managed to turn to starboard following the approximate direction of the other two.

I was almost on the sea and knew I must try and gain some height but the controls to the tail plane were becoming sluggish. We flashed over the harbour wall and, through the smoke in the cockpit, I vaguely saw a small hill in front on the spit of land beyond the harbour. The aircraft would not climb and somehow I shot between some trees to a little bay beyond the bluff. Beyond was a slightly bigger bay and I knew that this had to be it. I cut the throttles, and tried to lift the nose to bring the speed down but the response was practically negligible and at that moment flames swept across my face. From then on I seemed to do everything incorrectly. I thrust the control column forward so the nose of the aircraft hit the sea but it did not turn over on its back. It bounced dreadfully once, twice, perhaps three times and I was thrown about despite my straps. The next thing I realised was that the water was up to my knees and the aircraft was going down rapidly, nose first. My legs were trapped in the smashed nose but I eventually managed to wrench them free.

The escape hatch above my head was shut tight and my intercom was still plugged in. I managed to release the hatch as the nose of the aircraft went under but had to put my head down into the water to unplug the intercom lead to my helmet. By now the whole cockpit was submerged and I was surrounded by a pale green aura. I climbed out of the top hatch into the cool luxury of seawater and struggled to the surface just in time to see the fuselage and tail of the aircraft slide beneath the waves.

How quiet it was after all the noise of the previous two or three minutes. I could just see the other two aircraft, now a very long way off continuing with the sweep and gradually disappearing. I was to learn a lot later that they both reported 'a perfect ditching' - certainly not by me!

The shore was about a mile away. The rubber dinghy had been automatically ejected from its position in the aircraft's wing and was inflated and floating upside down. The emergency pack was a bit further away. I had hit my head hard on the gun sight - I should have stowed it to the side before ditching - and I had to keep ducking into the water to clear the blood. I swam to the dinghy and, thanks to my training in an Edinburgh swimming pool, I was able to right it and climb in. I was then able to recover the emergency pack and start paddling towards the shore.

Eventually I gained the shore and managed to climb onto rocks. Climbing the steep slope away from the sea was a terrible task but it was absolutely necessary to get as far inland as possible to avoid capture. I had a drink and felt dizzy and the next thing I recall was the barking of dogs and a rifle pointing at me.

A man claiming to be a doctor helped me and we returned to the shore where a boat was waiting with four German soldiers and two fishermen. It seemed very odd to return to the same harbour point from where the gunfire had brought the aircraft down. The Greeks and Italians helped me up the side of the harbour wall. More German soldiers, with an NCO, formed a guard either side of me and I was marched off into the tiny port of Fiskardo.

Ernest Thompson was in hospital in Greece for six weeks and eventually ended up in Stalag Luft III where he joined his pilot. Both men returned to England after the war in Europe.

Wing Commander Meharg remained in the RAF and was awarded a Bar to his AFC for his services as a squadron commander during the Berlin Airlift. Ernest Thompson returned to his pre-war job with the Metropolitan Police Force.

Sadly, Harold Yorke's navigator, Jack Shaw, did not survive when they were forced to ditch off Fiskardo. He was 21 years old and is commemorated on the Alamein Memorial. After his injuries were treated, Harold Yorke found himself on the way to Germany arriving at Stalag Luft 7 at Bankau on 22 August. In January 1945 he had to endure 'The Long March' as the POWs were marched west. He finally arrived home on 26 May 1945 and returned to live in Hertfordshire.

Harold Yorke's German prisoner-of-war card. (Mary Bite)

CHAPTER NINETEEN

THE GAMBUT DETACHMENT – SEPTEMBER 1944

Roy Butler and Ray Graham (left) display 46 Squadron's 'scoreboard' for the Gambut detachment. (Freddie Baldwin)

Towards the end of September 1944, 46 Squadron, based at Idku in Egypt, sent a detachment of Beaufighter VIfs to the forward airstrip at Gambut thirty miles east of Tobruk. During the approaching moonlight period, the crews of 'A' Flight were to fly intruder patrols over the Aegean islands. To assist them, an Irish packet steamer, the *Ulster Queen*, was positioned north of Crete and had been fitted out with a GCI radar and would be protected by destroyers of the Royal Navy. The ship was to act as a ground control station.

One of the pilots on the detachment was Warrant Officer **Roy Butler**. He and his radar/navigator, Warrant Officer Ray Graham, were starting their second tour in the Middle East having previously served on 108 Squadron. He describes the events of this short detachment.

Gambut was a typical desert airfield with sandbagged dispersal areas. The maintenance and flight offices were housed in tents. There were no runways and fine sand drifted constantly across the area. We arrived from Idku on 26 September and by late afternoon the four Beaufighters had arrived and were made ready for night operations.

After unpacking, we returned to the dispersal area where instructions for the night operations were posted. The four aircraft would be scrambled at ninety-minute intervals and we were to be the second away at 2000 hours. Allowing three hours for the transit, we would have ninety minutes on patrol.

At 1815 hours we made our way to dispersal just as the first pair were preparing to take off. It was dark and the dispersal area took on a different appearance. The moon was starting to rise and our all-black aircraft looked very menacing in the dim light. A truck was running across the airfield placing and lighting flares ready for take-off. The flares were made from used gasoline cans that had been cut in half and filled with sand. Gasoline was poured on the sand and ignited. About half a dozen were used for the take-off run and their main purpose was to give the pilot a straight line to follow. At best, it was a very crude type of flarepath, but it was sufficient and typical of desert practice.

We took off at 2010 hours and headed out over the Mediterranean. I levelled off at 6,000 feet and 230 mph and trimmed the aircraft to settle down for the 200-mile flight across the sea. After an hour we were seventy miles from the coast of Crete and I carefully lost height until I judged we were about fifty feet above the sea when I set the altimeter to read zero and trimmed the aircraft slightly tail heavy.

At fifty feet we were below the enemy's radar horizon. I armed the guns and turned on the gun sight and adjusted the brilliance. The theory was, that a wing span of forty feet would fit into the ring at a range of 250 yards, the range at which the cannons and machine guns were synchronised, making this range the most devastating.

At 2135 I called the *Ulster Queen* (call sign 'Trademark') and received a weather report and an altimeter setting. We climbed to 500 feet and began our patrol.

Communication between the controller and us now became relaxed. There were no verbal formalities during an interception and all that was required was quick, concise directions. This was also the case between Graham and me. During the two years we had been crewed together, we had developed and practised a certain patter to use during an interception. Typically, after the controller had given directions to get us to within ten miles of the target, Graham would expect to see the target on his radar. At this point he would follow the target until he was comfortable that he had it firmly established. Then he would tell me to inform the controller we wished to take over the interception. I would do this by using the code word 'Tally-Ho'. The controller would then follow the interception and be ready to help if needed, but he would not talk to us. Graham would continue giving me directions every few seconds until he had talked me into a position where I should be able to see the target. He would relay such information as slight changes of course to follow, the approximate speed of the target, the range as it diminished, and changes in height as required.

I had become so familiar with the way he presented all this data during an in-terception that I could easily tell by the inflection in his voice how the interception was proceeding. Sometimes, from the mental picture that was forming in my mind, I was able to anticipate the directions he was going to give me. As we got closer to the target, and before I could see it, I would tell him where I wanted the target to be in relation to us. This would depend on the weather conditions and was intended to keep us unobserved as long as possible.

The bond between pilot and radar/navigator was very important and was the reason why night-fighter crews liked to stay together. For me, it was exciting to be led blindly on a dark night and to suddenly see another aircraft appear. We had practised interceptions for hours with other crews on the squadron, taking turns to be fighter and the target, always hoping that some night our training would pay off.

At 2150 hours the controller told us to change altitude to 1,000 feet. An hour later we were beginning to doubt we would encounter any enemy aircraft. We had patrolled back and forth and nothing had come within radar range. Suddenly, as we were on our eastern leg, I saw two green lights cross our path from port to starboard on a south-westerly course. I turned hard to starboard to investigate. Trademark called and said there was a bogey in our vicinity. I replied that we were turning to intercept and had the bogey on our radar and were intercepting. He would now monitor our progress and be ready to give us assistance if required.

I could no longer see the lights, but Graham was directing me closer to a position where I could see and identify the other aircraft. We were slowly losing altitude and the target was coming closer. When we were 200 feet above the water, Graham said I should be able to see the target dead ahead. I turned my head from side to side, using my peripheral vision when, quite suddenly, another aircraft came into view about 300 yards dead ahead and 100 feet above me. When the range was down to 250 yards it was not necessary to go any closer to obtain identification. It was a Dornier 24 flying boat. I could clearly see the three engines and the twin tails. The Dornier had a wingspan of just over 100 feet and looked huge. I told Graham to take a look and he confirmed the identity.

It was at this stage of the interception that we started to receive gunfire from the enemy and tracer seemed to be lazily curling over us. I centred the gun sight on the middle engine and fired three short bursts of about two seconds each. It was a relief when all the guns fired because I had often imagined being this close and having the guns jam. I saw strikes on the port wing and engine and as our range was reducing rapidly I turned away to port. The enemy glided down, struck the water and immediately burst into flames. The time was 2250 hours, two minutes after sighting the enemy. I called Trademark and told him that the aircraft was down with many people in the water and he told me to go to Angels One and vector zero nine zero. I turned on to our new heading, somehow reluctant to leave the scene. It did not seem possible that we had caused such devastation.

We flew back and forth at the direction of the controller for almost fifteen minutes when we were told that there was a bogey crossing port to starboard at range five miles. I started to turn and Graham obtained a contact at three miles with the target below us. I started to lose height while Graham continued to give me directions until we were down to 100 feet. Although our airspeed was down to 140 mph, we closed in on the target rapidly. When our range came down to 400 yards the aircraft came into view. It was a three-engine Junkers 52 and we were closing very fast. I lowered the flaps a few degrees to give us more stability, but I could see that unless we acted quickly we were going to overshoot and probably lose the opportunity to get him. I told Graham to confirm my identification as I lined up to attack. Graham agreed that it was a Junkers 52 and I immediately fired a long burst. We were now very close and the effect of our attack was terrifying. The enemy exploded in a huge ball of flame. There was no way to take violent evasive action and the fact that I had lowered some flap was a lifesaver because it allowed me to turn slightly quicker than normal.

We flew right through the edge of the fireball expecting any second to be engulfed. We circled the burning wreckage for about ten minutes but there was no sign of life.

Graham and I concluded we had seen enough action for one night and it would be good if things remained quiet until it was time to return to base. However, at 2330 hours we had a call from Trademark. There were two bogeys north of us and we were to vector 035 degrees and investigate. We were just under 1,000 feet and closing nicely when the bogey disappeared hard to port and we were unable to regain contact. We had barely straightened out when Trademark called again and said there was another target eighteen miles west of us. He controlled us to within two-and-a-half miles and Graham got a contact hard to starboard of us.

I turned and the range started to reduce rapidly. I again lowered some flap to reduce the speed, but now the target was only 100 yards ahead of us. It was a Junkers 52 floatplane flying very slowly. To avoid colliding I pulled along the right-hand side of the enemy aircraft and could clearly see the unique corrugated skin and the swastikas painted on the side. Trademark called and told us it was time to return to base. I called back and told him we were in contact with an enemy aircraft and would talk to him later.

There was no way we could slow down enough to get behind him, so I told Graham that I was going to set my gyro to zero on our present heading and execute a 360-degree turn to starboard back to the same heading. If all went well, we should pick him up again a few miles ahead of us and have a chance for a more controlled interception. We agreed to try it, so I started the turn. As we completed our circle Graham picked him up at a range of four miles. We were both very excited because this was a manoeuvre we had not practised. It was a great job by Graham to pick up the target so quickly.

This time we made a good approach, but because of his slow airspeed we were still overtaking quite rapidly and I knew that we would only get one chance to attack him. The enemy was three miles off the coast of Trypete [sic] and appeared to be heading for a seaplane landing area. I got a visual at 300 yards and at 250 yards gave him one short burst of fire. I observed strikes on the starboard engine, which caught fire. I gave another longer burst and then went into a hard-climbing turn to port intending to try and come in for another attack. The enemy was losing height quite rapidly and as we completed our turn it struck the sea and burst into flames.

The time was 2340 hours and well past time to go home. We had been in the target area almost two hours and destroyed three enemy aircraft and had come very close to destroying ourselves. I called the controller and told him what had happened and that we were returning to base.

We didn't have enough fuel to return via the Straits of Kythera so had to fly direct over the mountains of Crete and hope that we were not engaged. We made a run for it and managed to get clear. Graham picked up the Gambut beacon at twenty-five miles and we landed after being airborne for five hours.

The ground crew met us and there was great excitement and a tonic since the squadron had not had any success for many months. Soon afterwards, we heard that Warrant Officer Terry Phelan and Flight Sergeant Freddie Baldwin, who took over the patrol from us, also shot down a Junkers 52.

We rested the following day and the following night the squadron increased its score to six aircraft destroyed and one damaged.

On the morning of the 28th, Squadron Leader Robbie Robinson, our CO, flew in from Idku and asked to see Graham and I. We presented ourselves and saluted. He shook hands with us and told us that His Majesty King George VI had graciously awarded each of us the Distinguished Flying Cross. We were unprepared for this and at a loss for words. We managed to stammer our thanks and I thought it would be appropriate to salute again, so I did.

46 Squadron Beaufighters over Idku. (Freddie Baldwin)

After having a night off, it was our turn to fly again. We were going to be the last away taking off around 2230 hours. We checked with the intelligence officer (IO) and discussed the possibility that the squadron's activities might prompt a response from the German night-fighters so we refreshed our memories on the characteristics of the Junkers 88 (their standard night-fighter) and the Junkers 188, which was a souped-up version of the Junkers 88. We must have been psychic because the discussion would stand us in good stead later that night.

It was a beautiful night and the flight to the western end of Crete was uneventful. We descended to fifty feet as we approached the enemy coast and made landfall at Cape Gramvansa just before midnight and contacted Trademark. We were told to patrol at 500 feet on a course north/south.

We carried out this patrol for just over thirty minutes when we received a call from Trademark telling us there was a bogey approaching on a northerly course and we should climb to Angels Five. I acknowledged and we started climbing as hard as we could. After ten minutes we obtained radar contact three miles ahead, to the right and high above us. We immediately started climbing and started our chase. Our speed was 200 mph and we were slowly closing on the target. This was obviously not a slow-moving Junkers 52. When we were at 6,700 feet and a range of 600 yards, I obtained a visual.

We kept gaining slowly until the range was 300 yards and I recognised it as a Junkers 188, one of the enemy's fighter/bombers that we heard was being used as a night-fighter. It was a very fast aircraft and could outrun us at heights above 6,000 feet. I opened fire from dead astern and saw numerous strikes on the fuselage and starboard wing. We were getting some return fire from the enemy's tail, but it was not very accurate. The target turned to the right and started to lose height rapidly and I followed him into the turn and tried a long deflection shot. To my surprise it worked, because black smoke started pouring from the starboard engine.

We regained contact when he was two miles away and below us. We followed him down and gained on him and at 300 yards I obtained a visual on him so I opened fire from dead astern scoring numerous strikes on the tailplane and starboard wing. Debris was breaking off the enemy and floating past us, and then the starboard engine caught fire. I broke away when we were directly above the badly damaged aircraft and turned starboard. He was diving steeply toward the sea just off the coast of Melos.

When we had completed our orbit, we could see no further sign of him. I talked to Trademark and he said the enemy blip had disappeared off his radar screen, which backed up our belief that he had crashed into the sea.

The journey back to Gambut was uneventful. We discussed the fact that we did not think it was going to be a piece of cake from now on, as it appeared the enemy was deploying night-fighters. We were lucky to have got the Junkers 188 as it had taken some violent evasive action. However, every time we needed help the controller stepped in, which of course was how it was supposed to work.

We landed after almost five hours and got our glass of brandy from the IO who told us that Phelan and Baldwin had got a Junkers 52. The squadron score was mounting – it was now eight destroyed.

We did not fly the next night, but Hammond and Harrison destroyed two Junkers 52s. Four crews flew on the night of the 30th when Bradley and Forrester destroyed a Dornier 24. Some of the other crews had opened fire before they were close enough to do real damage. It was very important to get to within 250 yards before opening fire. Hammond and I compared notes and agreed that the best attack was to get as close as possible and move the control column around slightly while firing. This had the effect of spraying the shells and meant that the cone of fire was larger. Crude but effective, as was born out by the results we were getting.

On the evening of 1 October we were first off. We headed for the *Ulster Queen* and made contact with Trademark who told us to patrol east/west at Angels One. We were sent off against a bogey but never made contact and Trademark told us to abandon the chase and vectored us to another contact flying at low level. We dived to 500 feet and obtained radar contact at a range of five miles. The target was slightly below us and Graham directed me to follow.

We closed to 250 yards and I recognised a Heinkel III flying at 200 mph at a height of 250 feet. I asked Graham to confirm my identification. At 200 yards I gave a three-second burst from dead astern. I saw strikes on the tailplane and pieces started to break off and float past us. Fires started at the starboard wing root and smoke poured from the starboard engine. The Heinkel did not return fire. As we broke away to port we watched the enemy glide down and strike the sea with a momentary burst of flame and then the water engulfed the wreckage. We did not observe any survivors.

We returned to Gambut and the following morning learned that Hammond and Harris had destroyed a Junkers 88 and Bays and Batiste had got a Junkers 52 and a Dornier 24. The squadron count had increased to fifteen destroyed.

We did not fly again until the 3rd but the patrol was uneventful. As we departed Trademark called and wished us goodnight. I did not realise that it would be the last time that anyone from our squadron would be talking to them. We later discovered that the *Ulster Queen* would be leaving the Aegean. They had done a wonderful job and it was a tribute to the Royal Navy for having kept them safe, especially during the daylight hours. As they had played such a key role in all that we had accomplished, it would be nice to meet them personally and compare stories.

The following day the *Ulster Queen* was withdrawn. At this point, 46 Squadron Gambut Detachment's final score was sixteen destroyed, one probable and four damaged.

Graham and I flew back to Idku on 5 October. After landing, and as I sat in the silence waiting for the hatch to be opened, I realised that a lot had changed since we had left a few days earlier. Ground staff and aircrew had proved we were an efficient night-fighter squadron (which we always hoped we were, but never knew for sure), four of us had been given a decoration by His Majesty, and most important, we had survived to tell the tale.

The next few days, after all the squadron had returned, were a constant round of parties. The highlight for me was when Air Marshal Sir Keith Park, Air Officer Commanding-in-Chief, Middle East visited us to offer congratulations.

Successful Gambut detachment crews pose in front of Roy Butler's aircraft. (Freddie Baldwin)

The press and photographers visited and one of the pictures taken during this euphoric period found its way into a British national newspaper. It was of Graham and I and described our recent exploits and that we had been decorated. This was how my family learned what had happened.

The final result of the Gambut Detachment was as follows:

- Butler/Graham,   Five enemy aircraft destroyed
- Hammond/Harrison,   Three enemy aircraft destroyed, one damaged
- Bays/Batiste,   Two enemy aircraft destroyed, one damaged
- Phelan/Baldwin,   Two enemy aircraft destroyed
- Chapman/Briginshaw,   One enemy aircraft destroyed, two damaged
- Irwin/Watson,   One enemy aircraft destroyed
- Bradley/Forrester,   One enemy aircraft destroyed
- Kirk/Carr,   One enemy aircraft destroyed
- Griffin/Green,   One enemy probably destroyed

CHAPTER TWENTY
ACTION OVER THE ADRIATIC

John 'Dusty' Miller trained as a pilot in the USA under the 'Arnold Scheme'. Assessed as above average, he was retained in the USA as a flying instructor and in 1944 he finally managed to get his wish to join an operational squadron.

On leaving the OTU at Charter Hall, John Dobson, my observer, and I were posted to 255 Squadron in Italy. After leave and going to the transit depot at Blackpool, we boarded the *Empress of Australia* at Greenock, bound for Algiers. From there, we boarded a smaller ship for Naples. Finally, we reached the squadron at Foggia some five weeks after leaving England.

The commanding officer of 255 Squadron was Wing Commander Charles Stewart. He was a charming man, shy and diffident and totally honest and straightforward. I immediately liked him. He explained that the squadron had not had a lot to do in the previous few months.

We lived in a tented camp on the edge of Foggia airfield. The mess was a large marquee and we slept one crew to a tent nearby. Ablutions were primitive but shielded.

Foggia was a joint user airfield with the US Army Air Force and had a medley of squadrons operating in different roles. Arriving in mid-September was 272 Squadron, also equipped with Beaufighters, but operating in the ground-attack role, using rockets as the main armament.

The squadron had been operating in the Western Mediterranean for some months and had lost a lot of crews, all whilst attacking shipping. The remaining crews were tired and had almost completed their tour of operations. The squadron's commanding officer had recently been posted away and it was being run by Squadron Leader Rose, who himself had completed his tour of operations and who was very tired and in need of a total rest. The squadron was clearly in danger of not being able to fulfil its assigned task of helping to clear the Adriatic Sea of the German navy and merchant shipping unless it received an influx of new crews.

The squadron had the important role of interfering as much as possible with the shipping that supplied the German army in Italy, sailing from Fiume, Trieste and smaller ports in the north and east Adriatic.

The message came down from Air Headquarters, Naples to 255 Squadron that 272 Squadron was in need of new crews and that any who wished to transfer would be allowed to do so. Charles Stewart put this to his squadron when two other crews and mine volunteered. I had a little difficulty in persuading John that this was a good thing to do. He had trained for months for the night-fighter role and was now an expert operator of the radar equipment in the night-fighter version of the Beaufighter. This particular skill was not needed in 272

A 272 Squadron Beaufighter TF.C over northern Italy. (Air Historical Branch CNA 3006)

Squadron where the task of the navigator was solely, but very importantly, to navigate. I was determined to leave 255 Squadron however, and eventually he agreed to come with me.

There was no difficulty in getting to the flight line of 272 Squadron from our tented camp since we were on the same airfield. We walked across and were made very welcome (understandably) by Squadron Leader Rose, the acting CO. We learned that he had just been awarded the Distinguished Service Order (DSO) and that seven other pilots had been awarded the Distinguished Flying Cross at the same time.

I had a demonstration flight of rocket firing on the day of our arrival and then flew one on each of the following three days – that was my training! It normally took three months at an OTU to train anti-shipping strike crews. On the evening of the third day, we made our first operational flight. The purpose of the operation was to sweep the north coast of the Adriatic from Venice to Trieste and to sink any shipping that we found. A Canadian pilot, Flight Lieutenant Chesney Rideout, was leading the flight of four aircraft. Naturally, I was at the back. The trip proved to be a fiasco.

We flew into a lot of flak from the coastline near Venice and again near Ravenna. This was my first experience of being shot at. It was dusk, and the tracer shells made a majestic slow-moving coloured line through the air as they came towards us. It takes a few seconds to realise that they are, in fact, meant for you. Nobody was hit on this occasion. For my part, I felt like ducking my head and flying off to anywhere at high speed just to get away from these pretty lines of streamers.

As we continued our search, it grew darker and darker. We were flying at fifty feet above the sea to avoid radar detection. I could barely see the aircraft in front of me. For a few minutes, I thought that I was at fault and was simply inadequate

Armourers prepare the armour piercing heads for fitment to the rocket motor. (Air Historical Branch CH 17880)

and inexperienced. Fortunately, this proved not to be so. Rideout gave the order to return to base and we returned individually. When we were on the ground at Foggia, he explained that the operations staff had made a mistake when they had looked up the time of darkness and, as a result, we had taken off one hour late. Little wonder that it seemed to get too dark very quickly!

Two evenings later we set off on a similar mission. Our technique when searching for targets in the anti-shipping role was to fly as low as possible over the sea, about fifty feet, to avoid detection by radar. When a target was sighted, we approached to within about a mile and then climbed quickly to 100 feet, lined up with the target, and, at the range of about half-a-mile, dived directly and steeply at the target. Using a modified gun sight, we fired the rockets, eight or sixteen, at a range of about 200 yards. Some rockets had a solid head and others an explosive head. The solid heads were the more accurate and could create large holes below the water line in a ship. The risk to us was the anti-aircraft fire from the target ship, from other ships with it and from the shore. We used a similar technique against land targets. The secret to survival in this form of operation, insofar as there is a secret, and aside from good luck, was to stay at around the 1,000-feet level for as brief a time as possible so that the anti-aircraft gunners had little time to judge speed, range and deflection.

It is perhaps not surprising that aircraft losses in low-level operations in the Royal Air Force show a preponderance of five to one caused by flak as against those caused by enemy aircraft.

On my second sortie two days later, the cloud base was about 200 feet and it was pouring with rain. It was difficult to stay in formation and impossible to carry out an attack if a target was sighted. Flight Lieutenant Tommy Grace, who was leading and on his last operational trip, decided to abandon. Unfortunately, the weather had closed in behind us at Foggia and we were diverted to Falconara, near Ancona. The weather stayed foul for two days and we were stuck, with not even a toothbrush. On the third day, we flew back to Foggia.

Foggia was in a truly bombed-out state. Much of the town had been flattened and fought through. Some buildings survived in a semi-derelict state. The block of flats we occupied was small and, although badly damaged, it was more or less waterproof. There was some running water at certain times of the day, but no heating. The officers lived in the two top floors and the aircrew NCOs in the bottom two of the block. It proved to be a good arrangement, since all the aircrews were readily available for call out and briefing.

The day after bedding down in the flat, we were operating again. By now we had a new CO, Wing Commander Park – a very quiet, efficient man. I was a flight lieutenant, and, although still junior in real terms, I was relatively senior amongst the few crews that we then had and the new arrivals from another night-fighter squadron. Rose explained that the officers of the squadron who had been there when I arrived were not going to fly any more operations. They had all done more than enough. Suddenly, we were largely a squadron of comparatively inexperienced crews.

Wing Commander Geoffrey Park DFC impressed very quickly. He was an experienced operator and soon began to take his full share of the flying. He was popular and respected. Unfortunately, only two weeks after his arrival, he was shot down. He and his navigator, Danny Edwards, were killed whilst attacking shipping outside Pula harbour on the Istrian Peninsula. Rose, still with us but not flying, took over again.

On average, given some consistency in the weather, and excluding any special operations, each crew flew every other day. The winter in Italy can be bitterly cold, windswept and wet and the one of 1944/45 seemed to us to be particularly bad.

I flew thirteen sorties in October, ten in November and eight in December, which indicates how the worsening weather reduced our activity.

A new commanding officer, Wing Commander R. N. Lambert DFC, arrived to replace Park. He was a quiet self-effacing man, and totally unafraid. He soon began to operate. Unfortunately, on 1 December, his aircraft was shot up and he received chest wounds from small-calibre bullets, presumably light machine-gun fire. He landed safely at the diversion airfield of Fano and was taken immediately to hospital. We never saw him again. Some waggish doctor at the hospital sent the offending bullets to the squadron adjutant. We took this in good part and put them in a small jar, labelled it 'Lambert's Folly', and hung it on the Christmas tree.

Our losses were steady and made us all a bit nervous. As we knew, they were caused by flak from ships, coastal and harbour defences and unseen guns that seemed to lie quite thickly throughout the occupied territory. We had aircraft attacked by fighters on only one occasion, when the pilot, Flying Officer Murray, escaped by twisting and turning within a few feet of the waves.

I was lucky. I was damaged only three times by anti-aircraft fire when none of the damage was serious. The nearest I came to pain was a bullet embedded in the parachute on which I sat. I saw only one enemy fighter and that at a distance. Presumably he did not see me.

By mid-January we had lost three commanding officers, either killed or wounded, within the space of about ten weeks. At this stage the experienced Squadron Leader Tony Mottram DFC took over as acting CO.

There were two main sources of fear in aircrew during the Second World War. The first, obviously, was when being shot at. This experience brings an immediate and hollow feeling to the stomach and a bit of panic to the mind and is common to all who fight in any kind of action. My reaction to these feelings was the same as that of the great majority; finish whatever the operation calls for and get out of the trouble spot as fast as possible.

The second source of fear, and the one that had the greater debilitating effect, was that felt as the operational tour progressed. The thought and fear of having to go on operations again and again until a rest was earned was almost constant.

In January 1945 I was sent to the Officer's Advanced Training School at Kalafrana, Malta on a course, which lasted three weeks. I returned to the squadron and immediately began operating again. By then, Tony Mottram was in charge. He was a sound and knowledgeable operator whom I liked and respected. I hoped that he would be promoted and become the commanding officer. This was eventually not to be, but he acted as such for two months.

A rocket attack against railway trucks and tankers at Banova Jaruga, Yugoslavia in February 1945. (Air Historical Branch CH 17880)

By now, February 1945, we had to spend a lot of flight time ferreting out shipping from the small bays and harbours that are dotted about the Istrian Peninsula and the islands and mainland of Yugoslavia. It was decided by Air Headquarters that the operations of the squadron should be carried out by a detachment of the squadron from Falconara, near Ancona, giving us a much shorter flying time to the operational area. I was given command of the detachment and Tony Mottram stayed behind at Foggia with the main servicing and administrative elements of the squadron.

This move gave me my first experience of commanding a complete unit. I carried out twelve strikes in the month of February, including one of twelve aircraft against shipping that had been sighted in the Arsa Channel on the Istrian Peninsula. It was very exciting. Attacking with twelve aircraft in a narrow channel dwarfed on each side by mountains concentrates the mind. We all survived, but almost all suffered damage from flak.

In early March, it was decided that I had had enough, and I was stood down, as the expression is, from operations. I had flown forty-three trips. Mottram had a good sense of humour, biased towards irony and wryness. I enjoyed my time with him. As he told me that I was tour expired, he added that, had I stayed, I might have been promoted. I replied that I was quite happy with the situation. He became a well-known Wimbledon and Davis Cup tennis player and remained a charming and modest man. He was later awarded a Bar to his DFC.

I stayed to command, but not operate, with the Falconara detachment until the whole squadron moved there in mid-March. John Dobson and I then went off to Rome for some rest and to see the sights.

We lost fifteen crews whilst I was on 272 Squadron. John and I were the only crew to complete a tour after September 1944. I was posted to the Beaufighter OTU at Nicosia in Cyprus as an instructor.

'Dusty' Miller (left) and his navigator, John Dobson, at Foggia after completing their tour on 272 Squadron. (John Miller)

John 'Dusty' Miller was awarded the DFC at the end of his tour, the citation concluding, 'he has displayed excellent leadership, a fine fighting spirit and great devotion to duty.' He remained in the RAF and had a distinguished career retiring as Air Commodore J. Miller CBE, DFC, AFC.

CHAPTER TWENTY-ONE

SILENTLY INTO THE MIDST OF THINGS

There does not appear to be any hard experience that the Japanese troops referred to the Beaufighter as the 'Whispering Death', although with its quiet 1,770-hp Bristol Hercules engines and its extremely low-level method of attack, it is quite feasible that it could be almost on top of them before they heard it. It is more likely that the sobriquet was coined by an imaginative war correspondent as the press used it extensively to describe Beaufighter operations over Burma.

However, the role of the Beaufighter in South East Asia Command (SEAC) was not just ground attack but also the night defence of Calcutta. Beaufighter Ifs of 'A' Flight of 89 Squadron were hurriedly flown in from the Middle East in January 1943 to counter Imperial Japanese Army Air Force (IJAAF) raids against the city. This detachment became 176 Squadron based at Dum Dum just outside Calcutta and it was soon in action.

On the night of 15 January 1943 a formation of Mitsubishi Ki-21 (Sally) heavy bombers were detected heading for Calcutta. First to sight the force was Sergeant Maurice Pring and his navigator Warrant Officer C. T. Phillips. In an engagement that lasted less than five minutes, the Beaufighter crew despatched three of the four aircraft. A few nights later, the Australian Flying Officer C. Crombie and his navigator Warrant Officer R. C. Moss RAAF destroyed two 'Sallys' but return fire forced them to bale out of their blazing Beaufighter.

These successes had an immediate effect on the morale of the citizens of Calcutta and also on the Japanese who stopped their night attacks on the city until the end of the year. Crombie was awarded a DSO, Moss and Phillips the DFC and Pring a DFM.

However, it was in the ground-attack role that the Beaufighter was to make such a major contribution to the eventual success in Burma.

Atholl Sutherland-Brown of the RCAF, and a pilot on 177 Squadron, provides an overview of Beaufighter operations.

The three Beaufighter squadrons of 901 Wing (27, 177 and 211) ranged all over Burma and the northern half of Siam (Thailand) engaged in ground attack of enemy transportation systems and airfields. Although part of the 3rd Tactical Air Force, their work was essentially strategic interdiction of supply. Mostly they flew at 100 feet or less above the jungles or plains on operations that were chiefly targets of opportunity ('rhubarbs') but which had direction regarding type of transport and area.

In response to air intelligence the principal targets and operational areas changed as the campaign unfolded. During the stalemate of 1943 the main targets were the large riverboats plying the Irrawaddy and Chindwin rivers. These shallow draft steamers could carry 1,000 troops. They were attacked and by the end of the year all were sunk, which compounded the enemy's reinforcement and supply problems. The squadrons were then directed to attack the airfields of central Burma and drove the fighters out of these and to the east. However, the Nakajima Ki-43 fighters, codenamed the Oscar, had a range of 1,000 miles, so they were still a threat from their rearward airfields.

Officers of 177 Squadron at Chiringa in November 1944. Atholl Sutherland-Brown is fourth from right in the back row. (Atholl Sutherland-Brown)

Coinciding with the airfield attacks, the Beaufighters turned to patrols of all the railways of Burma but especially the main line from Rangoon to Mandalay and on northwards to Myitkyina. By early 1944 trains were restricted to night movement, earth-filled locomotive shelters were constructed and major flak nests were developed along the railways. The Beaufighter squadrons reacted by carrying out ground attack at night during the moon periods and by using rockets to attack locos in their shelters. These changed tactics further inhibited and slowed Japanese troop and supply movements.

As Japanese intentions to mount offensives to capture India became known through intelligence in 1944 priorities again changed. The enemy, by using enslaved POWs, had completed the railway from Bangkok to Moulmein near Rangoon. About the same time, the Beaufighter squadrons were re-equipped with the long-range Mark X. Therefore, the trains of this railway came under intensive attack by Beaufighters, as the mainline ones had been before, and Liberators based in India and Ceylon (Sri Lanka) bombed the many bridges. The Bangkok railway also had many engineering problems, some caused by disguised forms of POW sabotage. Thus the railway never delivered more than a third of its designed capacity.

The Japanese offensive struck first in the Arakan along the indented coast on the Burma-India border. This was actually a feint to confuse the Allies and to absorb their reserves. Before the attacks developed the Beaufighters were directed to patrol intensively the road across the southern Chin Hills at Taungup Pass. This route was the enemy's only significant access to supply and reinforce the army in the Arakan. A month or so later, just before the onset of the monsoon, the main offensive struck around Imphal in the northern Chin Hills. It was tough for the Japanese troops filing through the jungle trails in the heat and rain of the early monsoon storms and impossible to move equipment or supplies except by mules.

The Japanese accomplished this so they gained tactical surprise when they arrived sooner and stronger than expected. Part of the reason for this was the use of new routes from China and Siam. Also, because the Bangkok railway and the sea route had come under intensive interdiction, they brought supplies in by using the Burma Road and the Lashio branch railway. The 14th Army repelled both offensives with bloody hand-to-hand fighting in the jungles, and the Allies were able to stand their ground without significant supply routes because of regular airdrops. Meanwhile, the Beaufighters were attacking the Lashio railway with great success.

At the end of the 1944 monsoon the defeated Japanese armies started fighting withdrawals from the Arakan and the Chin Hills. They were starving, ill and short of all supplies but still fierce and tenacious. The major battle of their retreat through the plains took place about the airfield complex of Meiktila, south-west of Mandalay. The retreat continued for 400 miles towards Pegu throughout the dry season until the onset of the next monsoon in May 1945. At the same time the retreating Arakan army, while trying to cross the wide lower Irrawaddy river, was continually strafed by Beaufighters.

Attack on the Irrawaddy against a fuel barge covered in foliage in a failed attempt at disguise. (Tony Rieck)

The Allies were preparing a combined operation with a landing near Rangoon called 'Dracula' to be launched just before the 1945 monsoon. The navy were terrified that the Japanese were building hundreds of wooden MTBs and hiding them in the delta of the Irrawaddy. The Beaufighter squadrons mounted dozens of rhubarbs to find and destroy these without success because they didn't exist. This is one of the few failures of air intelligence in the Burma campaign.

There are three examples of operations mounted on different target types that give a good insight into the importance of intelligence and the effectiveness of the Beaufighter in the Burma campaign.

Reinforcement and supply movements along the Lashio Branch railway were at its maximum in April-May 1944 preceding the Imphal offensive. I took part in several operations designed to strike this traffic and particularly a very successful one on 12 May. My observer was ill so I flew with Flight Sergeant F. J. Lumley as a replacement. We took off from Feni airfield south of Dacca, now in Bangladesh, in the late afternoon to begin our patrol at Mandalay as last light neared. I was flying as number two to Squadron Leader A. P. Willis DFC. Big storms crowned the Chin Hills, which had to be avoided, but fortunately the target area was relatively clear. We followed the steep road and railway switchbacks up to the Shan Plateau at Maymyo and continued towards the terminus at Lashio. We could hardly believe our luck for the area was full of trains and motor transports. Between us in a short time we severely damaged three locomotives under steam, shot up the carriages and attacked three locos that were stationary and possibly unserviceable. In between we encountered seven MTs and set four on fire.

Our style of attack was for the two aircraft to make separate dives on the targets, which was most effective and divided the attention of the flak crews. However, it required great concentration and awareness of the other's position in the melee. The failing light and the hilly terrain added to the difficulty. Soon we were both out of cannon ammunition so set course in the growing darkness for home where we landed after six hours aloft. This was my eleventh operation and the most destructive to the Japanese enemy transport to that date. The squadron record book during this period only had brief summaries of sorties but my logbook and nose camera photo are quite explicit.

On 10 September a flap developed when a sister squadron encountered and attacked a convoy of coastal freighters with naval escorts south of Moulmein near Kalegauk Island. Our squadron was ordered to press home the attack with armour-piercing rockets as the others rearmed for a third strike. We were quickly briefed and airborne again by mid-morning. We flew in a loose formation down the coast at wave tops to avoid radar and likewise across the Gulf of Martaban, which was like glass. In such conditions flying into the sea is a hazard but running out of fuel was a more serious one as the operation was at extreme range.

We arrived off the island to find one coastal freighter stationary at sea. Attacks were made *en passant* to try and sink it, but we continued around the lee of the island where six or seven ships were moored or beached. They opened up with flak as we dove towards them and the results were hard to confirm in the confusion except we had a number of direct hits. We had no time or inclination to linger so we again formed a loose gaggle and this time cut across the delta flying just above the trees. All our tanks were virtually empty as we landed safely at base after six hours and forty minutes in the air. If this was a Japanese experiment in reinforcement it was one they did not continue but it was scarcely the great victory in the Andaman Sea as reported in the *Calcutta Statesman* a few days later.

Operations to interdict motor transport across the Taungup Pass were frustrating both by day and by night. Streams of traffic moved across the pass to provide troops and supplies for the Arakan offensive and later to facilitate the retreat. During the day enough dust arose through the trees to reveal movement but attacking along the jungle road of the incised hills was extremely difficult. Given warning, the Japanese transports got off the road under the banyan and other great trees where they were no longer visible. The road was so tree covered and twisted it was challenging to follow at low level in fast aircraft. Destruction of vehicles was difficult to prove unless a lucky cannon burst ignited a fuel tank. At night everything was that much more demanding except for initial observation because the trucks in the convoys needed their masked headlights to stay on the road. At first attack they stopped, disappeared under the canopy and turned off their lights. Registering where they went to ground was difficult and manoeuvring low over the road to attack was fraught with hazard in the dark sky above the black jungle.

During the early retreat phase of the Japanese from the Arakan, my regular observer, Warrant Officer Alf Aldham, and I were briefed for a rhubarb on the night of 6-7 October along roads, railway and river in southern Burma. Our route was from Pyinmana on the main line south to Pegu, back up the Irrawaddy to Prome and then across the Taungup Pass. This multi-purpose offensive patrol covered the main line, river crossings and the route to Arakan. We took off from Chiringa airfield near the Bay of Bengal south of Chittagong in Beaufighter LZ 118 at 2200 hours. The weather was fair along the plains with a half moon but ground mist was common even on the pass. Flying south at about 100 to 200 feet we made four attacks on motor transport lights and claimed one damaged. Nothing was seen on the railway but about thirty-five parked railcars were attacked twice near Nyaunglebin without obvious results. Turning north nothing was seen on the river but following the road across the pass about thirty MT were moving west in groups of five or six. Four long attacks were made but the enemy trucks extinguished their lights quickly and it was difficult to assess results. We claimed several hits but no trucks exploded. We landed back at 0230 hours with only a few bullet holes from small-arms and light machine-gun fire.

All these operations found targets that might be expected based on Allied intelligence. Not all operations were so fruitful at interdiction or so free of opposition. The Beaufighter squadrons clearly benefitted from the intelligence work at Command HQ.

Warrant Officer **James Denny** joined 177 Squadron in September 1944. He had initially converted to the Beaufighter at 60 OTU followed by the Coastal Command course at Catfoss. He left for the Middle East soon to discover that his squadron was to head for India. On arrival at Jodhpur he learned that there was no immediate requirement for Beaufighter crews so he was sent to 42 Squadron where he completed a full tour, first on the 'dreaded' Bisley before they were replaced by Hurricanes. In September 1944 he received an urgent message to report to 177 Squadron. On 10 September he made his first operational sortie almost two years after completing his Beaufighter OTU course. As he explains, it was not quite what he expected.

This first trip was as number two to Squadron Leader H.B. Hunt DSO, DFC on a dawn patrol of the Mandalay to Lashio railway, which meant a 0415 hours take-off. Not having flown a Beau at night for two years, I was somewhat nervous of the take-off. Chiringa was a fairly narrow strip with tall trees in close proximity along each side. I managed to avoid a swing in the limited light and all went well. We climbed to 10,000 feet to clear the Chin Hills and then let down into central Burma. Dawn was breaking as we skirted Mandalay to the north at a height of about fifty feet. Flying at low level made it very difficult for Japanese fighters to spot us - our top camouflage blended in well with the terrain. We picked up the railway to Lashio and flew

James Denny, centre of the middle row, whilst at No. 2 (Coastal) OTU. (Kate Masheder)

along it, seeing no sign of activity until we came to a stationary train at Sedaw, which we duly attacked with cannon and received a lot of return fire. Nothing further was seen and we arrived back at Chiringa at 0830 hours.

My next trip was a solo patrol of the railway Shwebo-Sagaing-Monya on 15 September. Having seen nothing, I put a few cannon shells into a warehouse at a small station called Pankan a few miles north-west of Mandalay. I was surprised to see an explosion and a large petrol fire mushroom up into the sky. This effort made the *News of all India Radio* the next day.

On 22 September, my navigator, Flight Sergeant Joe Yates, and I were detailed to make a low-level patrol down the Japanese-held Arakan coast road, skirt heavily defended Taungup and then cover the Taungup-Padang road including the pass over the Yomas. Accurate navigation was vital on these treetop-height patrols in order to avoid known Japanese-defended positions and Joe had had little experience of this type of flying. Our first three trips together had been very exciting and we had already collected several bullet holes in our Beaufighter.

Take-off time was 1000 hours and we got off without mishap. It was the tail end of the monsoon period and still very hot and humid. Over-heating engines necessitated fast taxiing to the end of the strip and a quick take-off. In spite of this, we were, as usual completely sweat-soaked by the time we were airborne. Unfortunately, as the whole trip had to be carried out at low level, we would remain in this uncomfortable state for the whole six hours.

We headed out over the Indian Ocean from our Bengal base and then followed the coastline south, cruising at 220 mph at twenty feet above the waves. As soon as we had passed the front-line area we flew in over the land to pick up the coastal road along which the Japanese had to bring all their supplies. This long narrow coastal plain is covered by jungle and mangrove swamps, the road meanders and makes enormous detours and I had great difficulty following it at treetop height. There was no sign of life – even the few native villages seemed deserted and certainly there was no visible trace of enemy activity. Their transport usually moved at night and holed up in the daytime and their camouflage was excellent. In this way, we flew on for thirty minutes and then, as our orders were to avoid Taungup, I asked Joe for our approximate position. He, of course had been quite confused by our erratic progress down the coast road but was sure we could not be near Taungup yet. I could see a large village coming up ahead and decided to fly over it and try to identify it on the map.

We got to the outskirts of the place and then all hell broke out – it was of course Taungup! At that height I could hear the crackle of machine guns above the noise of the engines, tracer bullets were coming at us from all angles, then I heard the thud of light anti-aircraft shells and Joe reported shell bursts above and behind. I put the Beaufighter down to minimum height, gave it full throttle and we crossed the rest of the town desperately weaving to avoid huts, trees and telegraph poles. At the same time, I gave a few bursts on the cannons to add to the confusion. It seemed to take an age to cross that mile or so of scattered buildings and dumps and I crouched down in my seat, peering through the bottom of the windscreen and expecting to feel the rip of hot metal the whole way. Then, somehow, we were out of the town and its outskirts and I could no longer hear any gunfire although shells were still bursting above and behind us. I flew round a low hill, putting it between the town and us and for the moment we were safe. Then I looked around for damage to the aircraft and immediately saw five jagged holes in the port wing. They were roughly in line with the cockpit, the last one being some five feet away and had obviously been fired from almost directly beneath us. The one nearest to the cockpit seemed to be right where a fuel tank was situated but Joe reported no sign of any leak and I assumed the self-sealing system had worked. No other damage was visible from the cockpit so I decided to complete the patrol, after making a few caustic remarks to Joe about his low-level navigation capabilities!

I flew along the north side of the road, climbing steadily with it as it crossed the Arakan Yomas. As before, there was no sign of life and at the highest point of the pass I throttled back and put the nose down steeply to follow the road with its numerous S-bends. My last task on the patrol was to photograph the bridge at Padang where this same road crossed a tributary of the Irrawaddy at the foot of the mountains. With this object in view I opened up the throttles and hugged the tree-clad slopes in a steady dive. This bridge was known to have machine-gun posts at both ends. I switched on the camera and shot across the bridge. A few stray tracers came up as we reached the far end and then we were out of vision behind trees.

As we departed I noticed the tops of three sails on the Irrawaddy a mile or two to my right. I turned and approached the river and saw they were large boats of the junk type with square sails. Our orders were to attack any form of transport so I climbed to 500 feet, banked steeply and raked three of them with the cannons as I dived on them. Then I stayed low and turned north-west for base as I accelerated to get clear of a known danger area.

Soon I could see the Taungup-Prome road again, white in amongst the trees. At that moment, there was a tremendous bang in the cockpit, a harsh brittle sound accompanied by dust and smoke. I felt strangely numb for a second or two then my brain started to work again. My first thought was that a cannon shell had exploded right in the cockpit and yet there seemed no obvious damage. Then I felt numbness in my right forearm and, on raising the arm, I saw three blacked holes in the fleshy part, which started to bleed heavily. I called Joe and then saw that we were heading straight for a cluster of tall trees. Just in time I pulled hard on the control column with my left hand and cleared them with little to spare. I realised I was in no condition to return at low level and would have to take the risk of gaining some altitude. I trimmed the Beau in a steady climb and headed in the general direction of Bengal. By this time, Joe had crawled forward with the first-aid box. He made a fairly sound job of bandaging and then I noticed blood soaking through the left leg of my flying suit where I found several small wounds. The pain from my arm was now intense and I felt faint and sick with the heat and loss of blood. I had a drink of water and splashed some on my face and the faintness eased off.

I turned and looked at Joe behind me – he looked white and anxious. If I had passed out and he had managed to drag me out of my seat and get to the controls, he had no previous flying experience and could never have got us down in one piece. I pulled myself together and started to take a more intelligent interest in our return trip. I had a look around and found that a bullet had entered on the port side of the nose and smashed the top of the undercarriage lever and passed out through the Perspex canopy close to my right ear. Splinters of metal must have caused my wounds.

We were at 10,000 feet by this time and almost over the centre of the mountains. At this height we were in radio range of Chiringa and I called them up, reported the position and gave a rough estimate of our arrival time. After that there was nothing else to do but keep on course and wait for the strip to appear on the horizon, hoping no Japanese fighters appeared first, as we were still about 100 miles inside enemy-occupied territory.

The time dragged and my right arm throbbed painfully. The hand was numb and I found I could only use my forefinger and thumb. I began to worry as to how I was going to get us down safely.

At long last the strip came in sight and after a short call to the control tower, I lowered the wheels and made a hasty pre-landing check. I made the final approach fairly low and fast in order to do a wheelie-landing rather than a three-pointer. This would put less strain on my right hand and meant that I would fly the aircraft with low power until the main wheels touched and then whip the throttles closed and wind back the trim tabs with my left hand. Everything went smoothly until the wheels touched and began to take the full weight of the aircraft, then the port wing began to drop and we soon began a dangerous swing to the left towards the trees lining the strip. The tyre on the port wheel had been punctured, no doubt by a bullet. There was nothing I could do but apply full right brake, which was on the control column and normally applied by the right thumb. I managed to get my left hand across and applied

Cannon strike on fuel storage whilst strafing railway buildings. (Ken Waldie)

it as hard as I could. The swing checked and our speed began to drop. The good old Beau kept amazingly straight until near the end when it swung off the runway and skidded to a halt. I switched off and clambered wearily out of my seat and down the hatch. The MO was there and he took me straight to a nearby West African Rifles field hospital. On the 30th I was transferred to the RAF hospital at Chittagong where I spent the next five weeks and where they successfully operated on my arm to remove the worst of the splinters.

I finally arrived back on the squadron at the end of November to discover that the CO had been shot down together with five other crews.

Arriving on the squadron about this time was **Ken Waldie** RCAF.

I was a pilot with 177 Squadron and joined in November 1944. While the bombers dealt with the cities, docks and other concentrated areas, we covered the long stretches of roads, railways, rivers and the coastline with low-level patrols. Each of the three squadrons on the wing put up eight aircraft per day, so that there were always Beaufighters over some part of Burma at any hour of every day and on most moonlit nights. We think this was effective in discouraging movement on the roads and railways in particular. In addition, we tried to make life more difficult for them by damaging installations such as petrol and water tanks, small bridges and oil pipelines.

The main activity at this stage of the war, the Fourteenth Army had started its move south from Imphal and was heading for Mandalay, was to mount attacks south of Mandalay as far south as Moulmein, although we also went as far south as Tavoy at times and occasionally into Siam along the Burma-Siam railway. Aircrews were given specific areas to cover during a certain time period. It was left to our discretion as to how we did it, unless, of course, a specific target was tasked. On occasion, if the target justified it, we flew in pairs but single aircraft usually carried out the patrols.

A typical trip would last for four to five-and-a-half hours. The navigator (mine was Flight Sergeant Dan Whiteing of the RAF) did the long-distance navigation, but once on patrol we both map-read much as in the family car with all the usual arguments as to whether we should have turned left at the last town or carried straight on.

We flew at low level and kept jinking and when a target was spotted we made a quick climbing turn to about 600-800 feet at which point the turn would bring us into a position to make a dive attack. On these targets the 20-mm cannon was very effective, so much so that one could hit a petrol tank on a vehicle or puncture the boiler of a locomotive on the first burst. By the nature of the attack, any personnel, usually Burmese, had

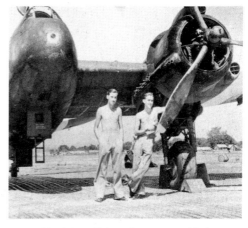

Ken Waldie (left) and his navigator Dan Whiteing. (Ken Waldie)

plenty of time and used it to find a safe hiding place. From our standpoint, we seldom encountered serious opposition in attacks of this sort. Japanese fighters had become scarce and we rarely encountered them and when we did, they found it hard to get at us at low level in spite of their better manoeuvrability and speed. The greater dangers were from low flying errors of judgement, or from light-arms fire from the tops of railway stations or other high spots, or from inadvertently straying over heavy anti-aircraft guns on the edges of cities.

The sturdy Beaufighter was very well suited to this type of work. While not as quick as some other aircraft of the time, it had other advantages such as excellent visibility at low level, long range and dependability under hot and humid conditions. The extremely quiet, slow-turning sleeve valve Hercules engines were a distinct advantage in approaching targets; in fact the 177 Squadron motto was based on this feature 'Silentia Medias Res' (Silently into the Midst of Things). I preferred the cannons for most jobs because of their accuracy and formidable power. On some targets, such as small bridges, or larger ships, rockets were more effective, but the dependability and accuracy of the rocket at that time left much to be desired.

I did twenty sorties between November 1944 and the end of April 1945 with a break of about six weeks recovering from a minor shrapnel wound. About the end of April it was decided that the Canadians, there were four of us, would be taken off ops and sent to the USA for re-training with the USAAF for service in the Pacific. Events

A supply train attacked with cannons near Kanbalu in Central Burma. (Air Historical Branch C 4480)

moved quickly so we never got away as planned. The squadron soon moved back to a base near Chittagong in June and was disbanded two months later.

> **James Denny** returned to operations in December 1944 but was still troubled by his right arm but by mid-January he was able to resume full operations attacking road, rail and river transports. One of his final sorties provides a graphic description of the weather conditions crews had to face flying in the Burma theatre.

On 2 May 1945 I made another night take-off for a dawn attack on Japanese guns in the Rangoon area. Two squadrons took part, thirty-six aircraft in all. Our course was south over the sea for about 300 miles and then east across south-west Burma, all aircraft to proceed independently. There was quite a lot of cloud around Chiringa with the moon shining through gaps but, after about thirty minutes flying over the sea at 2,000 feet, I ran into massive, towering black clouds with lightning flashes. I descended to try and get under them but found the cloud base was now well below 1,000 feet and it was raining heavily so I decided to climb and try to get over the tops. When I reached 20,000 feet, I could still see huge cloud masses well above me, so I abandoned the idea and started a descent with the idea of making another attempt to get underneath. There were now very few gaps and I made use of what there were but the last few thousand feet of the descent was in dense cloud with considerable turbulence. By the time I was down to 1,000 feet, and still in cloud, I was getting worried. Suddenly, at about 800 feet I broke clear and found myself in a small clear patch possibly half-a-mile across with towering black clouds all around. A ship engaged us, which could only have been one of ours, so I made a steep climbing turn back into cloud.

I headed west as we were buffeted around and then turned south and descended breaking cloud at 500 feet in pitch darkness and heavy rain. At that point I decided it was useless to press on any further and asked my navigator, Andy Anderson, for a course back to base. With all our cloud manoeuvres he was only able to give a rough estimate so I set off back to fly at 500 feet through intermittent heavy rain hoping conditions would improve before we were due to make landfall in about two hours' time. After about an hour the rain gradually lessened and then a few gaps appeared in the clouds allowing a little moonlight to appear. This was just enough for us to identify Akyab Island and alter course for Chiringa. Andy had not been far out in his estimate.

Dawn was breaking and it was quite light when we reached base. There was still heavy cloud about with rain and turbulence but nothing like that we had experienced over the sea. I landed safely, taxied to dispersal and switched off with a considerable feeling of relief at surviving the worst weather conditions I had ever encountered. Most of the thirty-six aircraft were forced to turn back and, surprisingly, we had no losses that day.

Nine days later I flew my thirty-second and final Beaufighter operations when I damaged a barge with cannon fire on the Sittang river.

> Denny spent the next few months in India before returning to England in October. Of the seven Beaufighter pilots and seven navigators who had set out with him three years earlier, only two pilots and one navigator returned.
>
> Atholl Sutherland-Brown was awarded the DFC at the end of his tour in Burma. He returned to Canada and became the chief geologist in British Columbia. Ken Waldie returned to live in his native Canada.

CHAPTER TWENTY-TWO
LOOKING BACKWARDS OVER BURMA

Warrant Officer Dennis Spencer and friend. (Ian Spencer)

Dennis Spencer outlines the techniques he used to navigate over Burma.

I was trained in Canada as a navigator/wireless (Nav/W). The syllabus was based on all aspects of air navigation, wireless operation, reconnaissance, aerial photography, bomb aiming and air gunnery. This qualified me to wear the coveted 'O' badge (observer), which originated in the First World War, rather than the new 'N' badge then being introduced for navigators.

After completing the OTU on Hampdens, my pilot Geoff Vardigans and I returned to the UK in the autumn of 1943 to find that we were to be trained on Beaufighters at 9 OTU at Crosby-on-Eden near Carlisle.

In marked contrast to the Hampden, the provision of accommodation for a second crew member on the Beaufighter seemed to me to have been something of an afterthought. "Let's cut a hole in the top of the fuselage towards the back and stick him in there with a Perspex cupola over his head", I imagined someone saying. "We'll give him a swivel seat and he can keep a lookout at the back, fire the rear gun, operate the W/T set. Oh, and incidentally, do the navigation. It won't matter that his forward view of the ground will be very much obstructed by those two bloody great engines."

True there was a chart table that folded down in front of you and those old friends, the T1154 and R1155 W/T transmitter and receiver, were within easy reach on the right. But there was no D/F loop aerial and no drift recorder, indeed there was nought else in the way of navigational aids except a handheld bearing compass – if you had remembered to bring it along. To swivel the seat round to face backwards it was necessary to first lift up the hinged chart table otherwise the back of the seat fouled it. Anything loose, like a pencil or protractor inadvertently left on the table, would of course fall off. Therefore, as a navigator, I did not like the Beaufighter at all but later I came to love it.

On completion of training we had expected to be sent to a Coastal Command strike squadron but instead we were posted overseas to South East Asia Command (SEAC) in India. To get there we were used as a crew to ferry a brand new Beaufighter from Cornwall to Allahabad in India. Thus my first service assignment was to navigate a Beaufighter on a journey of about 7,000 miles, which at the latitudes involved, was nearly a quarter of the way round the world. But we got there!

On arrival in India we were posted to 211 Squadron in the interdiction role. This involved sorties, mostly by single aircraft, penetrating deep into Japanese-held territory over Burma. None of this worried Geoff unduly except that low flying for long periods would call for continued high concentration – but what about me, the navigator? What methods should I use to keep track of where we were?

When I sought out the squadron navigation officer I discovered that he had been at navigation school with me in Canada. He had already been on several sorties and was able to give me some advice. "Best forget most of what we were taught," he said with a laugh. "The majority of trips are at low level with your pilot frequently taking evasive action. It is not practical to use charts for plotting or to use the standard navigator's log form." He went on to tell me that the technique was to plot tracks and make measurements on topographical maps and use a kneepad for jotting down times and other observations.

The RAF manual *Air Navigation (AP 1234)* then extant devoted only one-quarter of a page (Chapter XII, paras 40 to 54) to 'Low Flying Over the Land' and was mainly about which navigation technique was *not* practical. Clearly, low-level map reading was an art that needed to be learned by experience since, during my training, I had not done any low flying over land. So I would have to learn quickly, but over enemy territory.

It didn't help matters much when I studied the set of maps I was given. They were 1:1,000,000 scale topographical maps, a bit lacking in detail in some areas, which was not surprising since they were based on ancient surveys some as long ago as 1914. Even the colour keys used to denote contour heights were not the same on all maps. These were hardly the best aid for map reading over a country like Burma where rivers can change their courses over a period of time and where the appearance of the landscape can alter considerably with the seasons. Lush green valleys may become dried up riverbeds surrounded by parched brown countryside in a short space of time but these were the only maps available.

A 211 Squadron Beaufighter prepares to taxi. (Ian Spencer)

During my first couple of trips I encountered several problems. Handling and folding the several maps in the confined space was not easy, particularly when our track passed from one map on to another. Also orientating the maps was difficult, as I frequently had to face backwards to keep a lookout for enemy fighters in certain areas. This led me to adopt my own solutions. The maps were about twenty-four inches by eighteen inches and four of them covered the main area over which we normally flew. I stuck these four together, having trimmed the edges where necessary so that they butted up to form one large map. I then folded this with four horizontal and five vertical folds like a car road map. This gave conveniently sized panels and the map could be quickly folded so that one, two or sometimes four could be viewed at one time. Orientating the map in the line of flight was also made easier, whether you were sitting facing backwards or forwards.

Keeping a sharp lookout at the rear was vital, and when low flying the forward vision of the ground from my cupola was very restricted anyway, so I soon adopted the technique of map reading while sitting backwards. This called for close co-operation with Geoff over the intercom – with a sort of running commentary – warning him what was coming up next etc. We had little rules such as when we crossed a road or railway, perhaps en route to our target area; he would always look to port and I to the starboard side. By doing this there was less chance of missing telltale signs of dust from moving vehicles or a wisp of smoke from a locomotive. Of course deviations from our track to make an attack on a target of opportunity made my task more difficult, but careful pre-flight planning helped.

For most trips we were briefed in the late afternoon for a sortie the next day, because we would often have to take off before or around dawn so as to arrive in the target area about sunrise. This would give me time in the evening to study the intended tracks and note what land features I would use as position checks, not just along the track itself but on either side of it. Thus, if following some evasive action or unscheduled attack I was not sure of our exact position, I would know which was the best direction to turn to pick up some other feature such as a road or river that would lead us back to resume our original track. Of forty-nine operational sorties Geoff and I did together thirty-three involved extensive low-level flying over land and we always made it back. But I came to regard myself more and more as an observer rather than a practitioner of the science of air navigation. It was also my job to make reconnaissance notes of any enemy activities seen, what targets we hit and to assess the damage, to re-cock the 20-mm cannons if one jammed in addition to manning the rear machine gun if necessary.

I was, of course, a trained wireless operator but this skill was seldom used. At low level over Burma we were completely cut off from any R/T or W/T communication with base by the intervening Chin Hills. For most of our sorties that T1154 transmitter sat there like a useless passenger. I only used it twice and that was at high altitude over the hills themselves.

But I grew to like the Beaufighter better. Even the swivel seat, which I had found irritating at first, proved to be very useful. When we made an attack Geoff would climb up 300 or 400 hundred feet to make a shallow dive. As he put the nose down, I would swivel round to look forward because I could then see along the top of the fuselage and note whether we hit the target and with what effect. Then as he pulled up, usually banking steeply as well, I swivelled round to look backwards again to be able to make a further assessment. At the same time, I would be ready to man the rear gun in case there was any retaliatory fire from the ground. I became quite adept at manipulating that seat under adverse gravitational effects. The accompanying vibration and din from the 20-mm cannons made it feel like a ride at a fun fair – without the fun.

And as to low-level navigation in the Beaufighter? It was ironic that the RAF manual on *Air Navigation*, which I have said was of little help in this respect, headed each chapter with short amusingly apt quotations from Lewis Carroll's *Alice in Wonderland*. Can there be anything more reminiscent of *Alice in Wonderland* than the technique I adopted much of the time of map reading sitting backwards? I knew where I was going by knowing where I had been!

Dennis Spencer and his pilot Geoff Vardigans flew fifty-seven operations over Burma and both were awarded the DFC.

Pilot Officer Geoff Vardigans inspects damage to a propeller blade. (Ian Spencer)

CHAPTER TWENTY-THREE

FLYING ELEPHANTS OVER BURMA

The son of a Royal Flying Corps observer who was awarded the DFC whilst serving with 6 Squadron, Ulsterman **Robert 'Paddy' Sterling** was barely eighteen years old when he was accepted into the RAF determined to follow in his father's footsteps and be an observer. He was soon embarked on the long road to Burma.

After completing my training as an observer at 6 Air Observer School, Staverton, I was commissioned and headed for 3 School of General Reconnaissance at Squires Gate near Blackpool. It was here that we would polish our skills to fit us for the low-level flying and anti-shipping attacks we would be carrying out in the new Beaufighters. We felt we were getting near the coalface and most of our instructors had already completed operational tours in Coastal Command.

It was with considerable anticipation that I set out on my first flight on 2 May 1942 with several other trainee navigators. The aircraft was a Blackburn Botha about which we knew little or nothing but whose deficiencies we were about to discover. We headed out over the Irish Sea and as we got close to the Isle of Man, I noticed a substantial oil leak from the starboard engine. I alerted the pilot who immediately called for a course back to Squires Gate. We started to lose height and then Blackpool Tower came into sight and it looked as if we might make it but the pilot decided it would be too risky, turned into wind and ditched a few hundred yards off the shore. I inflated my Mae West and headed for the shore when a policeman stripped off and came and pulled me out of the sea. I went on to complete the course.

I still had one further course to complete and that was at 2 OTU at Catfoss where I arrived on 1 July. There I continued training in navigation, coding, meteorology, ship recognition, reconnaissance and signals. All extremely important for our kind of operation.

However, the most important part of the course was to crew up with a pilot. It was left very much to the individuals and, having survived one crash, I was fairly cautious about choosing a pilot and it was now that I met David Innes, an Australian who was to become my pilot for most of my flying career. I don't know what research he carried out on the new course but he approached me fairly early on and asked if I would consider crewing up with him. As we seemed to hit it off together I agreed and I never had cause for regret – indeed we have remained lifelong friends and I count our friendship as the greatest thing to come out of the war years.

We finished our training on 25 August and we were ready for operations. We were told that we were destined for the Middle East and sent on embarkation leave when we acquired tropical kit before leaving for Greenock where we embarked. We headed into the Atlantic and eventually arrived at Freetown in Sierra Leone before carrying on to Lagos in Nigeria. We boarded a magnificent BOAC flying boat and flew across the Belgian Congo and Sudan to Cairo.

The early crews of 27 Squadron with Paddy Sterling kneeling on the right next to his pilot David Innes. (Paddy Sterling)

Our stay in Cairo came to an end when we were told that we were not going to Malta but were to pick up our aircraft at Khartoum and fly to India instead where 27 Squadron was being reformed. We eventually left on 9 December and reached our destination at Kanchrapara near Calcutta on 12 January 1943 after suffering a series of delays. We met up with our colleagues and formed the new 27 Squadron, which went on to conduct a successful campaign through the monsoon in a series of low-level attacks against Japanese lines of communication in Burma.

> No. 27 Squadron went to France in 1916 equipped with the Martinsyde Elephant aircraft, and thus the elephant became the centrepiece of its official squadron badge. It was the first to use the Beaufighter in the ground-attack role against targets in the Arakan, although most of the squadron targets were in Central Burma, the other side of the Arakan Yomas.
>
> After being virtually wiped out in the shambles at Singapore and Sumatra, 27 Squadron reformed at Amarda Road in north-east India in October 1942. Five aircraft mounted the first operation on 25 December 1942 against the enemy airfield at Toungoo led by the commanding officer, the Australian Wing Commander H. C. Daish. During the next two months, the squadron moved first to Kanchrapara and then to the big airfield at Agartala in Assam.
>
> **Paddy Sterling** continues.

The task of taking on the might of the Japanese forces in the conditions, which existed, was a daunting one. But much was expected of us since we had brought a new range of weapons and capabilities. There were many problems getting the aircraft serviceable particularly with the poor supply of spares and with ammunition belting. The operational flying was strenuous as we had to cross mountain ranges between India and

Burma often surrounded by towering cumulonimbus before dropping down to our targets in the river valleys and on roads and railways in Central Burma. Operating at very low level reduced our chances of survival and the possibility of losing an engine was always a concern giving us only a fifty/fifty chance of getting back. However, Squadron Leader Bunny Horn managed to get back some 400 miles on one engine and was awarded a DSO for his efforts. His navigator, Flight Lieutenant Frankland, who had successfully steered him through the valleys, was awarded the DFC.

The environment was hostile, the weather was very hot and sticky giving rise to skin complaints such as prickly heat, which on occasions could cover the whole body and lead to boils. Various forms of fever were also common including malaria, dengue, sand-fly and occasionally blackwater. Dysentery was also a frequent visitor.

A Beaufighter TF.X of 27 Squadron over the plains of Burma. (Author's Collection)

Our station at Agartala was in the middle of Bengal and any kind of recreation was minimal and I found solace in reading. Every three months we were required to take leave usually to one of the hill stations. We visited Darjeeling a few times but towards the end of our tour we decided to go to Kashmir. This entailed a four-day rail journey from Calcutta to get there and it was a memorable experience. We lived on a houseboat on Lake Dal at Sringar and, after the heat of the plains and the stress of operational flying it was like heaven. All my prickly heat cleared up and the social life was very welcome.

It was the lack of social life compared to those colleagues who had been posted to squadrons in the UK that I envied. After flying they were able to visit local pubs, enjoy dances and also get home leave. Stationed in Bengal, all this was denied to us and while the life at the hill stations was some compensation, the lack of female company was limited as most were married and one dabbled with them at one's peril! This existence was to continue for three years, which seemed interminable.

In mid-March 1944 the squadron was taken out of the front line and our tour on 27 Squadron came to an end. We were at the station in Darjeeling and I was stricken down with a severe fever and admitted to hospital.

The squadron had been on constant operations for fifteen months during which time it had operated from four different airfields. During that period we had two commanding officers - Wing Commander H.C. Daish and Wing Commander J.B. Nicolson VC. In all, thirty-two aircrew were killed as a result of operations, another three survived as prisoners of war and three were killed in non-operational flying accidents. Awards to aircrew were one DSO, three DFCs and one DFM. The squadron undertook a total of 397 operations of which 337 were in daylight and sixty at night. To carry out these operations, 756 individual sorties were flown. David and I completed thirty-six operations.

According to official records the squadron caused much destruction and damage to Japanese lines of communication on rail, road and river, to aircraft and airfields, ground installations, stores and equipment, and had a significant effect on the morale of the Japanese troops. At the time, it was difficult for the aircrews - and even more difficult for the ground crew who were not personally involved

'Ground crew's pride'. (Ken Waldie)

with the enemy - to appreciate just what the combined efforts of the squadron were doing to disrupt the overall Japanese war effort in Burma. Without the ground crew's tremendous and unstinting efforts, the squadron would simply not have performed so successfully. To them, wherever they are, I know that I echo the sentiments of all of the aircrew who flew on 27 Squadron in the Burma campaign when I say, "Thanks fellows for your tremendous efforts".

> This account highlights just how demanding life was in Burma and the heavy price paid by everyone. It graphically illustrates how extreme the conditions were and the stoicism and determination needed to conduct and support dangerous flying operations.
>
> Flying Officer **Bill Rogers** RCAF joined 27 Squadron in March 1944 just as Paddy Sterling and David Innes were completing their tour and he takes up the story of the squadron's activities.

When I joined, the CO was Wing Commander James Nicolson VC. He was a little 'hairy' at times. During my second night on the squadron, I was sitting in our 'basha' officers' mess having a drink and minding my own business. The CO was also there with his .38 slung on his hip. Suddenly he drew his revolver and let four shots go at a rat that was running across a beam in the mess. It was a rather startling introduction to Wing Commander Nicolson!

Bill Rogers on his Beaufighter VI. (Bill Rogers)

At the time I joined 27 Squadron it had just claimed its 200th locomotive but there were to be very few more in the coming months. The squadron was equipped with the Beaufighter VIc de-rated for low-level operations with the two stage blowers removed from the sleeve valve Hercules engines, which made the aircraft very quiet. You could see one coming a mile away and not hear it until it was on top of you. At economic cruising, which was about 160 knots, they used about fifty gallons per hour per engine with a total fuel capacity of 680 gallons. To and from the target we cruised at 200 knots increasing to 220 knots in the target area with a further increase in the actual attack. Later, when targets became more distant, the .303 Brownings mounted in the wings were removed in order to carry more fuel and increase our range.

About a month after I joined, we moved to Cholavarum where we trained as an anti-shipping strike force and carried out a number of exercises against HMAS *Nizam*, an Australian destroyer. I made several dummy attacks against it, on one occasion flying as number two to Spratt and Adcroft when they had an engine failure and had to ditch. Both were picked up safely. I also spent some time on *Nizam* as an observer as squadron aircraft made dummy attacks.

From Cholavarum we went to Ranchi in September 1944 for training in rocket firing. By this time we were equipped with Beaufighter Xs with the more powerful Hercules engine. We could carry eight 3-ins rocket projectiles (RP), so we had really increased our destructive power. However, I cannot recall ever using rockets in attacks against targets in the Arakan.

Mick O'Brien, my navigator, was a Liverpool Irishman and an ex-City of London policeman. He was one of the original observer trade and did a lot to keep me alive. Early in our tour, I decided that he should learn something about flying in case anything happened to me. After crossing the bomb line on the way back I would get him to come up front and take over the controls whilst I stood behind him giving him instruction. I would get him to make a landing approach on a cloud top and give him the drill for approach and landing. He got quite good at it but I am glad he never had to use his new skill. We crewed up in August 1943 and flew our twenty-eight ops together.

One of my first operations after we got back from our rocket-firing course was to look for two squadron aircraft that had been mistakenly shot down by USAAF P-38 Lightnings of the 459th Squadron based at Chittagong. I located one on Ramree Island in a foot of water crewed by Trigwell and Chippendale. The fuselage was sitting there with the tail broken off and broken wings. There was talk of sending in some paratroops but with no sign of life there did not seem much point. Actually, both pilot and navigator had survived though Chips was shot through the body. Trig gave him what first aid he could, but after some mis-adventures the Japanese captured them. The Japanese were going to make them walk with Trig carrying Chips but they were holding up the column so the Japanese put the boots into Chips and killed him. We got Trig back from prison camp when Rangoon fell. The other crew were lost.

In the Arakan we took off and flew at deck level to the target area and any targets of opportunity en route were attacked. On trips over the Taungup Pass we flew at treetop height. Along roads and railways, which were usually lined with trees, we flew alongside just to one side to get a better view. On the rivers and chaungs, the Japanese had a nasty habit of stringing cables across rivers with some cable hanging down. One of our Beaus hit one and brought some cable back wrapped around the aircraft. These cables brought down some Hurricanes but the Beau was a much bigger and stronger aircraft. I still have my ops maps and marked on it are thirty-five trip wires, so they were not uncommon.

Our main opposition was 0.50-mm machine guns and 20-mm cannon, strategically placed at bridges, villages and airstrips. On one op I collected five 20-mm slugs in the mainplane, all in the tanks, and on other trips collected slugs in various parts of the aircraft. On another trip near a bridge, a heavy AA gun fired on me. I heard the initial bang as it fired and then successive bangs as the shells burst ahead of me.

The operational format was for the Form B [tasking signal] to come from the wing giving target details and the time to attack. Night ops were flown in moonlight but we never used any illumination but relied on our night vision. Trucks over the Taungup Pass usually had their lights on but you only had time for one pass before they went out. We often took off in the small hours to arrive at the target as dawn was breaking. The large river steamers had all been destroyed when I joined the squadron along with most of the locos, though I was able to blast one in Central Burma.

We attacked trucks and all types of small river craft. A 'laung' carried about twenty tons, a large 'sampan' about the same and a 'kisti' a smaller load. We knew that these craft carried ammo but it was always a surprise when one blew up in your face after you opened fire. I once came across some Japanese troops on the march but my gun sight was unserviceable; though I certainly scared the hell out of them, even if I did not inflict many casualties. Whenever we saw an oil installation we attacked it. Fuel was critical for the Japanese and they went to great lengths to camouflage installations but there was often a telltale sign such as a bund wall. On one occasion we had a spectacular success when we fired on what appeared to be a haystack and it exploded in our face.

Strike by 27 Squadron Beaufighter on a camouflaged oil dump at Sadaing. (Air Historical Branch CI 293)

On 8 January 1945 I saw what looked like a sampan factory and made several passes damaging twenty or more vessels. One pass was fairly prolonged and on the next, and my last, I could see that my rounds were hitting low. On return to base the armourers checked my cannons and found that I had prolonged my fire too long and the barrels had bent slightly from the heat generated.

A few nights later I was having a go at a barge in the Bassein delta region. As I was flying along assessing the situation, the barge opened fire on me so I went round and came in to make an attack. However hard I tried I could not get my nose down enough to get him in my sights and as I passed over him it opened fire on me. I had made five passes and never fired a shot – the barge had done all the firing – when I felt the cold steel of a revolver against my temple with my nav telling me to get the hell out of the area and get back to base. The aircraft was due for a major inspection and it had been reported as using an excessive amount of fuel. We had been airborne for almost five hours and the gauges were registering close to empty. We got over the coast and 100 miles out I called base to say that we were coming straight in...no circuit. I had everything sorted out on approach and we landed. Just as we got to dispersal, the engines died. When they refuelled the aircraft they found there was ten gallons spread over the four tanks; which was cutting it a bit fine! If I had played around with the barge any longer he would have won by default.

By mid-February, it was thought that the Japanese were evacuating Ramree Island and we were sent off to do a search between the island and the mainland. We were supposed to have fighter cover and to search from 1,000 feet. I saw two radial engine fighters climbing up in front of us and assumed they were our Thunderbolts and I told my nav to keep an eye on them. He asked "where?" and then, as the Japanese fighters hit us, he knew it was "there". He fired one burst before his gun jammed as he had forgotten to pull twenty or so rounds to remove any bent links from the belt, the first time ever that he had forgotten to do so. I pulled a stupid trick and got away with it. They expected me to turn towards them which was the standard drill, but I turned away and dived for the deck, with all the knobs and t**s out in the left-hand corner and headed out to sea. It was no contest and I just left them behind.

One of our squadron crews in the area saw the incident and the negative G as I started the dive, which cuts the engines momentarily and gives off a puff of smoke. He thought my engines had been hit and I was going into the drink. He shouted over the R/T, "Rogers just bought it". When I was straightened out and back under control I came back over the R/T, "He did like hell, but I've been hit and am heading home". The Japanese fighters had put seven .50 slugs into the aircraft. One hit a cylinder, knocking off a bunch of cooling fins, one partially cut the throttle controls, one hit my armour plating and another hit the nav's armour plate.

> By early April 1945, 27 Squadron was taken off low-level attacks and became a jungle search and rescue squadron and Bill Rogers left for a new appointment. Wing Commander Nicolson had left the squadron in April 1945 and joined the HQ RAF Burma. Anxious to experience the bombing operations he was responsible for tasking, he joined a Liberator crew of 355 Squadron for an operational sortie on 2 May 1945. En route to the target, the big bomber caught fire and crashed into the Bay of Bengal. A search found just two survivors and the gallant Battle of Britain fighter pilot was lost flying as a passenger who wanted to experience what he was tasking his men to do. Mick O'Brien was killed on a supply run to St. Thomas Mount when his Beaufighter crashed on the runway during a monsoon storm. At the end of the war, Bill Rogers returned to Canada.
>
> Paddy Sterling and his pilot David Innes were posted to 22 Ferry Control Unit at Allahabad, which included ferrying Beaufighters. On 2 May 1945 he was flying with Warrant Officer Jones when a Dakota obstructed their Beaufighter just as they were about to land. The aircraft crashed killing Jones and leaving Sterling severely injured. He recovered and finally returned home in early 1946 and was demobbed in June.

CHAPTER TWENTY-FOUR

MEMORABLE SORTIES IN BURMA

Bill Dickinson recalls three sorties that remained etched in his memory.

Memorable Sortie One

I served as a pilot on 211 Squadron flying Beaufighters during the Burma campaign in 1943/44. The squadron's main operational function was to attack Japanese supply lines, roads, rivers and sea-borne traffic to prevent supplies reaching their front line. These operations were known as rhubarbs and entailed climbing after take-off to around 11,000 feet to get over the Chin Hills and then descend to the Burma plain beyond to the allotted target area at zero feet to keep below the Japanese radar screen.

No. 211 Squadron in December 1944. Beaufighter squadrons had large complements. (via Don Clark)

On 19 March 1944 my navigator, Flight Sergeant Chatterton, and I were briefed to carry out a railway patrol on a branch line of the main Rangoon to Mandalay line. Two aircraft were involved, the other being piloted by the flight commander – a squadron leader. The plan was to fly out in loose formation and aim to reach the railway line at its midway point. We would then separate, and the squadron leader would turn south and take the southern half of the line and I would turn to do the northern half up to the terminus at Kyaukpadaung. Everything went according to plan and at a place called Nathauk the line went over a bridge across a dried-up riverbed. It was in the early days of my tour when we usually carried rockets and I decided to attack the bridge with the rockets. To my surprise, they were bang on the target and all at the brickwork supports but it was obvious that, although the rockets were fitted with 60-lb explosive heads, the only damage caused was to dislodge a few bricks. It was soon officially agreed that rockets were no use for attacking bridges.

We proceeded on our way up the railway line swerving from side to side and never flying in a straight line. When we arrived at the terminus of Kyaukpadaung there in the station was a locomotive. I could hardly believe my eyes because it was a rare thing to find one in the open in those days. The Japanese used to hide them during daylight hours and use them mainly on moon-less nights. The station was sited between two hills and I pulled up and round to begin a cannon attack on the loco. I got it well in my sights and gave it several good bursts of 20-mm and whilst concentrating on this I saw a vague blur out of the corner of my eye and automatically lifted the starboard wing sharply and there was a loud bang. Chatterton shouted, "Have you hit anything?" I replied, "Yes – I have hit a bloody tree". There was a tree growing on the side of one of the hills and I had not seen it in time. I climbed away from the area with much difficulty. The starboard wing kept dropping alarmingly and I had to hold the wheel hard over and put full opposite aileron trim to keep the aircraft level. I could see that the wing-tip was missing and part of a tree branch was sticking up through the upper surface.

Attack against a major rail junction on the Bangkok line at Anankwin with numerous spur lines into the jungle. (via Ken Waldie)

We eventually managed to limp back to base and as I eased the throttles back just before touching down, the starboard wing dropped again and we almost landed on one wheel and a wing-tip but the old Beau righted itself and we taxied into the dispersal area before a goggle-eyed ground crew. Apart from the damage already described, there were two large chunks of the leading edge of the starboard wing missing from each side of the oil cooler. The reason for the lack of aileron control was because the control cables, which ran along the inside of the leading edge had been jammed by the impact. If the oil cooler had been hit we most certainly would not have been able to return to base.

Very low flying often involved collisions with trees but the rugged Beaufighter survived. (27 Squadron album via Air Historical Branch)

I received a reprimand from the CO for 'bad flying' but the rest of the pilots congratulated me because none of them liked that particular aircraft. It was a rogue one with many recurring gremlins and they were relieved to see it written off.

Memorable Sortie Two

My next operational sortie following the tree incident was on 24 March, again with Chatterton. Unlike most of our operations this time we were given a definite target and it was a building being used as a Japanese HQ. There were four aircraft involved and we were briefed to take off consecutively and fly in loose formation. Unfortunately, my aircraft showed a large 'mag-drop' when testing the engines prior to take-off and I had to return to dispersal and transfer to the spare aircraft. By the time I was airborne I was nearly thirty minutes behind the other three.

During most of our rhubarb trips we stayed at low level all the time once clear of the hills and this gave us a certain feeling of security. This operation, however, was going to be different. The target building was situated in the hills on the other side of the Burma plain beyond Mandalay, which meant that we had to climb from low level when we were deep in enemy territory. An additional hazard was the fact that the target was dangerously close to Heho - a known Japanese fighter base.

Everything went according to plan and I climbed up from low level into the Shan Hills to around 4,000 feet and feeling horribly exposed at the same time. I followed the twisting road, which was more like a mountain pass and found our target. Our rockets were easier to aim accurately in a steep dive and I hit the building with all four of them. We were carrying only four because of possible difficulty in climbing and manoeuvring with a full complement of eight.

As I pulled up and away to starboard I looked up and saw four Japanese fighters approaching head on in perfect echelon formation about 500 feet above us, all glinting in the sun. I immediately pushed the throttles to full power and gave a violent push on the control column in a direction opposite to the fighters so that they would have to execute a 180-degree turn to pursue me. Chatterton wanted to know what was going on and I explained that we had been 'jumped' by fighters and to cock his machine gun and keep a lookout.

So, we went roaring down the valleys in a southerly direction with the Japanese in hot pursuit. I knew that the Beaufighter could outstrip the fighters at ground level but we were around 4,000 feet and I was uncertain. In fact we did not gain on them but they were not gaining on us. The distance I had achieved by my initial diving escape kept them out of firing range. My route home to base lay over to starboard so I needed to get to the edge of the hill chain and then on to the Burma plain before contemplating a course for base. I kept asking my navigator what the situation was and he usually replied, "They are still there but are not gaining on us". The four Japanese were all out on the starboard side so cutting off any attempt I might make to turn west and make a run for the far away Chin Hills and possible safety.

After what seemed an eternity, my navigator shouted excitedly, "They are turning back, you can turn now". I was taking no risks and gradually edged over to the west and as I got to the edge of the Shan Hills I put the nose down and went screaming down to the plains. Chatterton shouted, "It's all right, you don't have to go so fast - they are not chasing us anymore". We arrived back at base rather late to learn that we had been given up for lost. Fighters had chased the other aircraft before they could climb into the Shan Hills and one Beau was missing, presumably shot down. Another had seen us going in and tried to warn me on the radio but we never got the message. The chase actually lasted twenty-five minutes and I was at full throttle the whole time. A few days before the episode we had a visit from technical experts of the Bristol Aeroplane Co. and amongst other things we were told never to keep the engines at full throttle for longer than five minutes!

The Least Memorable Sortie

Towards the end of my tour I experienced my least memorable sortie but this was not an offensive operation but a flight to Calcutta and back, which we used to call a 'Hooch Run'. We used to take various passengers, some going on leave and others on official business, but the main and most important duty was to purchase liquid refreshments to re-stock the bars of the officers' and sergeants' messes and bring it all safely back to base at Chiringa. The aircraft I was allotted for this particular run was from 'B' Flight (I was in 'A' Flight) and I later learned that it was involved in an abortive sortie the previous night because the oil pressure warning light was illuminated. We took off for Alipore on 4 January 1945 and completed the outward leg with no problem.

When I attempted to take off for the return flight the following day there was a loss of power on the starboard engine and I had time to close it down and abort the take-off. The engine was checked and I made two further attempts with the same result. It was all very frustrating because we had to unpack our kit and find somewhere to sleep for the night. Eventually, the squadron engineering officer flew in to sort out the problem and he actually stood behind me when I made a successful test flight. I still felt there was something wrong with the engine but he assured me that what I had diagnosed as loss of power was just due to a faulty instrument. So we loaded up again, and with two passengers - Flight Lieutenant Einboden, the engineering officer, and Sergeant MacLellan, a dour Scottish fitter - I took off from Alipore for Chiringa. I have it recorded in my logbook as the 'diciest take-off of all times'. The engine lost power again but this time I was too far down the runway to shut the engine down and abort the take-off. We struggled into the air and wallowed crab wise about twenty feet above the runway. Out of the corner of my eye I could see the fire engine and ambulance following us at great speed. Ahead of us were the Calcutta docks with barrage balloons and we went straight between the masts of a ship berthed in the docks. I was able to make a gradual turn slap over the middle of Calcutta and miraculously the engine picked up and we flew serenely back to base.

When we landed the engineering officer personally supervised the check on the faulty engine and as the engine covers were removed, pieces of white metal fell out. He was man enough to tell me, "You were right after all".

That evening, Sergeant MacLellan invited me to his quarters and we sat on his charpoy (bed) and polished off two bottles of sherry that he had purchased in Calcutta.

CHAPTER TWENTY-FIVE

AUSTRALIANS OVER PAPUA NEW GUINEA

After making major gains in the Dutch East Indies in early 1942, Japanese forces landed on the north-west coast of New Guinea in April 1942 and quickly built up a base with stores, workshops and an airfield, confident that once the Japanese navy had landed more troops and taken control of the key town and port of Port Moresby it would have a base to launch an invasion of eastern Australia.

No. 30 Squadron RAAF aircrew with Keith Nicholson on the right. (via Peter White)

The Japanese navy suffered a severe reverse at the Battle of the Coral Sea leaving the Japanese ground forces in the north of the island to undertake the task of taking Port Moresby on their own. At the end of July this thrust was halted by fierce opposition from Australian ground forces in the Owen Stanley Ranges. A further attempt by the Japanese to establish 2,000 troops ashore at Milne Bay at the eastern end of the island was also stemmed.

To provide support for the two Australian infantry brigades, 30 Squadron, the first RAAF squadron equipped with the Beaufighter, moved to Ward's Strip near Port Moresby in August to begin operations against the Japanese and where it came under the control of 5th Air Force, USAAF.

The squadron had received its first aircraft in June 1942 at Richmond, NSW. Initially equipped with ex-RAF Mark Ic aircraft, ex-RAF Mark VIcs began to arrive in January 1943.

Twenty-year-old **Keith Nicholson** relates his time with 30 Squadron over Papua New Guinea in the South-West Pacific theatre of operations.

Ken Delbridge and I teamed up as a Beaufighter crew while we were on No. 3 Course at 5 OTU at Forest Hill near Wagga Wagga, NSW. He was a brilliant navigator and I was very fortunate in securing him.

At the end of the course we travelled to Brisbane and joined the other crews posted to 30 Squadron before going to Townsville by troop train. We spent a couple of days at the Personnel Pool at Aitkenvale and on 26 March 1943 we flew to Port Moresby in a Short Empire flying boat, alighting at Moresby harbour at midday.

Ken and I were allocated A19-74, which we regarded as 'our' Beaufighter. Being intensely interested in our aircraft, I spent a lot of time helping our ground crew. Each aircraft had an engine fitter, an airframe fitter and two armourers. Other specialist trades - electricians, radar mechanics instrument technicians, radio and so on - were part of the 'pool' in each flight.

No. 30 Squadron operated from Ward's Strip, a single bitumen runway with a parallel taxi/crash strip, as well as sealed taxiways leading to individual aircraft revetments. The strip was located in a narrow valley, with cleared flight paths over jungle to the north, and over low hills to the sea to the south. In addition to our squadron, Ward's was the base for the Bostons of 22 Squadron and numerous US squadrons.

Ground crew service the mighty Hercules engines and the cannons of a 30 Squadron Beaufighter. (Victoria State Library)

When we were not flying we spent a good deal of time in operations and the intelligence section reading the intelligence documents and operational summaries. Stan Hutchinson was the intelligence officer and I regarded him as having a genuine interest in his job. His briefings were spot on and he was always worth listening to. His debriefings were very methodical and he dragged every scrap of operational information from crews when they returned from an operation.

The army liaison officer (ALO) was an important fellow for we were doing quite a lot of work for the army. He always briefed us on which of the native tribes were friendly and could provide help if we were forced down. On 29 March, John Court gave all the new crews a lecture on army co-operation in New Guinea.

Ken and I took off for our first operation on 9 April with nine other Beaufighters to attack Alexishaven, but we had to turn back soon after take-off because the port engine started to smoke. However, we went out the next day to attack Madang. Bob Bennett was my section leader and George Gibson and Maurice Ball were Red Section. They did the strip over while Bob and I attacked a heavy anti-aircraft battery and then went on to strafe a launch and some native huts at Amron.

The squadron's first operation beyond the mainland of New Guinea took place on 14 May when, in conjunction with a squadron of USAAF Mitchells, eleven Beaufighters went across to New Britain to attack Gasmata. The boss's standing instruction was to the effect that we were to make one run only across any heavily defended target, and we followed his instruction on that day. We went in first and attacked the anti-aircraft defences and the Mitchells dropped their bombs along the strip.

We had flown across to New Britain at 500 feet and went through several weather fronts. The operation was a little scary as we had a lot of water to cross and if we either ditched close to shore or crash-landed on the island, I don't think we would have had much chance of survival as the Japanese occupied the entire island.

A long trip such as the one to Gasmata was not the most comfortable experience for a Beaufighter pilot. For one thing, his seat was in the centre of a rather crowded cockpit. Not only was he strapped tightly into his seat, but his behind rested on a dinghy, which was supposed to form a cushion but it was so rock hard that his thighs and backside became completely numb. Back at base, it took quite a bit of stamping and stretching to be able to walk again.

On 1 June we had a task to strafe the village of Bogadjim at first light so we staged to Dobodura the night before. It was an awful strip; the mud squirted up through holes in the pierced steel planking (PSP) as the aircraft rolled down the runway. While we were there all the aircrew did a two-hour spell of guard duty while our ground crew went off for their evening meal.

I was up at 0430 hours and took off in company with six other Beaufighters. I made four runs over the village, setting a hut on fire. I also attacked three flat-bottomed boats and a large bridge. Our expenditure of ammunition was 500 rounds of 20-mm and 4,000 rounds of .303. After picking up our ground crew at Dobodura, we returned to Ward's where we landed at 1430 hours.

Komiatum was our target on 8 June when I led Red Section. We had to go up to 18,000 feet to get above the clouds at the gap in the Owen Stanley Range and when we saw a break in the clouds near the target we descended some 10,000 feet in two minutes, which caused the windscreen to become fogged up. I made three runs along the tracks near the target, strafing huts and stores. There was no anti-aircraft fire or interception but the weather was lousy.

On 9 July, three of us, led by the CO, Wing Commander Glasscock, were briefed to carry out an armed reconnaissance along a coastal strip on the north coast of New Guinea. During our flight along the coast we suddenly came on a bridge across the Gogol river at Bogadjim and there were some fifty or so Japanese working on it. As we charged across they all took off and ran into trees along the river. We turned back and, as most of them had cleared the bridge, we just strafed the trees where they were hiding.

We didn't get another job, mainly because of foul weather, until 20 July when we went with

The permanent bridge and the replacement temporary bridge at Sulawesi destroyed by 30 Squadron. (Victoria State Library)

the CO to do a photographic reconnaissance of Gasmata. We made just one run down the strip while Ken operated his handheld camera. There was heavy anti-aircraft fire and I saw a Mitsubishi A6M 'Zero' on the strip.

Two days later, the CO led seven other Beaufighters in an attack on Gasmata, in which Bostons, Beauforts and Kittyhawks also took part. We went in first to strafe the guns, which was our normal procedure, and then we stooged around as low-level cover while

Beaufighter Ic A19-53 of 30 Squadron landing at Milne Bay. (Aviation Heritage Museum of Western Australia)

the others had a go. Graeme Hunt had a couple of feet of his port wing shot off by the anti-aircraft guns and three other aircraft were holed.

I led the formation back to Milne Bay, echelon right. I did the usual thing on arrival, shot along the strip at dot feet, pitched to port to do a very tight circuit, forgot to check if the starboard undercarriage was locked down, but I did see that the port one was down. I heard the hydraulic system relieving, and thus knew that it was up to full pressure. I didn't look at the fruit machine and it wasn't until I was on short finals that the klaxon went off and I found to my horror that the starboard leg was still up.

I tried to rectify the situation by using the hand pump, but that didn't work and no matter what I did the starboard leg would not come down. I had a go at forcing it down by climbing to a few thousand feet, diving down, pulling excessive G on the aircraft in the pull-out from the dive whilst selecting 'Down'. That did it and I saw the leg come down into the locked position.

Ken and I collected a replacement aircraft on 19 August and headed back to New Guinea. During the period we had been away, the squadron had moved to Goodenough Island to operate from the strip at Vivigani for the rest of our tour. We arrived back on 24 August, bringing with us food and grog we had collected at Amberley. A week later, the adjutant helped me to drink a bottle of beer to celebrate my twenty-first birthday.

During September, the squadron was given a lot of barge sweeps along the coast of New Britain in order to halt troops and supplies reaching the Finschaven area from Rabaul. A Catalina had reported that forty enemy barges were in Wide Bay so twelve Beaufighters were sent on a search and destroy mission. During an attack at Palmal we received a hit in the tailplane from an anti-aircraft gun.

During the flight back to Goodenough I carried out a slow speed handling check and discovered that I lost control at 135 knots. So when it came to landing at Vivigani I simply drove the aircraft in at 145 knots. The brakes had also been damaged and I had to steer the aircraft by engine power and turn on to a taxiway and let it roll to a stop. It might sound simple but it was a frightening experience and I was glad to get out of the aircraft.

The squadron had adopted the tactic of hunting in pairs. On 4 September Peter Fisher partnered Ken and me and a second pair were tasked for the same region. We went to Witu Island where there was a particular bay used as a staging post by the barges coming down from Rabaul. Steep cliffs were on three sides and the anti-aircraft defences were embedded in the caves on those cliffs and on that day their shooting was intense and accurate.

We went back to Garove on 9 September and found that the Japanese had increased their air defences. We received three .50-mm calibre shells in the nose of the aircraft and these spattered against the armour plate shield and threw back lots of shrapnel making the nose look like a colander. If that shield had not been there, I would not have survived. We diverted to Kiriwina airstrip.

On 13 September we were sent to search for a Boston, which had ditched between Gasmata and Vivigani but we found no trace. On the 18th, we were scheduled to go with three other aircraft for an attack on Cape Hoskins but we had to return to base because of engine trouble. That was our last flight in a 30 Squadron Beaufighter. The next day, the CO was lost when he was shot down during an attack on the same target.

Together with the last surviving crews who had joined at the same time as Ken and I the previous March, we left Vivigani at the end of our operational tour on 3 October 1943 in an American transport bound for Townsville.

> One of those crews was **Doug Raffen** and his navigator George Dick. Raffen made some interesting observations about tactics employed by the crews on 30 Squadron.

For operational flying the attack technique depended on the situation in the target area, the weather, the location of the air-defence guns, the presence of enemy fighters, concealment and camouflage measures and the ground features in the target area. I can use our attack on barges in Langemak Bay as an example.

The barges were hauled up close in-shore and well concealed under trees in a steep-sided inlet to the bay. It was only because we saw a couple of Japanese in a rowing boat near the inlet as we did a steep turn at low level that I happened to catch a glimpse of the barges under the camouflage. I wasn't in a position to attack them so I had to make another circuit and try to position the aircraft so that I could bring my weapons to bear on the target. But at our height they were not visible, so I had to memorise the details of the trees around the barges, manoeuvre the aircraft into position, identify the trees, dive at them and then make last-minute adjustments in line as I caught occasional glimpses of the barges. In the first dive I saw the barges too late for my fire to be totally effective, but in succeeding dives I managed to pinpoint them and pour cannon shells into them.

Doug Raffen (left) with his navigator George Dick. (via Peter White)

For our attacks on Cape Gloucester we nearly always made landfall at Arawe and flew across to the northern coast of New Britain, turned west and continued at low level down to the target. We approached the enemy airfield from behind the trees along the coastal fringe, popped over them from just north of the airfield, carried out our attack, and then scooted away to the south, jinking in the process. Had we attacked from the south, the Beaufighters would have had to get above the trees sooner, and therefore could have been seen earlier during our run-in and so exposed to the formidable anti-aircraft defences for longer.

For the most part we attacked targets such as gun emplacements, aircraft on the ground, buildings, supply dumps or barges. There were not many occasions when we actually saw any Japanese troops.

I never heard of anyone in our theatre baling out of a Beaufighter – we normally flew so low as to make this impossible. I always thought that if we were hit over enemy territory, I would try and get the aircraft as far away from Japanese forces as possible but finding a suitable spot for a crash-landing in the Highlands would be nearly impossible. However, I would try and put it down on the ground and hope that we could walk away. But walking away from a crash in the New Guinea jungle would also be well nigh impossible. Had I survived a crash, I would head for the coast by following a ridge or a river. There was always the possibility of coming across friendly natives who would help and might take notice of the Pidgin-English pamphlet we carried in our escape and survival pouch. Most of our attacks in New Britain were against targets along its coastline and if my aircraft had been hit and we had to make a forced-landing, I would have preferred to head out to sea and ditch the aircraft.

I had a very high regard for the Beaufighter. It was a rugged aircraft and terrific to fly. I never had any trouble with the engines except for one instance when there was an oil pressure problem after take-off. I suppose that I regarded the aircraft as such a sturdy machine that I never seriously entertained the idea that I might ever be forced down in enemy territory – although that was always a possibility.

Perhaps as a result of pre-flight briefing or hearing what other aircrews had said, there were individual occasions when I recognised that a dicey situation was coming up. There were times when I got an intense fright during an attack or a close call – and that probably relates to self-preservation. A few of our aircraft were shot down while I was with the squadron, but like most other people I tended to think that it was never going to happen to me. I gave it less thought in the later stages of my tour because most of our operations were rather tame barge sweeps, which might be exciting but not exactly dangerous. All in all, the possibility that I might never survive the war was something to which I gave only spasmodic thought.

Flight Lieutenant Keith Nicholson became a test and ferry pilot at No. 1 Aircraft Depot and left the RAAF in October 1945. Flight Lieutenant Doug Raffen completed No. 1 Test Pilot's Course at Laverton before being posted to No. 15 Aircraft Repair Depot. His final flight in the RAAF was from Port Moresby to Wagga in NSW in a Beaufighter in October 1945.

CHAPTER TWENTY-SIX

EARLY OPERATIONS OVER TIMOR

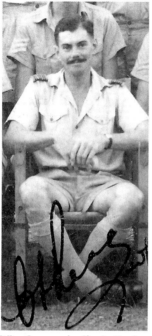

Wing Commander Charles Read, CO 31 Squadron. (Ian Madden)

With 30 Squadron based in Papua New Guinea to support ground forces facing the Japanese advance towards Port Moresby, the second RAAF Beaufighter squadron, No. 31, became part of a rapid build-up of Australian and American air and ground forces in the Darwin area of north-west Australia tasked to harass the Japanese forces and thwart any of their preparations for invasion.

The squadron was formed in August 1942 as a long-range fighter squadron and it was first equipped with ex-RAF Mk. Ic Beaufighters. Declared operational in November it moved to Coomalie Creek airstrip south of Darwin where it remained until December 1944 when it joined 30 Squadron at Moroati in the Moluccas.

The squadron's first commanding officer after it moved to the Northern Territories at the end of October 1942 was Wing Commander **Charles Read**.

The squadron was equipped with Beaufighter Mk. I and Mk. VI aircraft, some of the latter being fitted with extra fuel tanks. The maximum range worked on was 800 nm for the short-range aircraft, and 1,000 nm for the long range, and ninety per cent of sorties were up to the maximum range. The main difference between the Mk. I and Mk. VI Beaufighter was the performance, the older aircraft, the Mk. I, being superior in speed by 15-20 knots, which naturally made it popular as far as the aircrews were concerned.

Weather

A considerable amount of cloud and rain was encountered during the wet season. Even during the dry we usually encountered some rain en route to the target and over the target due to a persistent front 2-300 miles north of Darwin. However, the weather never really worried our crews except when it was raining over the target, which made accurate shooting impossible.

New aircrews found the towering cumulus and heavy tropical rain frightening at first, but we found you could always get a single aircraft through any weather, provided, of course, the pilot knew his instrument flying. Our problem was getting a formation to the target intact. The flight leader would always fly fairly low in the rain, avoiding the clouds, and the rest of the formation would stay in close even in the heaviest rain, but it was impossible to keep in formation through cumulus cloud with the reduced visibility and severe turbulence. During the entire nine months operations, which included the wet season, we only stopped flying one day due to the weather.

Quite a number of strikes on enemy bases were made at first light, but could only be undertaken successfully when the weather was clear as it involved approximately two hours night flying in formation. When the weather was known to be doubtful a rendezvous point was arranged thirty to forty miles from the target, and each aircraft circled this once it became separated from the formation. Usually, all the aircraft would turn up and could proceed with the attack. Fewer strikes were carried out at last light owing to difficulties in navigation and lack of fuel on the return to base.

Navigation

An astro compass and a drift recorder were installed in every aircraft and the observers used them extensively. All our operations were carried out over long stretches of sea and, as the last 100-150 miles was always carried out at fifty feet (to achieve surprise), accurate navigation was essential. The flight leader's observer did the final stages of navigation to the target as the other observers looked aft for any enemy attacks as the pilots concentrated on keeping formation fifty feet above ground level. The observer started his stopwatch as the formation crossed the

Beaufighter Ic of 31 Squadron landing at Coomalie Creek. (Victoria State Library)

coast, counted the time down to the target and told the pilot which side to expect the target. The formation, incidentally, was to attack in line abreast to dilute the anti-aircraft fire. After the attack, each aircraft had to be prepared to head back to base alone and we rarely managed to form up as an entire formation. Towards the end of my time we had better R/T between aircraft so the leader could exercise more control and try to gather up some of the other aircraft.

Compass swinging was a never ending and important job due to the deviation caused by the cannon firing. If the armament was used we left the aircraft for twenty-four hours to let the compasses settle down before re-swinging them. If extensive operations were carried out, when regular swinging was not possible, the rear compass or the astro compass was used. The average deviations experienced after cannon firing was twelve degrees for the front compass and three for the rear compass. When returning in formation, the observers compared notes to take an average course to steer.

Wireless Equipment

Our Beaufighters were equipped with the usual RAAF set, the ATR 58, and having only the one set we had to adopt a rather complicated procedure during attacks. On the way to the target, the flight leader listened on the primary reconnaissance frequency, and the remaining aircraft in the formation were tuned up for R/T on a suitable high frequency using crystal control. Thirty minutes before the target the leader changed to this R/T frequency and he remained on it until well clear of the target when he changed back to the primary reconnaissance for D/F bearings and information. Wireless silence was always observed prior to the attack.

We found very early that crystal control was the only reliable means of R/T communication. Using self-excited, slight differences in frequency between aircraft were sufficient to cause poor communication and we could not afford to have our observers with their heads down trying to adjust the sets in the middle of an attack.

The D/F loop on the Beaufighter had a Perspex cover and during the wet season this warped very badly, jamming the loop. Also, on several occasions during high-speed dives the cover and loop blew clean off the aircraft.

Throat microphones were used by all aircrews and were found to be satisfactory, although the average life of each microphone was six months, deterioration being caused by heat, dust and perspiration.

Armament

We used the following loading for our ammunition. The 20-mm cannon were all loaded with 50-50 ball and HE. Four machine guns were loaded with AP and the other two with incendiary. We never used tracer, as it tends to distract attention from the gun sight. The harmonisation was at 400 yards, rather far for air-to-air fighting, but our role was ground strafing and we opened fire at 1,000 yards and held it until we pulled out at about fifty feet. With a good burst of cannon on a parked aircraft it would explode into flames, up to 100 feet in the air, and well before the Beaufighter actually passed over it – it was quite an experience flying through such a wall of smoke and flame.

The .303 machine guns as aircraft armament were obsolete. A good example was an attack by one of our Beaufighters on a beached floatplane in the Aru Islands. The cannons had cut out so, while the observer was endeavouring to clear the stoppages, the pilot made five runs on the floatplane using the machine guns and failed to destroy the aircraft. Once the observer had cleared one of the cannons, a final run was made with the cannon and the floatplane burst into a mass of flames.

The cannons were very 'touchy' and needed constant attention, as the smallest amount of dust would cause stoppages. We kept toilet paper pasted over all the ejection openings to keep the dust out. This would blow off in the slipstream when the aircraft became airborne. However, it was a problem if we had to land at an advanced base to top up with fuel as they were always dusty so we tried to limit the amount of taxiing.

We carried out three major modifications to the armament:

1. Scare guns for the observer.
2. Bomb racks (American type).
3. Two extra .303 machine guns for long-range aircraft.

The observer's scare gun was loaded with tracer, and was effectively used by many observers against attacking fighters who showed a reluctance to close in the face of a stream of tracer. Unfortunately the observer's cupola is small and restricted effective aiming with the observer having to take care not to shoot through the aircraft's tail-plane and rudder. The bomb rack was a later modification and was fitted underneath the fuselage, carrying two 100-lb or two 300-lb American demolition bombs.

Enemy Anti-Aircraft Fire
The light anti-aircraft fire caused a lot of damage and after an attack, many of our aircraft returned with damage. One aircraft returned with 150 holes but some on this occasion were due to enemy fighter attacks. Several aircraft were hit in the wings by 20-mm shells, which exploded and did considerable damage. It was always quicker to replace the wing rather than repair it.

The Beaufighter's metal armour plate would not stop anything except shrapnel or 'sensitive' cannon shell used by enemy fighters. These exploded outside the fuselage on the slightest contact and did little or no damage. The windscreen was good and stopped .303 ammunition.

Convoy Operations
Shipping cover was our biggest job and all convoys approaching or leaving Darwin were given cover between 1000 and 1500 hours, the period during which enemy re-connaissance was experienced. In my period of command, the squadron flew 300 sorties covering convoys with each flight averaging five hours. Usually one aircraft at a time was employed, relieved as necessary. This was immediately increased if the convoy was attacked. We found it very difficult to sight the enemy aircraft before it dropped its bombs, especially with the usual broken cumulous cloud present. For this reason R/T between convoy and aircraft was essential. Only one enemy aircraft was destroyed during this period and several others were damaged, but the presence of a Beaufighter proved valuable in deterring enemy attacks. It was found that the time on patrol over the convoy should be no longer than one-and-a-half hours as aircrew efficiency deteriorated over a longer time.

Strike Operations
During the latter part of 1942, while the AIF were still present in force in Portuguese Timor, many attacks were made on enemy-occupied villages and roads. These were usually hampered by difficulty in finding targets. Villages generally were 'shot up' without seeing any signs of enemy activity but reports indicated that there were many Japanese casualties. The winding feature of Timor roads and the mountainous

country made strafing attacks difficult. On many occasions truckloads of Japanese troops were seen but could not be attacked because of the terrain. This made us wish we had bombs in the early days. However, these attacks were discontinued once Japanese airfields were developed in Western Timor and we began to concentrate on attacking them.

The aerial offensive from North-Western Area against targets in the east of East Timor, following the latest advancement of Japanese forces, was stepped up from 20 December. The squadron participated in this major burst of activity. Five attacks were carried out over a period of a few days on the main enemy airfield at Penfoei. The first four were successful and many enemy aircraft, gun posts, personnel and fuel dumps were damaged and destroyed. There was one outstanding reason for these early successes; the achievement of surprise. On the fifth occasion, because of their improved warning system, the Japanese knew of our approach. As soon as we pulled up from low level for the dive attack, intense AA fire was encountered. The Japanese also had fighters overhead as base cover and these chased and attacked the strike force for over 100 miles on the return journey. We sustained fifty per cent casualties and those aircraft that did return were all damaged. This highlighted the need to achieve surprise and also, the vulnerability of the Beaufighter once attacked by a fighter.

On the last day of January 1943, the squadron had a spectacular success. A probable ammunition dump exploded hurling debris to 1,200 feet, damaging one of the six aircraft engaged. Two buildings were fired, three grounded aircraft destroyed by fire and four bombers and one fighter probably destroyed on the ground. Motor transport was also strafed.

We encountered enemy fighters (Zeke, Hap and Rufe) on many occasions, always at low level when the only tactic was to turn into his attack as soon as possible, and then head for home at maximum speed. Getting a quick start gave the fighter a hard job, but both the Zeke and the Hap had a speed advantage, particularly the latter. The Beaufighter Mk. 1 could be 'wound up' to about 260 knots at sea level but still came under attack.

In several attacks on Taberfane, Beaufighters had to 'mix it' with Rufe or Pete, but it proved very difficult to close to effective range against such manoeuvrable opponents. They would pull up into a loop or roll off as soon as they were in danger of being attacked and, of course, it was impossible to follow them in our heavy Beaufighters.

By August it was noticed that the floatplanes in use had better performance than those previously encountered and they could keep pace with the Beaufighter. On 17 August, eight aircraft were briefed to attack Rufes at Taberfane. A lugger carrying Japanese troops was spotted on the Serwatoe river. It was strafed and set on fire and forty or fifty troops in the water were killed. At the same time, a thrilling dogfight ensued with five enemy aircraft – three Rufes and one Pete being destroyed and the remaining Petes damaged.

Good co-operation between pilot and observer, a sharp lookout by the observer and violent evasive action got us home from many encounters with fighters. Finally, every Beaufighter pilot was advised to treat Zeke and Hap with every respect, for in both of these, the Japanese had a good aircraft so combat was avoided whenever possible.

The squadron destroyed fifty-eight enemy aircraft and damaged sixty-one others. Those claimed as destroyed were seen to be burning furiously after an attack, while those classified as damaged were fired at but not seen to catch fire. The damaged aircraft were usually those attacked with machine guns only following a cannon stoppage. These figures show a good result during nine months of operations and the squadron was fortunate in having small losses on operations.

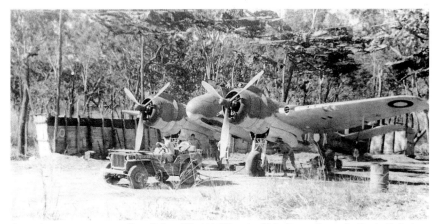

Ground crew prepare to tow Beaufighter VIc A19-152 to the flight line at Coomalie Creek. (Aviation Heritage Museum of Western Australia)

Losses

The squadron losses due to enemy action were sixteen aircraft and fourteen crews. The two crews to return to the squadron safely were, strangely, engaged on the same operation. Both aircraft were damaged by AA fire during an attack on a Timor village, one force landed a mile off the coast and the crew swam ashore where they were helped by natives and an AIF commando troop before returning to Australia. The other aircraft, with one elevator shot away, completed a hazardous trip back to Australia and the crew baled out safely over Bathurst Island.

A number of aircraft were lost in accidents on the landing strip, the most common being a swing to the right on take-off. There were a number of landing accidents due to damage sustained in action. Even experienced pilots (some ex-instructors) found difficulty in strip landings at first, especially when there was a crosswind blowing.

The squadron strength was twenty-one aircraft and in eleven months, twenty-eight were lost or badly damaged. This included those lost on operations. A further two burnt out on the ground following an air raid and the rest were flying accidents.

Charles Read was awarded a DFC for his time in command of 31 Squadron. He remained in the RAAF and rose to become the Chief of Air Staff, RAAF retiring as Air Marshal Sir Charles Read KBE, CB, DFC. AFC. He lived on the New South Wales coast.

CHAPTER TWENTY-SEVEN

SEARCH AND DESTROY IN TIMOR

Wing Commander Bill Mann, CO 31 Squadron, and his navigator
with their ground crew at Coomalie Creek. (Bill Mann)

Wing Commander **Bill Mann** assumed command of 31 (RAAF) Squadron
on 13 September 1943.

Air Headquarters had briefed us that they had received reports that the Japanese base
at Taberfane on the west coast of Aru Island had been building up its Rufe seaplane
strength. The Rufe was a Mitsubishi A6M Zero on seaplane floats, fast and nippy.
There was no airstrip on the islands where the Rufes were located, hence the use of
seaplanes, mainly to escort light and heavy bombers attacking Australia. The seaplane
base was established in a fairly narrow bay and from a low height there was only one
way in to attack the ground installations and the moored aircraft.

The operation order arrived two days before the strike was to be flown. I decided
to lead and called the flight commanders and section officers to my office to discuss
the plan. It was decided that the best tactic was to go in just above the water at first
light and try to catch as many moored aircraft as possible before they could get
airborne.

The Japanese base was almost fifty miles up the west coast of the island,
which added to the difficulty of a surprise
attack. Coastal lookouts were always on
watch and the strike force would be sighted before reaching the coastline giving the
defences time to be ready. The base was
heavily defended, and the Japanese were
well aware of the one and only possible approach for an effective attack to be made.
So, we would have to go through in a single
wave, doing as much damage as possible,

Bill Mann attends a debriefing of his sweat-
soaked crews on their return from a strike.
(Bill Mann)

and then fight our way out before any enemy aircraft could get airborne. A number of us had been to the target before and knew it was a tough one. Selection had to be of those crews best fitted for the task but also it had to be a mix of experienced and newer arrivals who had to build up their experience. The selection process for such an operation was always difficult and I was always aware that I potentially held the destiny of each of my crews.

Everything was readied, checked and rechecked and the briefing was thorough so all the crews were well versed on the details of the operation. An air of expectation permeated throughout the whole squadron.

The night before the raid coincided with the weekly issue of one precious bottle of beer, and though there was normally a relaxed air, this evening was subdued, not least because the participating crews could not draw their ration. The unwritten rule was that when engaged in a strike, there was no alcohol drunk the previous night. The realisation that some crews might not be back to claim their bottle was never far from our thoughts. But when they did claim it and imbibe in front of those who had done so the night before, it was some compensation for their ordeal and much humorous banter went with it.

It was an early retirement to our tents to try and relax, write letters and then try to get some sleep. Wake-up call was at 0100 hours, which gave us just enough time for a shower and breakfast, usually the despised baked beans on toast, then transport down to the strip with our gear.

At the strip, last-minute preparations were in progress. We sorted ourselves out, settled our gear and had the last-minute 'nervous pee'. It would be at least five hours before the next opportunity and there were no means available in the cramped cockpits. If you didn't last the distance, that was too bad. Sounds of someone being sick from behind some of the aircraft came at odd moments but no one took any notice.

My navigator, Ray Harber, and I strapped in, got the last instructions from the sergeant in charge and I cranked the huge engines into life. With both engines running, the hatch was closed and locked by the ground crew, the chocks waved away and we started to move into position. With the power increasing quickly, the Beau surged forward, the tail lifted and with rapidly gathering speed we sped off into the night. The strike had begun.

Cruising at economical settings to save fuel and to extend our range, we flew through a calm, clear starlit night, which allowed Ray to 'shoot the stars' from a steady platform with greater accuracy for his astro navigation. He had also dropped an aluminium flare into the sea to observe drift and get an indication of the wind speed and direction. The smooth air helped make the pilot's task much easier in maintaining an accurate course and speed towards a pinpoint arrival at the target area, so essential for surprising the enemy and giving him as little time as possible to man his defences. It was not always this way. Most times there was rain and low cloud and often storms.

Ray alerted me when we had about an hour to run and we let down to 100 feet to stay below the enemy radar. As we got closer I gave a wing waggle and we dropped a bit lower. Our concern was not the radar but the coastal lookouts. With ten minutes to go to the coast, night gave way to day (there is virtually no twilight at these latitudes) we cocked the guns and I turned the firing button to 'FIRE'.

In moments we had reached the southern shore of the bay and the odd trail in the smooth water suggested that some fighters were airborne. Then, all hell broke out. A mass of gun flashes and tracer erupted from the whole perimeter of the bay and then Ray called that there was a fighter closing in and his rearward-facing gun began chattering away.

With a sudden lurch of the aircraft a great round hole appeared on the outer starboard wing, which dropped steeply as the aircraft tried to turn and dive into the water. Only rapid instinctive action stopped the wing drop with hard left rudder and the two-handed spectacle control column rammed over to port to the absolute limit. The starboard wing still remained dangerously low and I had to take some power off the port engine in order to hold against the enormous pull.

With the aircraft still flying, though badly damaged, I was able to hold a straight course as I called to the formation that we had been hit and I handed control of the formation to my number two. Ray moved forward to assist but there was nothing we could do to relieve the pressure so he went back to work out a course to the nearest land. I adjusted the power settings and the trim to try and lift the wing and this took some of the pressure from the control column.

The wing continued to be down but the aircraft was now reasonably stable. The ailerons were obviously damaged and I wondered how much damage there was to the underside of the wing. A Bofors-type gun could only have caused the hole in the topside.

Ray estimated that it would take three hours to reach the northern coast of Australia and we had to do something to relieve the strain of holding the aircraft steady. We managed a gentle climb to 500 feet, which gave me a bit more scope to come up with a solution. With my left leg at full stretch to hold the rudder, I found that by using my 'free' right leg as a vertical prop with my right hand on the knee as a wedge, I could maintain the right height and stop the wing dropping further. To free my right hand, Ray found me a codebook, which we placed on my knee and below the controls and this worked.

Once well clear of the enemy area, we put out a short radio message to base to tell them of our problems and the likely need to ditch. I then noticed a streak of oil starting to emerge from under the port engine cowling and growing in size. Although it was only running at third throttle to balance the total power, it was helping and I did not want to lose it. We had climbed to 4,000 feet and Ray put out a Mayday call.

The streak grew steadily but the oil pressure gauge remained normal. With thirty minutes to go to the coast, the starboard engine spluttered before running normally again but it was obvious that we had used most of the fuel on that side. I had no option but to close down the port engine and cross feed from the port fuel tanks. The speed decreased slightly and we started to lose height gradually but at least some of the pressure on my leg came off.

I closed down the port engine until the propeller was idling under engine power. If I switched the engine off completely it would 'windmill', creating enormous drag so it was best to let the engine idle. Ray took an astro fix and came forward to tell me that we were getting near and would hit the coast on the edge of a vast area marked on the map as 'unexplored'. As the coast came into sight, the starboard engine coughed again before picking up.

We hoped to find a clear area but all we could see was a thick forest. Then we spotted a small clearing that looked like a marsh and I turned to make a wheels-up landing. The starboard wing was still down a bit, which was a concern but as I felt the aircraft settling I gave the aileron a violent wrench and the wings came miraculously level as we slammed into the swamp at 120 knots. For the second time that day, all hell broke loose.

The reeds and dark brown water completely obscured our vision of the outside world as we came to a stop. We got out through the top hatch and realised that the volume of water had probably doused any chances of a fire. Ray jumped down and came back to tell me that most of the underside of the wing was missing. The swamp was only a foot deep and I joined Ray to see that two thirds of the under-wing surface had gone.

Within minutes we saw a group of naked natives who came towards us laughing and gesticulating. We had landed in an unexplored area of Arnhem Land in the Northern Territory and we did not know what to expect. I approached the one who appeared to be the chief and offered him my Mae West, which he put on to the amusement of the others. Ray offered his to another. We gathered up our emergency kits and followed the natives to the edge of the swamp.

We gave them cigarettes and then worked out that we were some 300 miles to the east of base but only thirty from a forward strip we used occasionally and which was close to a mission station. To head for that seemed to be our only hope and by pointing and gesticulating we got the natives to understand which direction we needed to take. With eight natives we set off east towards the forests.

We marched, with breaks, for most of the day and spent the night in a clearing where our evening meal was of malted milk tablets and a bit of chocolate and dried fruit from our emergency pack. We had to accept the offer of foul-tasting brackish water.

The following day we came to a wide river. Thankfully we had taken the two dinghies from the aircraft and the natives were astonished when we inflated them. Halfway over a crocodile surfaced and the natives slapped the water and it disappeared but everyone got well clear of the river once we had crossed. At this stage, Ray, who was having trouble with his feet, became exhausted and had to be helped along.

During the afternoon, we thought we heard a shot. I fired my .38 revolver twice and this was answered by more shots and then out of the trees appeared a very big black man (he was a Fijian) with a half dozen natives. He held out his hand and in the most perfect and cultured English he said, "Wing Commander, I am happy to have found you, and I give thanks to the Lord that you are both alive". He briefly explained that he was the missionary in charge of Millimgimbi Mission. He said that they had set off to find the aircraft and he had shot a scrub turkey for their evening meal – the shot we had heard!

A rough bush stretcher was made for Ray and four natives carried him with ease. We soon reached the sea where we had a dip and then boarded a large dugout canoe. We said goodbye to our rescuers and left the Mae Wests and dinghies with them – they were delighted. We soon arrived at the camp near the mission where the warrant officer commandant looked after us, gave us some clean clothes and fed us a good typical meal of bully beef and dried potatoes.

The next morning an aircraft arrived to pick us up but not before we had visited the mission to bid farewell and thank the missionary for all his efforts.

> The two men quickly recovered from their adventure, collected a new Beaufighter and were soon back leading strike formations against targets in Timor. **Bill Mann** describes another incident that befell one of his crews and which typifies the dangers of operating at extreme range.

On 6 April eight aircraft were tasked to carry out a daylight sweep of Semau Island on the southern tip of Timor. Crossing one of the many channels, the lead aircraft, flown by Flight Lieutenant Boyd and Flying Officer Anderson, spotted what appeared to be a wooded island, which turned out to be a well-camouflaged vessel about 200 feet long. He was not in a position to attack and called to his number two, Flying Officer Dave Strachan and Flight Sergeant Jack Brassil – "Go for it, Dave!"

The oil barge found at Semau Island disguised as a wooded island attacked by 31 Squadron. (Bill Mann)

Weaving as the two aircraft approached, one behind the other, Strachan opened fire with his cannons followed shortly after by Boyd. Under this onslaught, the vessel blew up – it was an oil barge. The two aircraft jinked violently to avoid the explosion but ran into a hail of anti-aircraft fire from the shore.

Strachan's aircraft was hit and he saw some pieces fly off the starboard engine, which soon began to vibrate severely, failing completely about thirty seconds later.

Turning for the nearest land, other than enemy territory, the crew headed for Cartier, a small reef 160 miles south of Timor.

The reef was only a tiny atoll covered in sand, a few feet above sea level, with no trees or vegetation whatsoever. It was the only spot where a crash-landing could possibly be made and a rescue effected.

After flying on the port engine for a short time the fuel gauge light began to flutter and the engine coughed. By cross feeding fuel from the starboard tank, the engine recovered. This committed them to Cartier so they jettisoned all the ammunition and the fuel remaining in the port tank and this allowed them to gain some height.

The lightened aircraft responded with a slow steady climb to 3,000 feet. A message was passed to base of their intentions and a rescue plan was put in place. After an hour Cartier came into view and they circled to make a thorough inspection. After a couple of circuits the best spot was chosen and the aircraft glided in to a belly-landing on the soft sand.

Boyd and Anderson, who had accompanied the stricken Beaufighter, remained overhead the reef for two hours as the rest of the formation went back to base to refuel. Once Strachan and Brassil were down the rescue plan was initiated. A Catalina flying boat based at Darwin took off and headed for Cartier. Two Beaufighters had also taken off and they overtook the Catalina and took over the top cover for the downed crew.

As the afternoon wore on, Strachan and Brassil started stripping valuable items from the Beaufighter. The Catalina glided in and in the fading light taxied as close to the reef as possible. The crew paddled out in the dinghy with the recovered instruments, camera and other portable items and were soon aboard the flying boat and on their way back to Darwin. The two Beaufighters overhead then strafed the wrecked aircraft on the reef and set it on fire.

Flying Officer Strachan and Flight Sergeant Brassil crash-land on Cartier Reef. (Bill Mann)

Finally, **Bill Mann** concludes by describing one of his last sorties.

During the morning a strike formation had attacked two large freighters in the sea-lanes around Timor. On return they reported that one had been left on fire and the other had probably been damaged. I gathered the strike leader, his navigator and the squadron intelligence officer and we decided that the two damaged ships had no option but to seek a safe haven. They were large ships and would need a deep and protected harbour. The only one within range was at Lautem. This was strongly defended with large and medium AA and heavy harbour defences.

We decided that we could get them if we mounted another strike at first light the following day. Eight aircraft were tasked, four carrying semi-armour-piercing bombs with the other four acting as close escort since the fighter base at Fuiloro was near Lautem. I intended to lead the strike force with OC 'A' Flight leading the fighter cover.

The targets were at our maximum range so it was a case of straight in and out. Operations approved the plan and the aircraft were prepared. Ray had not been well and was in sick quarters but when he heard about the operation, my last before handing over command of the squadron, he insisted on coming with me despite my protestations.

The take-off in the small hours and the long flight across the sea through the night had been routine. As dawn broke we got the pungent smell of the island jungle, which was a warning that landfall was not far off. Ray had been repeatedly checking our position but the most difficult decision was identifying the tight valley to enter, with no second choice available. It was a mammoth task to make a 'spot on' landfall across 500 miles of sea by dead reckoning, relying largely on the astro compass and drift sight.

Ray warned me to look out for two peaks close together two miles inland, which we had briefed the previous evening. Shortly afterwards I picked them up slightly starboard and Ray reminded me to aim for the one on the left, which would be at the entrance to the valley we needed to fly down. I called, "Astern" and the three strike aircraft slipped in behind me. We entered the valley, guns cocked and ready and the bombs fused.

The squadron had not been through the valley before. It was narrow with a few wider channels and wound its way across the island. It took us five minutes to cross at treetop height and we passed Fuiloro where we saw some aircraft taking off. They closed on the rear of our formation but still out of range. The race was on.

As we approached Lautem harbour we saw a column of black smoke and I broadcast to the strike force that it could be our target and I ordered the cover force to climb as we accelerated. The valley was wider and we were able to fly line abreast. There were several gun emplacements on the hills that marked the end of the valley on the edge of the bay. We were too close and low for the gunners to bring their sights to bear. At the same time Ray called me that fighters were approaching and to weave as his gun started chattering.

A large bay confronted us with the burning ship in the middle. Beyond it at a thousand yards was moored another large ship. Incredibly it was broadside on, in perfect position to attack, and it was unloading. The four attacking aircraft opened up with all guns and sprayed the decks as troops endeavoured to disembark. Anti-aircraft fire was all around us with tracers streaming from every direction accompanied by black puffs from the heavier batteries and our own guns blasting away.

As we closed on the ships, we released our bombs into the black hull facing us, then swept up and over the ship to clear it. The bombs hit and exploded after the eleven-second time delay.

Once over and clear of the ship, the formation dived down again to sea level, made a wide left turn and headed away from the island. It was in that instant that there was a huge explosion along the entire length of the ship. We could hear the cover flight still engaged in a melee at a higher level. I called them to break and re-join and soon the two teams were back together again leaving devastation behind us, together with a crashed and burning Japanese fighter, which Squadron Leader R. Gordon DFC, leader of the cover force, had shot down. A second had been damaged.

Glad that the formation had all survived in spite of the intense opposition, there was mostly silence amongst the crews on the long flight home.

It was later confirmed that both ships were troop carriers bringing in a new garrison with 3,000 Japanese troops aboard. The majority were killed.

Both men left 31 Squadron at the end of May 1944 when their tours finished and shortly afterwards they were awarded the DFC. Bill Mann headed for England where he served until the end of the war on special duties with the invasion force in north-west Europe before returning home to Australia. He retired from the service as a wing commander.

CHAPTER TWENTY-EIGHT
OPERATIONAL SWANSONG

Aircrews of 45 Squadron at Kuala Lumpur. Michael Robinson is in the middle row second from the left. (AVM Michael Robinson)

The RAF's last operational Beaufighter squadron was 45 Squadron, which exchanged its Mosquitos for Beaufighters at the end of 1946 whilst based in Ceylon (now Sri Lanka). Once established in Malaya it became heavily involved in the Malayan Emergency, Operation Firedog, the fight against the communist terrorists (CT). The squadron flew its first operations in August 1948.

Amongst the new crews to join the squadron was **Michael Robinson** who had graduated from the RAF College Cranwell in April 1948. He outlines his experiences.

My perspective of the Malayan Emergency is that of a junior pilot on 45 Squadron. I joined them at Negombo in Ceylon in October 1948 to fly the Beaufighter TF.X. The senior crews of the squadron were already at Kuala Lumpur in Malaya where the rest of us joined them in May 1949. The KL runway had a laterite surface, 1,400 yards long and thirty-three yards wide with a batik factory at one end and a high railway embankment at the other. The squadron's dispersal, of pierced steel planking, was forty yards or less from the runway so, under those conditions, our Beaufighters could not afford to swing on take-off!

The aircraft was the last of the line and Malaya was nearly the end of the supply line so spares, particularly for engines, were at a premium. Much reliance was placed on the judgement of our senior NCO fitter who assessed the amount of metal swarf in the oil filters to decide the probable remaining life of the engines. Formation positions were decided by which engine was the more vulnerable. A four-ship flight from Butterworth to KL at the end of an armament practice camp was decided using this formula and, as the junior pilot, I was allocated the number four position - for obvious reasons. i.e. both engines were suspect.

The Beaufighter's armament was two 500-lb bombs, one under each wing, eight 60-lb rockets and four 20-mm cannons. We could also carry 20-lb anti-personnel bombs and this became necessary when our use of 500-lb bombs exceeded supply. Pilots Notes of those days, which I have tried to refer to, gave absolutely no detail on armament other than to point out the various switches, so one had to go to other sources to be reminded of what was carried.

Originally intended as a torpedo fighter, the Hercules engine of our aircraft had a rated altitude of 1,500 feet, which is to say that at above that height the power decreased, so an engine failure during a strike, or a training flight to the east of the hilly spine of Malaya dictated a transit to Singapore. Target identification at the time depended on the best available photographs. Primary and secondary jungle could be distinguished but target positions were often little better than a bearing and distance from the edge of a patch of secondary jungle. Except for the populated west coast, maps were usually of little value and could be seriously inaccurate.

The afternoon thunderstorms played a significant part in our routine and flying in Malaya. Our CO, Squadron Leader Alec Blythe DFC, who had previously served at the Instrument Flying Flight at Changi, introduced us to flying cloud penetrations in formation.

He described the cloud-break technique:

> On approaching the cloud the formation was brought in close, so that each pilot could check his heading with the leader's compass. This was to allow for compass deviation. Then numbers two and three turned five degrees away from the leader for five seconds and climbed 500 feet. Numbers four and five turned ten degrees and descended 500 feet before resuming the leader's heading. The aircraft was carefully trimmed for straight and level flight before entering cloud and once in it were allowed to ride the storm with the minimum interference from the pilot. All he was required to do was to maintain heading as far as possible without harsh use of the controls.

This was fine except that I switched on the cockpit lighting and lowered my seat to lessen the distraction of the associated lighting. One particular experience was when I was flying in my usual number three position to the left of the leader. I came out of the storm and looked to the right to see where the other three aircraft were. No sign! So I looked to the left and there they were. In the storm I had unwittingly and involuntarily swapped places with my number two.

We did have some early successes, in terms of confirmed kills of CT, such as a series of attacks by Beaufighters and Spitfires in a forested area of Selangor, just to the south of KL, in April 1949 when air was credited with thirty-seven out of forty-five kills - but these were rarely repeated. Nevertheless, air strikes in my time did discourage the CTs from camping near the fringes of jungle to sustain their protection rackets on the local populations for food, money and intelligence. The strikes may also have spared the land forces from having to make deep inroads into the jungle but I recognise that eventual victory was achieved because our army, with the help of the Malayan police and armed forces, was prepared to hold ground over which control had been achieved – none of this firepower demonstration and then retire at nightfall – the answer was to secure the base and then hold it.

I do not know if the quality of target information given to us in those early years could have been improved, but it was only after the arrival of General Templar as high commissioner and director of operation in February 1952 that the proper integration of police and military intelligence was achieved. That, however, was after my tour, which finished in April 1951 by which time I had done 175 strikes in the Beaufighter and later in the Brigand.

Some reflections on the effectiveness of offensive air, and here I hasten to add that these reflections are not by a pilot officer but by a senior officer with the benefit of hindsight and much more experience. In his 1966 book, *The Long, Long War*, Brigadier Richard Clutterbuck, as he then was, considered air transport and its ability to bring government services to control remote areas, to be the most effective use of air support. Offensive strikes were, he thought, the least effective. He placed proper value on the helicopter, which the RAF was late in developing, a troop-carrying capability not being available until about 1953.

Whilst I agree with Clutterbuck's listing, I would certainly question his assertion that offensive air strikes did more harm than good. He accepts the terrain was mainly responsible for the lack of tangible success and, during my tour, there were no effective means of target identification, such as bearing and distance from ground beacons

The port engine of Beaufighter TF.X RD784 starts up. (via Jeff Jefford)

or smoke, a technique that was established successfully later. Aiming relied on a best assessment of map, or photo, reading and the Mark 1 eyeball. Neither the Beaufighter nor the Brigand was fitted with a bombsight and our technique involved a simple rule of thumb assessment of a thirty-degree dive. An attempt to produce a concentration of bombs by flying in close vic or finger four formation at 250 feet, and all releasing on the leader's call was short lived. Our bombs were allegedly fitted with eleven-second delay fuses but dropping them through the jungle canopy disproved that theory when we got instantaneous explosions.

Bombing and strafing *did* make a positive contribution, albeit perhaps not directly in relation to the effort expended, but not to indulge in offensive air would have been military nonsense. The judgement was that bombs, particularly if they were concentrated, could play a part in adversely affecting the morale of the CTs by forcing them to stay in the inhospitable jungle, short of food and medicines, and not receiving any hoped for reinforcements of men and material from other Far East communists who were, at the time, having some success. However, in the early years of Operation Firedog it was certainly a close run thing, as many of the local population were far from convinced that the security forces would win through and it took an uncomfortably long time for the political powers to appreciate the seriousness of the threat and the scale and effort and quality of intelligence necessary to succeed.

The squadron moved to Tengah in December 1949 and I flew the last Beaufighter out of KL. The expenditure of weapons during the sixteen months at KL highlights the scale of the squadron's efforts. Almost 800 500-lb bombs and 859 of the small 20-lb bombs were dropped. There were also 3,718 rockets and 148,181 rounds of 20-mm fired. A few more strikes were flown from Tengah before we started converting to the Brigand. The squadron flew its last Beaufighter strike on 7 January 1950 – the very last operational sortie flown by the aircraft almost ten years after it first came into service.

Mike Robinson had a long and distinguished career in the RAF flying Canberra B (I) 8s and later commanding a Victor strategic bomber squadron. He was the station commander at RAF Lossiemouth and retired as Air Vice-Marshal M.M. J. Robinson CB.

ABBREVIATIONS

AA	Anti-Aircraft
ADGB	Air Defence of Great Britain
AFC	Air Force Cross
AI	Air Intercept
AIF	Australian Infantry Force
ALO	Army Liaison Officer
AOC	Air Officer Commanding
AP	Armour Piercing
CT	Communist Terrorist
DFC	Distinguished Flying Cross
DFM	Distinguished Flying Medal
DR	Dead Reckoning
DSO	Distinguished Service Order
ETD	Estimated Time of Departure
E/V	Escort Vessel
GCI	Ground Control Interception
IJAAF	Imperial Japanese Army Air Force
IO	Intelligence Officer
MO	Medical Officer
M/S	Minesweeper
MT	Motor Transport
M/V	Motor Vessel
OTU	Operational Training Unit
PRU	Photographic Reconnaissance Unit
PSP	Pierced Steel Planking
RAF	Royal Air Force
RAAF	Royal Australian Air Force
RCAF	Royal Canadian Air Force
RNZAF	Royal New Zealand Air Force
R/O	Radar Operator
R/P	Rocket Projectile
SYKO	Cyphers and Codes
QDM	Question Direction Magnetic
USAAF	United States Army Air Force
WAAF	Women's Auxiliary Air Force
WOP/AG	Wireless Operator/Air Gunner
W/T	Wireless Telegraphy

BIBLIOGRAPHY

Allen, Michael, *Pursuit Through Darkened Skies*, Airlife, 1999

Barnes, C.H., *Bristol Aircraft*, Putnam, 1995

Bingham, Victor, *Bristol Beaufighter*, Airlife, 1994

Bowyer, Chaz, *Beaufighter*, William Kimber, 1987

Bowyer, Chaz, *The Flying Elephants*, Macdonald, 1972

Braham, J.R.D., *Scramble*, William Kimber, 1985

Burrowes, David M., *489, An Unofficial History*, Private, 2006

Golley, John, *John 'Cat's-Eyes' Cunningham*, Airlife, 1999

Goss, Chris, *Combat over the Mediterranean*, Frontline Books, 2017

Goulter, Christina, *A Forgotten Offensive*, Frank Cass, 1995

Innes, David, *Beaufighters Over Burma*, Blandford, 1985

Jefford, Wg Cdr C.G., *The Flying Camels*, Private, 1995

Kane-Maguire, Leon, *Lost Without Trace*, RAAF Air Power Centre, 2011

Kitching, T.W., *From Dusk Till Dawn*, FPD Services, 2001

Nesbit, Roy, *The Strike Wings*, William Kimber, 1984

Odgers, George, *Air War Against Japan*, Australian War Memorial, 1968

Onderwater, Hans, *Gentlemen in Blue*, Leo Cooper, 1997

Parry, Simon, *Beaufighter Squadrons*, Red Kite, 2002

Pike, Richard, *Beaufighter Ace*, Pen & Sword, 2004

Pitchfork, Graham, *Airmen Behind the Medals*, Pen & Sword, 2015

Ross, David, *The Greatest Squadron of Them All*, Grub Street, 2003

Spencer, Dennis, *Looking Backwards over Burma*, Woodfield, 2009

Sutherland-Brown, Atholl, *Silently into the Midst of Things*, Book Guild, 1997

Thomas, Andrew, *Beaufighter Aces of World War 2*, Osprey, 2005

Willis, G.R.T., *No Hero; Just a Survivor,* Private, 1999

Young, Douglas, *The Dangerous Sea and Sky*, Avon Books, 1994

INDEX